Mornings with
JESUS

Mornings with Jesus

ISBN 978-0-8249-4504-6

Published by Guideposts
16 East 34th Street
New York, New York 10016
Guideposts.org

Distributed by Ideals Publications, a Guideposts company
2630 Elm Hill Pike, Suite 100
Nashville, TN 37214

Guideposts and *Ideals* are registered trademarks of Guideposts.

Acknowledgments

Every attempt has been made to credit the sources of copyrighted material used in this book. If any such acknowledgment has been inadvertently omitted or miscredited, receipt of such information would be appreciated.

All Scripture quotations, unless otherwise noted, are taken from The Holy Bible, King James Version. Other Scripture references are from the following sources: The Amplified Bible, (AMP), © 1954, 1958, 1962, 1964, 1965, 1987 by The Lockman Foundation. Used by permission. www.Lockman.org. The Common English Bible (CEB), © 2011 by Common English Bible. All rights reserved. The Holy Bible: Contemporary English Version (CEV), © 1995 American Bible Society. The Holy Bible, English Standard Version® (ESV), copyright © 2001 by Crossway Bibles, a publishing ministry of Good News Publishers. Used by permission. All rights reserved. *The Message* (MSG). Copyright © 1993, 1994, 1995, 1996, 2000, 2001, 2002 by Eugene H. Peterson. Used by permission of NavPress, Colorado Springs, CO. The New American Standard Bible, (NASB) copyright © 1960, 1962, 1963, 1968, 1971, 1972, 1973, 1975, 1977, 1995 by the Lockman Foundation. Used by permission. www.Lockman.org. The Holy Bible, New International Version® (NIV®). Copyright © 1973, 1978, 1984, 2011 by Biblica. All rights reserved worldwide. The Holy Bible, New King James Version (NKJV). Copyright © 1997, 1990, 1985, 1983 by Thomas Nelson, Inc. The Holy Bible, New Living Translation (NLT). Copyright © 1996, 2004, 2007 by Tyndale House Foundation. Used by permission of Tyndale House Publishers, Inc., Carol Stream, Illinois 60188. All rights reserved. The New Revised Standard Version Bible (NRSV) copyright © 1989 by the Division of Christian Education of the National Council of the Churches of Christ in the U.S.A. Used by permission. All rights reserved. The Revised Standard Version (RSV), copyright © 1946, 1952, 1971 by Division of Christian Education of the National Council of Churches of Christ in the U.S.A. Used by permission. *The Living Bible* (TLB) © 1971. Used by permission of Tyndale House Publishers, Inc., Carol Stream, Illinois 60188. All rights reserved. The Holy Bible, Today's New International Version (TNIV). Copyright © 2001, 2005 by Biblica. www.Biblica.com. All rights reserved worldwide.

Grass/sunset in cover photo by Chris McGuire / Masterfile
Cover design by Lookout Design, Inc
Typeset by Müllerhaus

Printed and bound in China

Introduction

WHEN JESUS WAS PREPARING HIS disciples for His departure and ascension into heaven, He tried to comfort them. They were understandably confused and upset. And Jesus urged them not to be worried; He assured them that He would come back and was preparing a place for them. The famously doubting Thomas said what many of us have thought: "Lord, we don't know where you are going, so how can we know the way?" (John 14:5, NIV). And how did Jesus respond? "I am the way and the truth and the life. No one comes to the Father except through me" (John 14:6, NIV).

These are heady words, yet they are the same way that Jesus responds to us today, when we have doubts and fears. How will we know the way to forgiveness, to compassion, to better loving our families? Jesus Himself is the way. Follow His teachings, imprint His words on your heart and mind, draw near to His presence, His comfort, His love…be still in His presence.

The stillness that Jesus promises is abundant, but we must seek Him to find it. *Stillness* is a word and concept that is foreign to our modern, scheduled ears. But Jesus is all about stillness, He's all about resting the weight of our worries and stresses on Him—He says, "Come to me, all you who are weary and burdened" (Matthew 11:28, NIV) and "Do not let your hearts be troubled" (John 14:1, NIV).

You will recognize the easy-to-use devotional format of this book. There is a one-page reading for every day of the year. A Bible verse opens each day, followed by a devotional by one of seven specially selected writers, who connect the Scripture to a moment in their lives, sharing their wisdom and insights in hopes of encouraging you. A "faith step" ends each day's reading. It's a practical way to apply what you've read to your life, and to continue to mull over the day's lesson by implementing its truth. The faith steps will challenge you to look at a Scripture passage in a new way, ask a question that will help you make a change in your life, or simply encourage you to praise and thank your Savior.

Discover more of who Jesus is through these devotionals, which will bring to life His encouraging teachings, parables and promises. Walk alongside Him as you spend your *Mornings with Jesus*.

January

JANUARY 1

"Very early in the morning, while it was still dark, Jesus got up, left the house and went off to a solitary place, where he prayed." Mark 1:35 (NIV)

*M*y day planner was bursting at the seams. Each small square on the calendar was crammed with conflicting responsibilities: children's music lessons or play practice, church meetings, work deadlines. Even brief moments of social life required budgeting well in advance. I was so busy that I resented the time I had to spend sleeping. And in the midst of my overscheduled life, God continued to call me to spend daily quiet time with Him.

How could I fit in one more thing? Didn't He understand how important all my activities were? The work of the day insisted on its own urgency, so I often rushed through a token devotion and hurried prayer.

Reading through the Gospels, I discovered that Scripture mentions many times how Jesus went away to pray—sometimes early in the morning, sometimes overnight.

When life is overwhelming, setting aside time for prayer feels counterintuitive. Surely diving into the work of the day will bring more progress than stepping aside for prayer. Jesus understood the pressure of time. His brief years of ministry were limited, and there were so many people who needed truth, forgiveness, healing. His disciples needed to be taught. The Father's plan needed to be carried out. Yet He made prayer a priority.

As busy as my life might be, I will never carry the weight of responsibility that Jesus did. He came to redeem the entire human race. Yet instead of frantic urgency, He consistently modeled a life of prayer, of retreat, of seeking a quiet place.

Martin Luther said, "I have so much to do that I shall spend the first three hours in prayer." That level of commitment, along with the consistent example of Jesus, inspires me to find my own solitary space and time each day to spend time in prayer.

FAITH STEP: *If your day feels too full, take a risk and schedule some extra prayer first, trusting Jesus to provide what you need for all the other responsibilities.*

—*Sharon Hinck*

JANUARY 2

"Give us today our daily bread." Matthew 6:11 (NIV)

In ancient days, God fed his people with manna: bread from heaven that appeared each morning with the dew. Each day, they could only gather enough for that day, because any excess would rot overnight. Hoarding was not only prohibited but also impossible. Centuries later, Jesus taught His followers to pray, not for lottery winnings or fat 401(k)s or even a week's worth of provisions, but for "daily bread."

During his time on earth, Jesus chose to live in poverty. His human family was not well-off. As an itinerant rabbi, he depended on the hospitality of strangers and the financial support of several wealthy women (see Luke 8:1–3) and other benefactors. He trusted that His heavenly Father would provide daily bread.

Daily bread is so, well, daily. There's not a lot of security in it. You have to be grateful each day, and then get up the next day and say, "Do it again, God!" You have to learn to live with a manna mindset. It is at once frightening and exhilarating, scary and joyful.

You have to pray for that bread (or mortgage payment) each day, and trust that it will be provided, that there will be enough. To pray for daily bread is to be willing to gather only enough manna for this day. In our self-indulgent world, "enough" is a powerful but unpopular word. And yet, it is a word of freedom.

What's true of physical resources is true of spiritual resources as well. Each day, we must ask for and receive spiritual nourishment, and trust that Jesus will provide enough love, enough strength, for us to continue our journey of trust with Him.

FAITH STEP: *Ask Jesus to give you a manna mindset—and enough of whatever it is that you need this day: love, strength, money, food. Thank Him for knowing your needs and generously meeting them.*

—*Keri Wyatt Kent*

JANUARY 3

"'This is where the Israelites crossed the Jordan on dry ground.'
For the Lord your God dried up the river right before your eyes,
…just as he did at the Red Sea." Joshua 4:22–23 (NLT)

"*M*om, Cali has a bad surprise for you!"

My son's announcement rang from the hallway to the kitchen where I was fixing breakfast. A moment later both kids appeared, Paxton leading the way for his sister. Two-year-old Calianne had taken off another messy diaper and was shuffling behind him, holding out the stinking offender.

I cringed, but then had to smile at my precious pair—Cali in her innocence and Paxton in his element as her guide. I could almost hear him whisper to her, "Don't worry, I've got your back. I'll tell Mom for you."

And once again Jesus reminded me how He truly "has our backs" through our ups and downs and how He also walks ahead of us to shield us from what's to come.

Joshua 4 tells how God prepared the Israelites to conquer Jericho. Have you ever wondered why He parted the Red Sea *and* the Jordan River? Surely He wasn't yawning in heaven: "Well, that parting the waters trick worked once; I may as well do it again."

Hardly.

God parted the Red Sea to save His people from Egyptian tyranny—an act in their *defense*. He parted the Jordan River to prepare them for an *offensive* move—to claim victory of the life He had promised them. Sandwiched between the miracles were forty years of wilderness waiting.

Through any "stinking" circumstance, Jesus is constantly acting in our defense and leading our offense, for His glory and our good. As 2 Thessalonians 3:5 says, His guidance helps us become loving and patient as He is—if we'll follow His lead.

FAITH STEP: *Buy a small windowsill plant as a reminder that Jesus' presence helps you thrive in any circumstance, just like sunshine grows your plant. Each time you water it, think of Jesus parting your troubles to see you through to His promises.*

—*Erin Keeley Marshall*

JANUARY 4

"While he was in Bethany, reclining at the table in the home of Simon the Leper, a woman came with an alabaster jar of very expensive perfume, made of pure nard. She broke the jar and poured the perfume on his head. Some of those present were saying indignantly to one another, 'Why this waste of perfume? It could have been sold for more than a year's wages and the money given to the poor.' And they rebuked her harshly. 'Leave her alone,' said Jesus. 'Why are you bothering her? She has done a beautiful thing to me.'" Mark 14:3–6 (NIV)

*W*hen I worked as a choreographer, I marveled at the dedication of ballet dancers. They invested years in daily training, making huge sacrifices of time and effort to develop the strength, grace and skill needed for their art. And that was just the first step. Once they were in a production, they poured out more of themselves—repetition, discipline and a constant attempt for perfection. All for a fleeting performance.

Dance is an extravagant art form. It requires a huge offering of love. For the dancers I know, every strained muscle, each disappointing audition, every sacrifice of other activities is worthwhile because they are creating a work of beauty and power.

The woman with the alabaster jar understood that sort of extravagance. She gave beyond what seemed reasonable to the onlookers: a year's wages for one moment to demonstrate her love for Jesus.

My life is full of activities on which I could lavish time and attention, and many of them don't provide much return on the investment. But when I spend time alone with Jesus, pouring out my love and praise, breaking open the alabaster jar of my heart to share with Him, I can never be too extravagant. Nothing I offer Him is wasted.

There will always be important needs that could benefit from my attention, just as there were poor people who could have benefited from the money the perfume could bring. But there are also times when the gift Jesus most wants from me is worship. I long to hear Him say, as He did of the woman in Bethany, "She has done a beautiful thing to me."

FAITH STEP: *Play your favorite worship music and pour your heart out to Jesus, telling Him how much you love Him.*

—*Sharon Hinck*

JANUARY 5

"Haven't you read this passage of Scripture: 'The stone the builders rejected has become the cornerstone; the Lord has done this, and it is marvelous in our eyes'?" Mark 12:10–11 (NIV)

My oldest son has been addicted to Legos ever since he received his first set at age four. Growing up, he had a plastic tub filled to the top, and daily he'd sit down and start sorting through the pieces with a special design in mind.

In those early years, taller was better. He'd stack those little blocks on top of each other, in a single row, determined to create a tower as tall as himself. The problem was, he didn't have a strong foundation. No matter how determined he was, his tower soon toppled.

For many years I tried to live without Jesus as a foundation. To say my life toppled like Legos is an understatement. Determined to build something with my own hands, I soon found myself crashing and breaking. The foundation I tried to build on didn't work.

In biblical times, the cornerstone was the stone that united two walls. It was the visible corner, and everything else was built upon it. It cost the most because of its beauty and strength. Builders refused to build without a cornerstone because if they did, their efforts would be futile. This is a good reminder not only for my life but also for every day. Everything in my life must be built upon Jesus—His truth, His grace, His plans. Like my son eventually learned, the better the foundation, the higher we can reach—for Jesus' glory.

FAITH STEP: *Write a list of ten ways Jesus has been a firm foundation in your life. Pray and thank Jesus for each of these ways.*

—*Tricia Goyer*

JANUARY 6

"...The Spirit helps us in our weakness, for we do not know how to pray as we ought." Romans 8:26 (NRSV)

"If we live by the Spirit, let us also be guided by the Spirit." Galatians 5:25 (NRSV)

"The wind blows where it chooses, and you hear the sound of it, but you do not know where it comes from or where it goes. So it is with everyone who is born of the Spirit." John 3:8 (NRSV)

*J*esus' will for His children is like a river. It flows toward and through the desires and plans He has for us. If we throw ourselves into that river, we will be carried toward His designed destination for our lives. We might float toward shore occasionally and get tangled in the weeds of sin, or get hung up by an outcropping branch of enticing worldly temptations—but He will guide us in His ever-flowing stream.

We cannot know all Jesus knows about our faith journey, so it is best to rest back in the buoyant river of His will and be carried by Him.

FAITH STEP: *Pray that Jesus' will be done in your life, whatever that may be. Cast your lot with Him and relax into the soothing waters of His guidance. Ask Him to navigate your life from now on. Check in with your Captain often and take His direction.*

—Judy Baer

JANUARY 7

"But I have calmed and quieted my soul, like a weaned child with its mother; like a weaned child is my soul within me." Psalm 131:2 (ESV)

When our children were babies, my husband loved to hold them and play with them. His favorite game with our daughter, when she was only a few months old, was to stick out his tongue at her. She'd gaze at him, and then stick out her tongue back at him.

"Look what I taught her to do!" he'd boast, as only a deeply smitten new father can. But when that same darling baby got hungry, she had no further interest in making faces. She'd turn toward her daddy's chest and begin rooting, pushing her mouth against him, looking for food. Unable to help her, he'd hand her over to me. Any woman who has ever nursed a baby will tell you—when those children want to eat, they want to eat! They are not content with a parent's mere presence.

I loved the miracle of feeding my children, keeping them alive, really. And yet, once they were weaned, there was a new kind of closeness that developed between us. My son would toddle to the rocking chair, tattered blankie in one hand, and pat it invitingly while looking at me with sweet blue eyes. "Cuddle, cuddle," he'd say. I'd sit down and he'd climb in my lap, wanting nothing but my arms around him, my presence. He no longer rooted for food in the desperate way of a nursing baby, but simply leaned up against me, content. In a way I never had before, I understood the phrase "like a weaned child."

Do I come to God like an infant, rooting, restless, wailing to be fed, demanding that my needs be met? Or can I come to Him like a weaned child, wanting only Jesus' presence?

FAITH STEP: *What would it take for you to calm and quiet your soul? Take some time to sit, imagining yourself leaning against Jesus' shoulder, like a weaned child, content.*

—*Keri Wyatt Kent*

JANUARY 8

"Many are the plans in a human heart, but it is the Lord's purpose that prevails." Proverbs 19:21 (TNIV)

It should have been a great Saturday afternoon of bowling. The youth group, with which I volunteer, was planning a major tournament of staff versus kids, and competition was going to be fierce. Trash talking abounded, and we adult staff members had our reputations to defend.

But that day turned out to be very rainy, and when we arrived at the bowling alley, not only was there a birthday party there, but other families had also come to bowl since the weather was bad. There were no lanes available.

Instead, we recruited a few parents and some college students who'd shown up to be drivers, and everyone went to Nickel City, a video-game arcade. It ended up being a fun outing.

I admit I got kind of frazzled with the last-minute organizing, and I remembered ruefully how our plans are not always God's plans. I always thought the verse referred to "big plans" such as what career to go into or whether to buy a house. A foiled bowling trip seemed like something too trivial for God to want to bother Himself with, and something I could handle by myself.

But I think the point of the verse isn't about big plans or little plans. God wants us to realize that in life, there will always be change, and that He is the one in charge. And sometimes we have to relinquish our sense of control and be flexible.

Jesus talked about the rich fool who built barns for his abundance of grain, making plans to eat, drink, and be merry, but died the next day. His plans took a major U-turn. His plans weren't God's plans.

FAITH STEP: *Whether you're a planner or not, are you able to graciously accept changes in plans? Are you flexible? Pray for Jesus to help you relinquish control and practice flexibility.*

—Camy Tang

JANUARY 9

"I saw the Lord always before me....
Therefore my heart is glad." Acts 2:25–26 (NIV)

*I*t's finally here! I wanted to dance and shout for joy. Instead, I sank onto the new mattress, this treasure I had yearned for after sleepless nights on our old, worn-out mattress. Oh, the promise of rejuvenating sleep and pain-free wake-ups. I could almost hear heavenly trumpets rejoicing with me.

I could see it now.... This mattress would launch my morning workouts to new levels. My children would arise and call me blessed because good sleep would grant me unending patience. This mattress would change our lives.

Anticipation...what a great gift from our ever-wise God.

Even before I spent a night on my new mattress my spirit was given a lift. And that's the great thing about anticipating—we can revel at the promise of a desire coming true.

Anticipation is timeless. The ancient Israelites anticipated the coming Messiah. Hannah, Elizabeth and Mary anticipated God's promises of children (1 Samuel 1:17–20; Luke 1:11–55). David rejoiced in his victory over Goliath before he ever flung the stone (1 Samuel 17:32–50). And we long for perfect eternity with our risen Jesus.

In addition to those big hopes, Jesus gives us reasons to anticipate the little things, like comfy mattresses. We can always look ahead of this moment's frustrations and find encouragement. Consider the joy of rest after a long day or finding new blooms in the flowerbed or the scent of a new season.

Expect more from this day; expect Jesus to show up.

FAITH STEP: *Think of something Jesus wants you to anticipate about tomorrow, believing that your hopes placed in His care will enrich this moment. Memorize Romans 15:7–13 (MSG): "May the God of green hope fill you up with joy, fill you up with peace, so that your believing lives, filled with the life-giving energy of the Holy Spirit, will brim over with hope!"*

—*Erin Keeley Marshall*

JANUARY 10

"For me to live is Christ, and to die is gain." Philippians 1:21

I teach literature classes at a local university, and one of my favorite things to teach is short fiction. There's a class in which we discuss "The Jilting of Granny Weatherall," a short story by Katherine Ann Porter, and "The Death of Ivan Ilyich," by Leo Tolstoy. The two stories illustrate perfectly the contrast between life and death.

On the surface, the stories are similar because in both, the main characters are dying of an incurable disease. However, in "The Jilting," Granny Weatherall also dies a spiritual death. She's a woman who has "weathered all" and lived a good life on earth, but in the end, her religion deserts her. Her death is described as a slow descent into night. In fear and bitterness of heart, she finally chooses to blow out the light, which represents her hope of salvation, and succumb to total darkness.

Ivan Ilyich has a pathetic physical life compared to Granny. He has no good relationships, and has lived mostly to make money as a lawyer in upper-class Russia. However, on his deathbed, he finally learns to live. His regrets are swallowed up in love. His fears are overcome by peace. He moves out of a dark tunnel toward the light, and he finds Jesus.

Every time I read these stories with my students I am struck by the choices the main characters make. At each of their critical moments, they are given the same choices I have every day: I can choose bitterness or acceptance. I can choose fear or I can choose peace. I can choose light or darkness. And my choices mean the difference between life and death.

FAITH STEP: *When you encounter the choice between life and death today—as you inevitably will—ask yourself: what can I do to choose Jesus, to choose life, today?*

—*Gwen Ford Faulkenberry*

JANUARY 11

"'Whoever serves me must follow me; and where I am, my servant also will be.'" John 12:26 (NIV)

*H*aving a baby at seventeen years old was hard. I had little money, I depended on others to babysit while I took college classes, and my boyfriend and friends continued enjoying their teen years without me. But with the hardship came an unexpected change—I dedicated my life to God. Once I felt God's love and forgiveness I wanted to serve Him with all that was in me, especially after I married and had more children. I volunteered in Sunday school and Vacation Bible School. I cooked at church. I led Bible studies and mentored young women.

Reading the story of Jesus' triumphal entry during the Passover festival, I understand the celebration. If I had been in that crowd, I would have been waving my palm branch the highest and singing praises the loudest. Yet it wasn't the people's excitement or service that Jesus valued.

Through the crowd, rumors spread about how Jesus had raised Lazarus from the dead. Visiting Greeks approached Jesus' disciples, wanting to rub shoulders, but the words out of Jesus' mouth weren't what anyone expected. Jesus didn't thank them for the praise. "Whoever serves me must follow me," He said.

I pause when I read those words. Those who serve must follow…not the other way around? In the years since I was a teen mom I've become a person who likes to "do" things for God. Serving means picking out activities that I can do in my own strength, like volunteering in the church nursery or making a meal for my pastor. Those things fit my schedule. The "following" has been harder. It means stepping out of my comfort zone and sharing the good news of Jesus with others.

With boughs in hand, those in the crowd were forced to make a decision—God's way or theirs. I've had to learn the same thing. I do celebrate that Jesus saved my soul when I was seventeen, but I also try to follow Him every day of my life. When I follow I'm not only doing something for God; I'm also allowing Him to work through me in amazing ways.

FAITH STEP: *Write down three things you do to serve God. Are you doing those things because God asked you to? Cross out any you're doing because someone asked and you didn't want to say no. Now, fill that space with an activity or mission God's asked you to follow Him in.*

—*Tricia Goyer*

JANUARY 12

*"What good is fasting when you keep on fighting and quarreling?
This kind of fasting will never get you anywhere with me." Isaiah 58:4 (NLT)*

As I write this, my stomach growls. For the fourth year in a row, our family is participating in what our church calls "the Five-Day Challenge," a modified fast in which we eat a diet similar to that of most of the world's poor: small portions of oatmeal, rice and beans, the occasional tortilla or handful of veggies. We add a small amount of chicken to our dinner portion.

Last night, day two, we got home late. My husband sat at the table, waiting for me to make dinner. I felt angry and resentful, stirring the beans, which overcooked and turned to mush. We got into a silly argument. My anger seethed and boiled over like the pot of beans. I am ashamed to admit that at one point I yelled at my husband, "Get off my case! Just give me some grace!"

Hunger makes you cranky. So this morning, I tried to remember why I engage in this annual modified fast. Isaiah 58 says we fast to share our food with the hungry, which is the idea behind this challenge—we take the money we would spend on groceries and donate it to provide food for the poor.

Fasting provides Jesus a little housecleaning opportunity, to clear away the clutter in your soul. This morning, I read Isaiah 58:4, and wept into my oatmeal. My fasting had led to quarreling. I was still trying to depend on my own strength to get through the day. I need Jesus to help me. I need to depend on Him like I typically depend on food.

FAITH STEP: *Try this challenge for only one day, where you eat a cup of plain oatmeal for breakfast, and a small portion of rice and beans for lunch and dinner. Read and meditate on all of Isaiah 58 during the day. Take the money you would have spent on meals for that day and donate it to a food pantry.*

—*Keri Wyatt Kent*

JANUARY 13

"The Lord is with you!…Go with the strength you have….
I am sending you!" Judges 6:12, 14 (NLT)

*I*t was one of my first speaking engagements to a crowd of strangers. I felt eleven again. Awkward. Self-conscious.

As I waited to be introduced, I tried mind over matter to calm my heart. Problem was, my mind wasn't feeling very confident. I scanned the audience of women—my peers—and reassured myself that I was one of them. I fit in fine. Even if that woman to my left looked so together…and the one over there looked a bit stern…and the woman next to her exuded such casual confidence.

No turning back, though. I stepped to the podium that was too small to hide behind, breathed a *Help me, Jesus*, and turned on the enthusiasm.

Why does insecurity come so much easier than confidence? No matter how old we get or how varied our life experiences are, none of us is ever far from our inner adolescent. Remember that gawky middle-school phase? If not, you're in the minority.

But you know what? Jesus loves the inner child in each of us, and He thrills to show Himself strong when we need a boost. In 2 Timothy 2:1 (CEV), Paul speaks of Jesus' caring nature when he encourages his young protégé, Timothy: "My child, Christ Jesus is kind, and you must let him make you strong."

As I cast my nerves aside during my talk, I felt spiritually hugged by Jesus. I found myself actually engaging the audience and even got a few laughs, which were at the appropriate times and—wonder of wonders—not at my expense!

Jesus' strength was enough for me that day, and He and I together accomplished the job He gave me to do.

Will you let yourself bask in His spiritual hug and watch as He does His work through you?

FAITH STEP: *Ask Jesus to challenge you today. Then feel His arms holding you and follow His lead.*

—*Erin Keeley Marshall*

JANUARY 14

"He took him outside and said, 'Look up at the heavens and count the stars—if indeed you can count them.' Then he said to him, 'So shall your offspring be.'" Genesis 15:5–6 (TNIV)

*D*espite living in Hawaii for my childhood—I know, lucky me!—I only saw the Milky Way once.

It was late at night—or rather, early in the morning. I happened to be outside in our backyard, staying up late with my parents' permission. The lights of our suburb were dimmed. I looked up…and drowned.

You know the feeling, right? Suddenly feeling so incredibly small, so incredibly *awed*. There were millions of stars, stretching from the roof of my house to the lychee-tree branches on the other side of the yard. I'd never seen so many in my entire life (all of ten years).

Before, I'd seen the night sky and stars through the little window in my room. But this sky was different. It wasn't as close to me as when there were rain clouds on a murky day. The sky was deep and fathomless, but adorned with the Milky Way draped across its shoulders. Suddenly, the sky was the limitless black of the universe, and I was just a speck.

And suddenly, God was so much *bigger* than how I'd thought of Him before.

This was the God who took on human flesh. I realized that Jesus was like the Milky Way cramming itself into my small body, instead of stretching across the black of space and time.

With a Lord like that, is there anything Jesus can't do for us?

I'd been trying to cram God into that little window in my room, thinking that was all He was. I had to go outside, like Abram, and see the majesty of God's universe.

FAITH STEP: *When we see God's limitless nature, rather than trying to limit Him in a window frame, we can trust Him more. We can believe in Him more. Where in your life can you trust your Jesus more?*

—*Camy Tang*

JANUARY 15

"Do you not know that you are God's temple and that God's Spirit dwells in you? If anyone destroys God's temple, God will destroy that person. For God's temple is holy, and you are that temple." 1 Corinthians 3:16–17 (NRSV)

Though Paul was speaking these words to the church at Corinth, they speak to us as well. We live in a body-conscious world populated with diet gurus, exercise clubs and beauty salons. Whole magazines are dedicated to healthy eating, stylish clothing and movie stars. As Christians we have another aspect to consider about our bodies. We are literally temples of God. The Holy Spirit dwells in us. We are His households!

The Old Testament temple was built with great care and expense. Gold, silver, bronze, iron, onyx and precious stones were used in abundance. Why? Because God dwelled there! It was His house. There would be nothing but the best for the King.

He also lives in us. "Those who love me will keep my word, and my Father will love them, and we will come to them and make our home with them" (John 14:23, NRSV). "And I will ask the Father, and he will give you another Advocate, to be with you for ever" (John 14:16, NRSV).

Think of it: God lives in me! I must be careful where I go, what I do and what I think about. Just as David made careful plans for the temple, I will tenderly care for the vessel I am for the Holy Spirit.

FAITH STEP: *Begin by choosing one thing to do that will improve the temple that is yours—exercise, positivity, healthy food—and make it a regular practice.*

—Judy Baer

JANUARY 16

"'Are you the king of the Jews?' asked Pilate. 'You have said so,' Jesus replied. The chief priests accused him of many things. So again Pilate asked him, 'Aren't you going to answer? See how many things they are accusing you of.' But Jesus still made no reply, and Pilate was amazed." Mark 15:2–5 (NIV)

$\mathscr{I}$ couldn't be more excited. After working with teenage mothers for years I decided to write a book to help them. I couldn't travel the country and personally help each young mother as I wanted to, but I hoped my words—in a small way—could do that for me.

After the book was published I e-mailed out a sample chapter to a group of young moms I had met online. For some reason, they assumed I'd stolen quotes from their online chats without permission. They accused me of many things and didn't listen when I tried to explain that the moms I quoted had known about the project, saw how their words were being used, and had approved.

After a few days of trying to explain myself, I was encouraged to keep silent. "You can talk until you're blue in the face but their minds are already set," an adviser told me.

It's hard when others accuse you. Our first reaction is to deny people's claims and try to explain what really happened. We want others to know we are right. We want to be justified, but sometimes that doesn't happen.

Jesus understood that no matter what He said or how much He tried to explain, Pilate wouldn't understand. Pilate's mind was focused on an earthly kingdom. Jesus' mind was on a final solution to the problem of sin and on a heavenly reign.

Jesus *not* defending himself got Pilate's attention. Jesus did have a point to prove, but He didn't do it with words. He did it by walking to the cross and spreading His arms wide.

Even though I'll never be a fraction as blameless as Jesus, I can follow His example. I can speak words that will share hope with others when it's needed, and I can stand silent during times when nothing I can say will change a disbelieving heart.

FAITH STEP: *The next time someone doesn't believe you, don't allow an argument to erupt. Instead follow Jesus' example—be silent and allow your actions to speak louder than your words.*

—Tricia Goyer

JANUARY 17

*"Another angel, who had a golden censer, came and stood at
the altar. He was given much incense to offer, with the prayers of
all God's people, on the golden altar before the throne. The smoke
of the incense, together with the prayers of God's people, went up
before God from the angel's hand." Revelation 8:3–4 (TNIV)*

There are many times that I feel like my prayers are useless. I repeat the same thing, day after day, and see no answer from God, no results.

Other times, I treat prayer like the least and last thing, when there's nothing else I can do: "I'll pray for you." I say it when I'm feeling helpless and hopeless.

When did prayer become like this for me?

Jesus prayed constantly. He would sometimes stay up all night to pray. He went away to lonely places to pray. He experienced everything we do, so I'm sure there were times He felt like God wasn't hearing Him. In the Garden of Gethsemane, He prayed for the cup of suffering to pass from Him, and His prayer wasn't answered.

In Revelation, the prayers of God's people are offered with incense on the altar. Our prayers are like incense—an aroma before God, pleasing Him, moving Him. The aroma becomes stronger the more we pray or the more intensely we pray.

Our prayers rise before God's throne. Our prayers reach Him.

So even if I feel like my prayers are worthless, or I've become repetitive, I have to remember that they're valuable; they can please God and move Him.

FAITH STEP: *Is your prayer life stagnant? Give it a new jolt of energy. Remember that your prayers are treasured, that they rise to God where He sits on His throne. Devote yourself to a certain amount of prayer every day this week, and make your prayers incense before God.*

—Camy Tang

JANUARY 18

"As Jesus looked up, he saw the rich putting their gifts into the temple treasury. He also saw a poor widow put in two very small copper coins. 'Truly I tell you,' he said, 'this poor widow has put in more than all the others. All these people gave their gifts out of their wealth; but she out of her poverty put in all she had to live on.'" Luke 21:1–4 (NIV)

"*L*et me throw in my two cents." I've said it often in conversation. Sadly, my best often feels like two cents' worth, especially when the needs of others seem mammoth. A friend battles cancer. A child has a learning disability. A spouse loses a job. A parent faces Alzheimer's. I want to help, but can my quiet prayers, meager strength and tiny acts of love really make a difference?

By myself, what I have to offer seems insignificant. Yet when the poor widow gave her two copper coins, Jesus saw the love and sacrifice and praised her gift. In fact, Jesus often reminds us of the value of small things.

I love the fact that God's economy is upside down. Whether it's a few pennies, or fishes and loaves, or a minuscule mustard seed, Jesus is able to take small, ordinary things and multiply them into more than we can imagine. The widow could have felt paralyzed by her poverty. She could have made excuses, could have justified not giving. Yet she put all she had into God's hands. Today when I'm faced with a problem or need beyond my ability to solve, I want to put my two cents into Jesus' hands and offer all that I am for His use.

FAITH STEP: *Prayerfully choose a ministry in your church or community and send a contribution, even if all you can share seems tiny. Ask God to multiply your efforts.*

—*Sharon Hinck*

JANUARY 19

"When Jesus' followers saw what was going to happen, they said, 'Lord, should we strike with our swords?' And one of them struck the servant of the high priest, cutting off his right ear. But Jesus answered, 'No more of this!' And he touched the man's ear and healed him." Luke 22:49–51 (TNIV)

I've been struggling with insulin resistance. It means my cells don't respond to insulin and don't intake the sugar in my bloodstream into the cells, and so my cells are starving. Poor cells!

At first I felt frustrated and alone, because I felt I had to heal my body myself. Granted, it was my terrible diet that caused the insulin resistance in the first place, but I still felt alone. After all, no one else can eat or not eat the right foods for me.

As I wallowed in self-pity and tried not to think about chocolate-chip cookies, I prayed half-heartedly. *Please, Lord, heal me from my insulin resistance.* Saying the prayer felt silly to me. It's not like I had cancer or a heart attack or a stroke. Why would Jesus care to heal me from my insulin resistance, which I had caused myself?

But then I remembered the priest whose ear Jesus had healed. An ear isn't huge like cancer, and the man wasn't deathly ill or particularly beloved like the other people Jesus had raised from the dead. This man was Jesus' enemy. And he wasn't an important man; he was simply a servant. But Jesus healed him anyway.

If Jesus healed a servant from a cut ear, He can heal my insulin resistance. Jesus cares about me. Jesus cares about my body.

FAITH STEP: *What are things in your life and your body that need healing, big or small? Jesus cares about you and your problems, no matter how trivial they might seem. Pray to Jesus about the small things in your life, and let Him help you.*

—*Camy Tang*

JANUARY 20

"While walking by the Sea of Galilee, he saw two brothers, Simon (who is called Peter) and Andrew his brother, casting a net into the sea, for they were fishermen. And he said to them, 'Follow me, and I will make you fishers of men.' Immediately they left their nets and followed him." Matthew 4:18–20 (ESV)

*I*n the Sunday-school classroom with the flannel-graph Jesus and the orange plastic chairs, I stood with the other "primary" kids and belted out the words, "I will make you fishers of men, fishers of men, fishers of men…" Our enthusiasm for singing was rivaled only by our passion for motions, which for this song included pantomiming casting our rods, and then reeling them in, over and over.

It may have been fun and burned off some six-year-old energy, but our exaggerated casting and reeling motions were woefully inaccurate. Unfortunately, such experiences shape us. This and other conversations about witnessing pointed to the idea that evangelism was meant to be undertaken individually, that it was akin in some way to hunting.

Peter, Andrew and their father never owned a hook, rod or reel. They fished with nets. And when Jesus used the metaphor of fishing for people, the image that would have come to Peter and Andrew's mind was just that—of a net. A net was typically cast over the side of a boat by two or three people. Fish were scooped, not hooked.

Francis Schaeffer once said, "Community is the final apologetic." What if he was right? What if winning others to Christ involves casting a net—with the help of others? And that net—cast by a community—gathers others into that community, where they experience life-changing love and grace? What if we thought not of "hooking" unbelievers, but of scooping them up into community where they are convinced not by arguments, but by seeing and experiencing the love of Jesus lived out?

FAITH STEP: *Today, pray about and engage in community that intentionally draws others in.*

—Keri Wyatt Kent

JANUARY 21

"Anyone, then, who knows the right thing to do and fails to do it, commits sin." James 4:17 (NRSV)

"If we confess our sins, he who is faithful and just will forgive us our sins and cleanse us from all unrighteousness." 1 John 1:9 (NRSV)

"Give thanks in all circumstances; for this is the will of God in Christ Jesus for you." 1 Thessalonians 5:18 (NRSV)

I confess that sometimes I treat the Lord like a heavenly ATM. I come to Him with a list of requests and expect Him to fulfill my needs in the same way I punch my PIN number into my bank's ATM and anticipate the cash I want to mysteriously appear. I neglect to talk to Him when things are going well, but I come running to Jesus when things go wrong and blurt out my requests.

I'm getting it all backward, am I not? I must learn to praise Him first, to tell Him how much I love Him. I don't say it nearly often enough. He is the King of Kings and Lord of Lords and He cares about me!

This is astounding. I'm a sinner. I've done things that don't please Him. I need to confess them to Him—both the things I did and the things I didn't do, the sins of commission and those of omission.

I usually thank Jesus for the good things in my life but neglect to thank Him for the troubles I have. It seems counterintuitive to be grateful for losing a job, for illness or distress, but Christ has His hand on that as well. He is able to redeem every situation and convert what is troubling into something positive. He asks me to trust Him and to give thanks in every circumstance.

First I will praise. Then I will give thanks and confess my sins. Only then will I come to the Lord with my appeals and entreaties. He is able to make my prayers less about myself and more about others, deepen my prayer life and bless the time I spend with Him.

FAITH STEP: *Organize your prayer with intention today. Praise Him first. Thank Him second. Confess. Then bring your appeals to Him.*

— Judy Baer

JANUARY 22

*"Dear children, let us not love with words or speech
but with actions and in truth." 1 John 3:18 (NIV)*

*I*t's not about me. It's not about me. It's not about me.

Sometimes, though, at 2:00 am, I want it to be about me. Even if it's my sweet little kiddos waking me because they need something.

Before I became a mother, I had heard other parents say they didn't know the depths of their own selfishness until a child entered their life. I had heard them say that, but I still didn't get it…until I got it.

Take last night, for instance. The first wake-up came from my son's sneezing fit. As I dragged myself from beneath the warm covers, exasperation at myself for forgetting his allergy medicine blended with compassion for him and his suffering nose. After another couple of stirrings to refill my daughter's water cup and comfort dreams of monsters, I was tuckered out.

Every time I have to get out of bed at 2:00 am, I know my body and mind will pay for it in loss of energy and clear thinking the next day. I wonder how I'll be able to get things done that need doing.

However, through the blessings of family, Jesus is growing another blessing in me—the ability to experience Him providing for me as I provide for others. When I release my frustrated moments to Him, trading them in for a quieted heart, He proves Psalm 23 to me. He miraculously calms me and spreads a table of abundant mercy before me. He smoothes the day, and toxic, selfish emotions don't suffocate my limited resources. As hard as selfless giving can be, heart growth is a sweet experience.

As He blesses me, He is making me a blessing to others. And while I have a long way to go, I can't help but be thankful to be stretched.

FAITH STEP: *How did Jesus model selfless living? How is "selfless loving" redundant? See 1 Corinthians 13:1–13.*

—Erin Keeley Marshall

JANUARY 23

"I am the light of the world. Whoever follows me will never walk in darkness, but will have the light of life." John 8:12 (NIV)

*N*ot long ago I was sitting at a ballgame when a woman I barely knew sat down beside me. I smiled at her and said hello, just being polite. She seemed to want to talk, but I tried to make it obvious that I didn't. I wasn't there to make friends. I was there to watch my kid play basketball.

The woman finally got the message around halftime. She turned to someone else—anyone else—who would listen and act as if they cared what she had to say. I pushed her further to the periphery of my brain as our team went on to win the game. Harper ran over to me to celebrate his victory, and we hooted and hollered all the way home.

The next day at church a friend of mine spoke about Jesus being the light of the world, and how when He comes into our lives He doesn't provide just enough light for us. Instead, He gives us all He has, and that's enough light to share with everyone. We read the Scripture, "Do not forget to do good and to share with others, for with such sacrifices God is pleased" (Hebrews 13:16, NIV). I thought about that lady at the ballgame and how needy she was. And I thought about how I just turned away, not even considering what Jesus would do with her.

It's not that I believe He wanted me to ignore my child's ballgame; I don't. But I'm pretty sure He wouldn't have ignored that woman's need. Being Jesus, He'd have found a way to manage both, even if it meant inviting her and her kid for ice cream—or perhaps a little tea and sympathy—after the game.

FAITH STEP: *Is there someone in darkness who needs to see the light of Jesus in you today?*

—*Gwen Ford Faulkenberry*

JANUARY 24

"Work willingly at whatever you do, as though you were working for the Lord rather than for people. Remember that the Lord will give you an inheritance as your reward, and that the Master you are serving is Christ." Colossians 3:23–24 (NLT)

*W*hen I was in elementary school, star charts and contests motivated me. One summer I read more books than any other kid in our town and my picture made it in the newspaper. In Girl Scouts, I got a certificate and a stuffed animal for all the boxes of cookies I sold. During Vacation Bible School, I won a board game for learning the books of the Bible.

It has been hard not to focus on rewards in my ministry. My attitude can change like the tide if I get a good review or a bad one. Sometimes I'm bummed if I've poured work into a project and others don't notice as I think they should.

I don't get a certificate or another trinket as I serve Jesus. An eternal inheritance is my reward. And Jesus, of course, doesn't put a star on a chart for the things we do right. Instead, He is the one who will shine bright in our lives now, and for eternity. I need to remember that. I need to remember that He is the one I work for, and pleasing Him is enough.

FAITH STEP: *When is the last time you worked hard and didn't get the reward you deserved? Think about that time and consider Jesus looking down on you with approval. "Well done, good and faithful servant." Write a prayer committing to Him your work and your desire to serve others for His approval.*

—Tricia Goyer

JANUARY 25

"Stoop down and reach out to those who are oppressed. Share their burdens, and so complete Christ's law." Galatians 6:2 (MSG)

*B*ecause of where I live, it is easy for me to avoid "the oppressed." I know there are welfare families living within a ten-minute drive of my suburban neighborhood, but I usually drive past, not into, those apartment complexes. Usually. But not always.

Last winter, I got to know a welfare mom. Her husband had died of cancer when she was pregnant with her fifth child. Her story was sad, even horrific.

We ended up taking this mom's one- and two-year-old sons into our home for a couple of weeks. Our quiet, steady home became chaotic, our world tilted, and we fell in love with those two little boys. The younger was happy-go-lucky, the older more temperamental. We were his fourth foster home in less than a year—a year in which his father had died. When frustrated, his limited verbal skills became even more limited, so he would simply scream. For five or ten minutes straight.

But in the mornings, when I'd be up writing, he'd climb out of the portable crib he slept in, and wander down the hall to my room, peeking in cautiously. I'd always greet him with a gentle "good morning, buddy," and he would scurry over and climb onto my lap, cuddling against my shoulder.

The boys are now back with their mother. But sharing their burdens for a while forever changed us. Loving them gave me a chance to love Jesus. When we stoop down to help the oppressed, we are the ones who are lifted. When we love the poor, we complete Christ's love. This truth you learn only by doing. When you touch the oppressed, you touch Jesus.

FAITH STEP: *How can you help the oppressed? Perhaps the first step is to figure out ways in which you avoid those in need, and to begin to change that.*

—Keri Wyatt Kent

JANUARY 26

*"Therefore, if anyone is in Christ, the new creation has come:
the old has gone, the new is here!" 2 Corinthians 5:17 (NIV)*

As an author, I've made it a point of studying the inner thoughts and feelings of people. To create a good character in a novel you need to understand a character's flaws and motivation.

In my own life my flaws and ungodly motivations are things I didn't think too much about. In fact, I wanted to forget them. There are times in my life where I've stumbled and bumbled. There are things in my past I wish I could forget for good.

The good news is that even though I can't forget, when I confess my sins to Jesus, those things are remembered no more. Isaiah 43:25 says, "I, even I, am he who blots out your transgressions, for my own sake, and remembers your sins no more" (NIV).

In every novel there is a turning point. It's a moment when the character makes a drastic decision that turns the tide of the story. Jesus turned the tide when He sacrificed Himself for the sins of all men. My turning point came when I realized that sacrifice was for me.

I can't change the past, but I can accept who I am now. I am a new creation. Jesus Christ is in me. My inner thoughts and feelings, even my motivations, will forever be changed because of that.

FAITH STEP: *Think about your life before Jesus. If it was a book, what title would you give it? Then, think about your life after Jesus; what would the new title be?*

—*Tricia Goyer*

JANUARY 27

"The whole town gathered at the door, and Jesus healed many
who had various diseases.... Very early in the morning,
while it was still dark, Jesus got up, left the house and went off
to a solitary place, where he prayed." Mark 1:33–35 (NIV)

Life gets crowded sometimes. The needs of family, the pressures of work, the delicate drama of friendships—all create a pressure on us that can feel overwhelming.

Jesus experienced and understood this. His days were full, and He took it in stride when the whole town showed up at His doorstep looking for help and healing. He willingly gave them what they needed.

But the next morning, He did something some of us might consider selfish, if we dared to do it ourselves. He escaped from the people and their demands. He walked out (for a little while) on even His closest friends.

Jesus came to earth to die for us, but also to live in front of us. If we want to be close to Him, the only way to do it is to imitate Him—to live as He would in our place, to make His spiritual practices ours.

Throughout the Gospels, this refrain echoes: "Jesus went to a solitary place." Jesus regularly engaged in the spiritual discipline of solitude. What drove Him away from the adoring but demanding crowd? Certainly not obligation or guilt. Rather, He valued His relationship with the Father more than the approval of people.

When it feels like the whole town is gathered at your door, asking for your help, it can be seductive—we love being needed, even if it wears us out a bit. When we follow Jesus to a solitary place, we are replenished, paradoxically, by the privilege of being needy ourselves—and realizing that only God can meet those needs. In Jesus' presence, we gain proper perspective on what really matters.

FAITH STEP: *Tomorrow, get up early to spend some time in solitude, alone with Jesus. Enjoy His presence in a simple and quiet way.*

—Keri Wyatt Kent

JANUARY 28

"For the accuser of our brothers and sisters, who accuses them before our God day and night, has been hurled down." Revelation 12:10 (TNIV)

One thing I really struggle with is guilt, and I see this often in other women as well. It seems sometimes that I'm prey to guilt more than I should be. I rehash things I should have done. I feel like a failure. The guilt comes back every hour to haunt me, to make my stomach feel like it's full of lead.

I know we're all human, we're all imperfect. And yet I find myself striving to do absolutely everything right. When I fail, or when I fail someone I care about, it eats away at me. I don't think about how I can learn from my mistakes; instead, I revisit what I did wrong, over and over again.

Sound familiar?

I'm starting to realize that when guilt keeps returning to me, it's like a voice accusing me inside my head over and over. And Satan is the Accuser. Revelations 12:10 reminds us that Jesus, the Lamb of God, has triumphed over Satan, our enemy and accuser.

It doesn't mean Satan doesn't take potshots at us. But if I remember Jesus' victory and love, the guilt and accusations melt away. I am covered by Jesus' blood—it forgives and transforms me.

FAITH STEP: *What guilt is plaguing you? Pray to God to be able to release it, to trust in Jesus' blood that has washed you white as snow.*

—*Camy Tang*

JANUARY 29

"His master replied, 'Well done, good and faithful servant! You have been faithful with a few things; I will put you in charge of many things. Come and share your master's happiness!'" Matthew 25:21 (TNIV)

*J*esus' parable of the three stewards talks about bags of gold that the master gave to his servants for safekeeping. But when praising the servant, the master uses the word things rather than specifying the bags of gold—he's praising the servant for being faithful with the responsibilities given to him, not the money given to him.

Jesus has given me many "things." I have my job, which I love. I have my husband and family. I have my marathon running, which I recently started. I have my work with the church youth group. None of these requires gold so I never equated them with the things the master talks about in the parable. But then I realized that he didn't specify gold. He praised the servant for being faithful with a few things.

I started being more faithful and responsible with what Jesus has given to me. I strive for more discipline and efficiency at work. I try to more deliberately love my family. I am faithful in my running routine and will schedule around it when I can. I give 110 percent to my youth group.

And Jesus started blessing me even more. I got more responsibilities at work. My family dynamics are stronger. I'm getting better at my running, and my youth group work has expanded to college students too. My life is full of "things" I love.

FAITH STEP: *What has Jesus given to you? How can you be more faithful with those "things"? Pick three of them and work on being more faithful this week.*

—*Camy Tang*

JANUARY 30

*"You're blessed when you're content with just who you are—
no more, no less. That's the moment you find yourselves proud
owners of everything that can't be bought." Matthew 5:5 (MSG)*

*"But if we have food and clothing, we will be content with that. Those who
want to get rich fall into temptation and a trap." 1 Timothy 6:8–9 (NIV)*

*M*y husband and I both have cell phones that are several years old.
They still work, much to the chagrin of my children, who work and save
to upgrade their phones regularly. My husband's even once fell out of his
shirt pocket and into a tub of water, but even that couldn't destroy it.

I'm happy with my old phone—it can make calls and text, and that's
sufficient. I can use my laptop or desktop to send e-mail or surf the Web.
I've attained phone contentment.

In other areas of life, contentment is incomplete. I'm content with our
house—I don't want a bigger one. But I long to fix ours up a bit, to replace
the carpets or the old furniture, upgrade the kitchen. I'm happy with my
thirteen-year-old Toyota, but I'd kind of like a newer SUV.

Everything in our culture pushes hard against the value of contentment.
Advertising's goal is not to inform us about products so much as it is to
make us discontent with the products we already own, possibly even the
one we bought last week.

Lisa Graham McMinn writes in *The Contented Soul*, "Being content
does not mean we are satisfied. In fact, to be content is to know we will
always be groaning this side of eternity. Yet when we believe that fullness
will come, that there is more than this life, we live with contentment."

The "more" she writes of is Jesus. His love and grace are sufficient. Resting in Him, we can be content.

FAITH STEP: *In which areas of your life do you experience the most discontent-
ment? What would it take for you to be content?*

—Keri Wyatt Kent

JANUARY 31

"This is how we know that we live in him and he in us:
He has given us of his Spirit." 1 John 4:13 (NIV)

"I don't have it in me," I whispered to God yesterday.

Several friends had shared happy news about successes, achievements and blessings. I longed to celebrate with them. But in my secret heart, the contrast with my own recent loss and pain kindled an ugly temptation to self-pity.

I could keep my voice bright and fake it. I could say the appropriate things. But I wanted to coax my heart to match, to find sincere joy for my friends.

How does a man who is out of work celebrate when his friend gets a fantastic new job? How does a woman grieving a miscarriage attend a friend's baby shower? How does someone crippled with pain wholeheartedly rejoice over another's miraculous healing, without that whisper deep in the soul: "Lord, what about me?"

But as I confessed, "I don't have it in me," the recognition filled me like a deep breath of peace. Of course, I didn't have the power in myself, just as I didn't have the power to forgive those who hurt me, or sing a song of praise through a throat raw with tears, or to serve day after day in small ways that seemed to offer no evidence of results. I can't do any of it.

But Jesus can. And He lives in me.

My prayer changed. "Lord, love them through me. Change my heart to be more like yours. Lift my eyes off my needs so I can rejoice for my friends. It's not in me…but it's in You."

And He answered. He helped me celebrate the good things He is doing in the lives of others, enabled me to respond genuinely, even to take a few actions to support and promote others.

I don't know what moral challenges I'll face today, but I hope I'll remember not to face them in my own feeble power. It's not in me. But it's in Him.

FAITH STEP: *Ask Jesus to empower you to celebrate the blessings of another today.*

—Sharon Hinck

February

FEBRUARY 1

" 'Go,' Jesus replied, 'your son will live.' The man took
Jesus at his word and departed." John 4:50 (TNIV)

*H*ave you ever noticed how sometimes, when Jesus heals someone, He asks the person to do something first? For the official whose son was sick, Jesus told him to go home.

Can you imagine being that poor man? Just go? Just walk away? This healer wasn't even going to come see his son to heal him? What was up with that? Didn't He need to touch his son or say an incantation? Instead He was telling him to go home? Home was a day's journey away. What if his son wasn't healed? He'd have lost all that time going back home when he could have gone to get another healer.

Jesus might have captured the man's eyes with a level stare, waiting to see if he would do what He told him to do. The official's feelings would be warring inside him. Could he trust this man? Should he insist Jesus come back to his house with him?

In the end, he took Jesus at His word and did what He told him to do, and his son was healed. Sometimes, Jesus asks us to take Him at His word, to act on faith, to walk out and believe that He will do what He says He'll do. The miracle comes after we act, not before.

FAITH STEP: *Pray for Jesus to help you to be able to take Him at His word, to act on faith when He wants you to. Ask Jesus to help you trust Him and see His power in your life.*

—Camy Tang

FEBRUARY 2

*"Come to Me, all who are weary and heavy-laden,
and I will give you rest." Matthew 11:28 (NASB)*

*H*ave you ever been bone-tired? I don't mean just sleepy. I mean drained in your spirit. At the point of exhaustion all the way down into your bones.

I'm feeling that way right now. I've got a husband, three little kids, extended family, church, a full-time job and a writing habit. This past week we've been practicing for a musical at church and I'm the director. My husband hurt his back and has not felt well. We have a big yard and lots of farm animals to tend. My two oldest kids have had tests in school and several extracurricular activities. We went camping—without my husband— over the weekend, and I did not get much writing done when we got back, as I had planned. Other duties called. My deadline is fast approaching, and I can barely hold my head up.

As I ponder how to inspire others, it is clear I need some inspiration myself. I close my eyes and listen for the still, small voice. Faithful as always, He speaks to me from the pages of my memory: Come to Me. I will give you rest.

The kind of rest Jesus is talking about here is not sleep, although sleep is necessary to physical and emotional health. But what the weary person needs goes much deeper than that. He speaks to us on a spirit level and says, "Come to Me." In Him we find the source of rest and peace.

FAITH STEP: *Come to Jesus. Take His yoke and learn from Him, and find rest for your soul.*

—Gwen Ford Faulkenberry

FEBRUARY 3

*"Listen to the Lord who created you.… The one who formed you says,
'…I have called you by name; you are mine.'" Isaiah 43:1 (NLT)*

"Woo-hoo, Mommy!"

I blinked away tears of joy at my little ones' cheers, unsure what I had done to earn their accolades. Maybe I had got us out the door without losing my cool, or possibly it was that extra cookie after lunch, or maybe I'd finished vacuuming.

I didn't have time to bask before a familiar voice nagged: "It's about time you showed more patience…. You're a bad mom for giving them too many sweets…. You ought to vacuum twice a week—and dust daily."

Why is it so hard to accept acceptance? You know that voice too, don't you? Society and human nature tell us to work, work, work to earn, earn, earn.

But Isaiah 43:1 breathes fresh air! Although spoken to the Israelites, it holds a truth for all God's followers.

"The Lord who created you." That phrase catches my spirit in a cozy embrace. My Maker didn't just toss me together, and He still takes personal interest in who I am becoming.

I get even more excited about what comes next: "I have called you by name; you are mine." I'm His! Jesus echoed His Father's sentiments in John 10:3, 7–10. I'm not perfect, but He claims me as His own. He accepts me, all the while helping me grow to be like Him.

Do you really get that He accepts you if you are His? Go ahead and accept His acceptance of you—bask in it!

FAITH STEP: *In pencil, list circumstances that trigger the wicked voice of self-criticism. Then in ink (never to be erased!) list how your life would be changed by truly accepting that Jesus accepts you.*

—*Erin Keeley Marshall*

FEBRUARY 4

"Love one another as if your lives depended on it." 1 Peter 1:22 (MSG)

*Y*esterday my husband and I worked outside preparing a place for our new chicken coop. We cleared a spot at the edge of the yard that had previously been wild. I thought it was just woods and underbrush, but we discovered that it was primarily a patch of briars. Mean ones. I have the scratches to prove it.

Stone had a rock rake, and as he raked the briars and underbrush into a burn pile, my job was to clip the briars loose from the ground; otherwise they could not be raked. While doing this job, I was amazed at the range of the briars. They were a tangled mess. Almost impenetrable.

Several spiritual applications came to me as I was playing pioneer woman. At one point, I was reminded of my favorite poem by William Blake, called "The Garden of Love":

> I went to the Garden of Love,
> And saw what I never had seen:
> A chapel was built in the midst,
> Where I used to play on the green.
>
> And the gates of this Chapel were shut,
> And "Thou shalt not" writ over the door;
> So I turned to the Garden of Love,
> That so many sweet flowers bore,
>
> And I saw it was filled with graves,
> And tomb-stones where flowers should be:
> And Priests in black gowns were walking their rounds,
> And binding with briars my joys and desires.

If we think of the community of faith as a garden of love, the idea of briars choking out joy is pretty scary. Sadly, a lot of people experience this. Sometimes we get so caught up in doctrines and rules that we forget what the garden is for. Peter reminds us in the above verse that we're supposed to be all about love.

FAITH STEP: *What's your contribution to the community of believers? Determine today to be a flower, not a briar, in the garden of God's love.*

—Gwen Ford Faulkenberry

FEBRUARY 5

"When he arrived at the house of Jairus, he did not let anyone go in with him except Peter, John and James, and the child's father and mother. Meanwhile, all the people were wailing and mourning for her. 'Stop wailing,' Jesus said. 'She is not dead but asleep.' They laughed at him, knowing that she was dead. But he took her by the hand and said, 'My child, get up!' Her spirit returned, and at once she stood up. Then Jesus told them to give her something to eat." Luke 8:51–55 (NIV)

I was just out of college when my father died after a torturous battle with cancer. Surgeries, chemo, remissions and reoccurrences had created a rollercoaster of dread in our family. I knew the promise of eternal life, but even so, as I stood by his side in the ICU as the monitors marked his life ebbing away in remorseless numbers, death was no longer a theological discussion but a devastating reality.

During the immediate grief after my father's death, and after other losses I faced, I sometimes felt a flare of anger when I read about Jesus raising Jairus' daughter. He has proven Himself stronger than death, so why not return my loved one? I wondered if there were others in that village who had lost a child or a spouse, who marveled at this miracle even as a tiny part of their hearts cried, "What about my loss?"

One day I brought my confusion and longing to Jesus. "You've healed. You've raised the dead. My father fought so hard. Why didn't you defeat death for him?"

And His soft whisper spoke to my heart: "I did."

Jesus granted Jairus' daughter a few more years on earth, but one day she would face death again. And then He would defeat it permanently, as He did for my father. As He offers to do for each of us. Now when I read this story I celebrate this foretaste of the day He will take my hand and say, "My child, get up!" and welcome me into eternal life.

FAITH STEP: *Have you watched Jesus do something marvelous in someone else's life and wondered if He's overlooked your need? Tell Him about your pain, and let Him comfort you. Then send a compassionate note to someone you know who is grieving a loss.*

—*Sharon Hinck*

FEBRUARY 6

Jesus replied, "Go back and report to John what you hear and see: The blind receive sight, the lame walk, those who have leprosy are cleansed, the deaf hear, the dead are raised, and the good news is proclaimed to the poor." Matthew 11:4–5 (NIV)

I have a confession. I often wonder what God is up to, like when my husband and I finally decided to adopt a baby girl from China and then the wait extended from one year to three and beyond. (We're still waiting.) Seriously, God, you placed adoption on our hearts only to have us wait?

Jesus' friend John wondered what God was up to too. "When John, who was in prison, heard about the deeds of the Messiah, he sent his disciples to ask him, 'Are you the one who is to come, or should we expect someone else?'" (Matthew 11:2–3, NIV).

Jesus' answer to John wasn't something He pulled out of thin air. When Jesus spoke of the deaf hearing and lame walking John no doubt remembered the words of the prophet Isaiah: "Your God will come...then will the eyes of the blind be opened and the ears of the deaf unstopped. Then will the lame leap like a deer, and the mute tongue shout for joy" (Isaiah 35:4–6, NIV).

For someone who understood Scripture as John did, Jesus' message was powerful.

There are times in my life when I've questioned, "Jesus, are You the one?" Are You the one who called us to adoption? Are You the one who can take away my disappointment over the wait and wipe away my tears?

In my moments of doubting, Jesus gave me an answer similar to John's: "Haven't you seen what I've done?" Memories stirred in my mind of the times in the past He showed up. His Word reminded me to expect Him in this situation too. As I relinquished my plan and timetable to God, another miracle happened—a birth mom approached us about adopting her baby. So even though we're still waiting for one child, in the end we will be blessed with two!

Jesus came performing miracles not for His sake, but for mine. I can relinquish my will, knowing He has the perfect plan. When I look to Him I don't need to worry about getting my hopes up. Believing in Him, I will never be disappointed.

FAITH STEP: *When is a time you saw God do something amazing in your life? Before you go to sleep tonight find at least one person to share that story with.*

—*Tricia Goyer*

FEBRUARY 7

"Everyone who is called by My name…whom I have created for My glory, whom I have formed, even whom I have made." Isaiah 43:7 (NASB)

$\mathscr{I}$ was reading from Denise Austin's newest diet book, and I began to tell my children about our menu for the week. We were all going to follow Denise's plan. It would be new and exciting!

They looked at me as if I were crazy. "Who's Denise?"

I showed them the picture of the fitness guru, flexing her abs in a two-piece bathing suit on the cover of the book. "This is who I'm going to look like. I'm going to eat like Denise so I can have a body like Denise."

"Good luck with that, Mommy." Grace grinned at me. At age ten, she's been around the block, and is old enough now to take my fitness experiments with a grain of salt.

"You scoff, but soon you will call me Mommy Denise."

My two younger kids were appalled.

"I don't want you to look like her," Harper said.

Adelaide chimed in. "Me neither Mommy! I like you for my mommy. Not Denise!"

I assured them that even if I lost weight I would not become Denise. (Alas!) But they would have none of it. They even went so far as to confiscate my book.

I'm not sure what they had against the woman—after all, she helps lots of people. But I suspect the reaction came from a place of deep loyalty and love for what is theirs. Chunky, soft, imperfect, but devoted to them nonetheless—Mommy.

Their desire was to see me stay the same, even if changing would be an outward improvement.

What a picture of God's unwavering love. While I recognize that He is always inwardly transforming us into the image of His Son, the truth is that He made us. He sees His creation and calls it good. There are no mistakes. He loves us just the way we are!

FAITH STEP: *Spend some time today meditating on the truth: In Jesus, you are loved. Valued. Accepted. You don't have to be anything else except what He's made you to be.*

—*Gwen Ford Faulkenberry*

FEBRUARY 8

*"Don't pick on people, jump on their failures, criticize their faults—
unless, of course, you want the same treatment. That critical
spirit has a way of boomeranging." Matthew 7:1–2 (MSG)*

It's unfortunate in our culture that many people outside of the church say they would rather stay outside of it. Why? Because they perceive Christians as judgmental or critical.

Jesus' words in Matthew are often translated "judge not, lest you be judged." It's easy for me to skim over this command, checking it off my list without really examining my attitude—I'm not judgmental. I am merely standing up for what is right, calling sin what it is. I'm loving the sinner but hating the sin.

Really? As I reflected on this verse, I had to ask myself: What do I think of people who vote differently than I do? Who live a different lifestyle? And how do I treat my family? Do I point out their flaws? Criticize?

I love this translation because it spells out the specifics of what judgment is: being unkind and critical. And it also tells us that judgment is like a boomerang—it will come back to us. I realized that sometimes, this pretty accurately describes how I treat those closest to me. I can be critical of other's faults—and then I can pretend I'm doing it to help them grow into a better person. Ouch. That hits a bit closer to home.

I've been judged by other Christians, and it hurts. But rather than moaning that other Christians are judgmental, I need to ask God to show me where I am being judgmental, and repent of that.

FAITH STEP: *Today, choose not to criticize anyone—even if they make a mistake. Notice how they respond to you. Is there a connection?*

—Keri Wyatt Kent

FEBRUARY 9

"God, who said, 'Let there be light in the darkness,' has made this light shine in our hearts so we could know the glory of God that is seen in the face of Jesus Christ." 2 Corinthians 4:6 (NLT)

"Mom, things just aren't working out for me today."

Since we had spent the day together and it had seemed to be a pretty good one, my curiosity was piqued. "What hasn't worked out for you, hon?"

"I didn't get to go to the jump house, and then I didn't get to play at the playground."

I stifled a smirk. If all the world could have such troubles…

"Well, sweetheart, I didn't know you wanted to do those things. What about all the fun things we did instead?"

My offer of a different perspective was met with a weary sigh. So he wasn't quite ready to look at the day in a new light. I had to admit I understood his slump. After all, I often miss out on joy because I let my focus wander off track.

Perspective is a powerful thing, isn't it? For good or bad, we choose how we see the world. Perspective can be an asset or a liability to our health, relationships, work, even our spirituality. Especially our spirituality.

Jesus is the great perspective-shifter. Through His life and death, He offers us the ability to see through any depth of darkness. 2 Corinthians 4 describes how those who don't know Him as Savior are unable to see His light and enjoy His perspective.

If you belong to him, take a moment to celebrate the soul freedom he offers from whatever drags down your thoughts; look through the clouds at the Sonshine.

FAITH STEP: *Read 2 Corinthians 4, and ask Jesus to help you see His light more clearly in your circumstances.*

—*Erin Keeley Marshall*

FEBRUARY 10

"A bruised reed he will not break, and a smoldering wick he will not snuff out." Isaiah 42:3 (NIV)

My wedding ring was bent into a strange oval shape from doing chin-ups as part of an ill-conceived burst of fitness fervor. For months I tried to ignore the chafing and poor fit, telling myself, "It's not that bad. It's almost round." Then for the next few months I kept hoping the ring would ease back to its round shape somehow, as if gold could remember its intended design and compensate for being squashed. The ring didn't cooperate, and reminded me of the damage each time I washed up for dinner or glanced down at my hand.

Our budget was tight, and I was afraid to bring the ring to a jeweler for repairs we couldn't afford.

Finally, while wandering a mall on our date night, my husband and I stopped at a jewelry store, timidly asking what would need to be done to fix the ring. After I pried it from my finger, the jeweler slid the gold band onto a tapered post, tapped it gently with a mallet, and handed it back—good as new. No charge.

Months of discomfort and worry could have been avoided if I'd only known how easily the ring could be fixed. It made me realize how often I've held back from God with my warped habits, bent intentions and lopsided motives that needed repair. I'm ashamed of the damage I've caused and afraid of the cost of restoration. But when I finally face Him, bringing the crookedness of my life, His forgiveness is instant—and already paid for.

I can place my mistakes and failures into His hands and trust His gentleness.

FAITH STEP: *Are you feeling bent or bruised in some aspect of your life? Invite Jesus' gentle hands to bring restoration today.*

—Sharon Hinck

FEBRUARY 11

*Peter asked, "Lord, why can't I follow you now?
I will lay down my life for you." John 13:37 (NIV)*

I wanted a boyfriend badly. I was in my early twenties and horribly lonely. All my friends had found nice guys and I was the only one without a love interest.

So I did what other hormonal, immature, desperate women do—I settled for a guy who was interested in me. It didn't matter that he wasn't a Christian and didn't even want to understand my faith. He was available; he was cute. That's all I cared about.

It ended up being a colossal mistake. I'm sure you can see the ending—regretful woman struggles to break up with a guy who's leading her to do what God doesn't want her to do. It took a lot of time and several mistakes, but I finally did break up with him.

It caused damage to my relationship with Jesus that took a long time to heal. And isn't that always how it is when we jump the gun rather than waiting on God?

Peter asked Jesus why he couldn't follow Him—why he couldn't do what he wanted to do. But sometimes that waiting period is exactly what we need.

Sometimes we can see why that waiting period is necessary, but sometimes we can't, and that's when we get impatient and try to run ahead of God. I know how hard and frustrating it can be, but we have to hold steady and wait for God to move first. Otherwise, the consequences of jumping the gun can be a pile of regrets.

FAITH STEP: *Are you impatient in a waiting period of your own? Pray to Jesus—be honest and vulnerable, lay it all out before Him. Ask Him to help you to wait and just trust in His timing.*

—*Camy Tang*

FEBRUARY 12

"The Word became flesh and made his dwelling among us." John 1:14 (NIV)

As a novelist, I've always appreciated the power of words. Words can immerse a reader in a setting, evoke emotion, and establish connections. One of the key skills that fiction writers discover is that it's more effective to "show" rather than "tell." If a writer paints a scene where the hero pauses to help a child with a skinned knee, we get a more effective glimpse of the character's kindness than if the narrator spent several sentences telling us about the hero's sensitive and caring qualities. The slump of a mother's shoulders by the hospital bed of her child invites us deeper into her emotional state than a line telling us, "She felt sad."

Teachers also know the importance of showing rather than just telling. Students might yawn and let their attention drift to the closest window during a long lecture. Visual aids help keep them engaged. Hands-on participation helps even more. A sixth-grader who builds a topographical model of South America, listens to pan flute music, and tastes recipes from Brazil and Peru will remember more about what he learned than a student who reads a chapter of facts about the continent.

Words have power—God spoke the universe into being. But words also have limitations. Our attention drifts. We misunderstand. Or we struggle to sort out the vital words from among the clamor of voices around us.

So God did what the best novelists and teachers strive to do. He brought the truth to life. Jesus, the Word, came to show us—not just tell us—God's love and plan of redemption. The embodiment of grace walked among us. He touched lepers, embraced disciples, broke bread. He laughed and cried and prayed. And He died and rose again. The tangible incarnation of God's story of sacrifice, mercy and love.

FAITH STEP: *Think of one way to show others your love today.*

—Sharon Hinck

FEBRUARY 13

"Then Jesus stood up again and said to the woman, 'Where are your accusers? Didn't even one of them condemn you?... Neither do I. Go and sin no more.'" John 8:10–11 (NLT)

I pulled my protesting son off the kitchen chair and headed to the "sit stool," which was out of everyone else's hearing. Discontent with only half of his friend Gracie's graham crackers, he wanted all of them and his own as well. It was time for a talk.

Madder than ever at the embarrassment of a timeout, he continued his complaints while I sat him on my lap, determined to be the adult and handle this calmly.

"Paxton, you're a kind boy."

Suddenly he was listening.

"Now I want to see you act like it."

His thumb went in his mouth, a sure sign that my sweet boy was back. He relaxed into me for a moment before responding. "Mom, Grathee can have all of my cwackers," he managed with a thumby lisp.

Stunned, I explained that he didn't have to give all the crackers away; he just needed to share as Gracie had shared with him.

As I saw into my little boy's heart, Jesus allowed me to witness a picture of mercy's shocking power and the importance of appealing to someone's basic desire to avoid condemnation. Instead of being pulled away to be told he was acting naughty, Paxton had been shocked and transformed with a positive approach.

Jesus is a master of the positive approach. Even though He has every right to condemn us, He handles us with merciful care, which gently transforms us into creatures who can reflect His beautiful character. He doesn't let us get away with wrongs; He just guides us to the bar that He sets high instead of smacking us over the head with it.

FAITH STEP: *Who needs your positive approach instead of condemnation today? Perhaps yourself?*

—Erin Keeley Marshall

FEBRUARY 14

*"And so we know and rely on the love God has
for us. God is love...." 1 John 4:16 (NIV)*

$\mathcal{G}$od is love. What a statement. Imagine it! Everything He does is love. He can't not be loving toward us; it's not in His character.

As people, we know love and show it sometimes, but even in our best efforts we are limited. We're not always loving; we don't always act in love. My husband and I have a great marriage, but we still disappoint one another. I'm crazy about my kids, but sometimes I make parenting mistakes. And I try to be there for my friends, but sometimes I let them down.

I want to love, and I'm growing in it. Because of Jesus I can be successful at loving, but there is no way I can ever be love. Neither can you. As human beings we have our limitations.

However, the Bible says that with God there are no limits. God is in all of the expressions of love that we experience in the greatest moments of our human existence—like the love of a husband or wife, a parent, a child, a true friend. But He is also so much more.

Imagine the deepest part of the ocean, where it's too dark to see. His love is deeper than any ocean of loss or longing we might feel. Imagine the Grand Canyon, or a wide gulf. God's love is wider than any vast open space of loneliness or grief. And even if we're facing the Himalayas, God's love is higher than the tallest mountains of tests and trials.

Should we lose everything else, in Him we would still have all we need. For we can never lose His love—and it is enough.

FAITH STEP: *Today, rest your heart in the security of Jesus' love.*

—*Gwen Ford Faulkenberry*

FEBRUARY 15

"Abraham took the wood for the burnt offering and placed it on his son Isaac, and he himself carried the fire and the knife. As the two of them went on together, Isaac spoke up and said to his father Abraham, 'Father?' 'Yes, my son?' Abraham replied. 'The fire and wood are here,' Isaac said, 'but where is the lamb for the burnt offering?' Abraham answered, 'God himself will provide the lamb for the burnt offering, my son.' And the two of them went on together." Genesis 22:6–8 (NIV)

Growing up in America, it's uncommon to come across people who have never heard about Jesus. That isn't the case with international students. I learned this when I was asked to speak at a weekend retreat for foreign-exchange students. When I asked if there were any who'd never heard about Jesus Christ and his birth, life and death, most of the Asian students raised their hands. My heart started pounding. How can I share the good news in fifteen minutes with someone who's never heard?

I met them where they were. I spoke of the various religions—including ones common in Asia—and talked with them about what people must "do" to make their god happy. The list was long. Then I shared about God the Father, who loved us so much that He provided. He did the "doing" part in Jesus Christ.

Sin must be reconciled. In the Old Testament God demanded the death of a lamb or a goat. In the New Testament Jesus Christ took all our iniquity upon Himself once and for all.

Unlike other religions that require followers to strive toward salvation through works, I'm thankful that my God provides. He provided for Abraham and He provided for me and you. As I ended my time with the exchange students, I could see tenderness on their faces. Many thanked me for sharing my faith and beliefs. I was thankful, too, that God had provided me with the message they needed to hear. Who knows how the truth of God will continue to grow in their hearts? I can't wait to find out in eternity!

FAITH STEP: *Think of someone in your life who might have never heard the truth about Jesus Christ. Pray for a way to share God's truth whether it's through a book, a video or your testimony.*

—*Tricia Goyer*

FEBRUARY 16

"He brought me out into a spacious place; he rescued me because he delighted in me." Psalm 18:19 (NIV)

*W*eary, beat-up and burned-out, I had reached a point where I was questioning everything. Especially the persistent whisper of God to write, of all things, Christian books.

I was still the mom of young children. I had written one book, but wasn't sure what was next. My husband was wondering why I didn't find a job in PR or some other more lucrative form of writing. I was overcommitted at church and at my kids' school—hemmed in by a fence I'd built myself.

On the advice of a mentor, I scheduled a day of solitude at a retreat center. I needed some time with Jesus, just the two of us.

I prayed, searching the Psalms for the comfort they always bring. I lingered in Psalm 18, making its laments my own, longing for its promises to be true. Needing fresh air, I took a walk, following a path through a small woodland, praying as I went. Don't you have enough Christian book writers? I asked Jesus. I'm pretty busy.

The path through the woods led to a huge open field bordered on all four sides by ancient woods. I stood in that spacious place, which Jesus had brought me to. I listened, recalled the words I'd read. And believed— He delighted in me. I had been rescued by Jesus, who'd saved me for a purpose. Did I trust His calling? Could I rest in that spacious place, enjoy the fact that in spite of my questions and doubts, He delighted in me?

In that spacious place, God gave me a picture of what my life could be if I said no to all the things that cluttered it, so I could say yes to His purpose for me.

FAITH STEP: *Is there an area in your life where you feel crowded by questions and doubts? Where you are questioning God's calling? Ask Him to bring you to a spacious place, where you can feel His delight in you.*

—*Keri Wyatt Kent*

FEBRUARY 17

"I have chosen and consecrated this temple so that my Name may be there forever. My eyes and my heart will always be there." 2 Chronicles 7:16 (NIV)

*L*oving others can be a hard thing because it involves risk. It means extending our hand with the risk of it being slapped away. It means opening ourselves up to the risk of being hurt by a person who doesn't reciprocate our love.

Yet Jesus asks us to love other people as we love ourselves. That's a lot of love, because we're programmed for survival and self-preservation.

But Jesus Himself was an example of loving despite risk. He loved Judas, whom He knew would betray Him. He loved Peter, who denied Him three times.

We don't often think of God the Father as loving with risk, but He did. When Solomon built the temple, God promised that His eyes and His heart would be there. That meant He would see the people who sacrificed to Him and prayed to Him. That meant He would feel the hurt of their unfaithfulness.

I think He felt it when invaders raided and looted His temple—after all, wouldn't you feel upset if someone raided and looted your house? And He felt it when the temple was burned to the ground, because He had set His heart there, to love His people. He brought them out of Egypt because He chose them to be His people. He chose to love them, just like Jesus chose to love us.

FAITH STEP: *Look again at the familiar verse about loving others. Yes, it might involve risk and hurt, but Jesus thought the risk was worth it. God thought the hurt was worth it. If you're fearful, that's okay—bring it before Jesus and ask Him to help you to love others the way He loved us. Despite the risk of hurt.*

—*Camy Tang*

FEBRUARY 18

"Be tolerant with each other and, if someone has a complaint against anyone, forgive each other. As the Lord forgave you, so also forgive each other. And over all these things put on love, which is the perfect bond of unity. The peace of Christ must control your hearts—a peace into which you were called in one body. And be thankful people." Colossians 3:13–15 (CEB)

I'm a very tolerant person—of people who agree with me. People who don't agree with me, however—people who question things I do, vote differently than I do, interpret the Bible differently than I do—these people annoy me. Since they haven't done anything specific against me, I don't feel any need to forgive them; I can merely harbor a low-grade animosity.

One group of people who bug me a lot are those who skip over this verse on tolerance and seem to highlight the Bible verses about correction and rebuke. How can they be so judgmental when the Bible says don't judge, but forgive?

I hope you're laughing at the irony here! After all, if I'm not tolerant of people whom I think are intolerant, I'm just as intolerant as they are. Not to mention hypocritical.

Jesus asks His followers to be deliberate in how we relate to other people. We can't simply hope for good feelings toward others; we need to "put on love" and choose to forgive. We have to surrender control of our hearts to Jesus. This verse asks us to take specific, deliberate actions that will allow us to behave as Jesus would.

So often, in our churches or small groups, we long for unity, but we want it to happen without our effort. It doesn't until we "put on love"— that is, deliberately choose to take loving action toward those who we need to forgive.

FAITH STEP: *How do you truly feel about people who disagree with you, or someone you have a complaint against? Ask Jesus to help you honestly forgive that person.*

—Keri Wyatt Kent

FEBRUARY 19

"With them indeed is fulfilled the prophecy of Isaiah that says: 'You will indeed listen, but never understand, and you will indeed look, but never perceive. For this people's heart has grown dull, and their ears are hard of hearing, and they have shut their eyes; so that they might not look with their eyes, and listen with their ears, and understand with their heart and turn—and I would heal them.'" Matthew 13:14–16 (NRSV)

*B*lindness is a spiritual metaphor in Scripture for the darkness in which those without Christ exist.

Just because our eyes are open doesn't mean that we can see. Sometimes we cannot perceive things that are in plain sight because we aren't paying attention. We focus on a task, event or object so completely that we don't see what's right in front of us. Perceptual blindness means that if we aren't paying attention, we can miss even the most obvious events.

We don't even know what we don't know. Only as things are revealed to us, as we learn, are we able to fill in those gaps in our knowledge. How much of Jesus have we missed while focused on someone or something else?

We must put our antennae up to be aware of the Lord. That is how we see Him in the sunrise, hear Him in the laughter of a child, touch Him in the downy softness of a baby chick, smell His fragrance in the freshly washed air right after a rain, and yes, even taste Him in the sweetness of a juicy orange. All good things are from the Lord. How dark our lives would be without Him!

Do not let another day go by without looking for the Lord in it.

FAITH STEP: *Slow down. Jesus manifests Himself in ways both small and large. Take notice.*

— *Judy Baer*

FEBRUARY 20

"So when you give to the needy, do not announce it with trumpets, as the hypocrites do in the synagogues and on the streets, to be honored by others. Truly I tell you, they have received their reward in full. But when you give to the needy, do not let your left hand know what your right hand is doing." Matthew 6:2–3 (NIV)

One year, as my special project during the season of Lent, I decided to do a secret kind act each day. Selecting a small kindness was the easy part. First, I sneakily did chores that were the responsibilities of others in the family—laundry, dishes, garbage. Then I waited for them to notice and rejoice. Instead, my husband and children hurried along with their day and didn't realize someone had lightened their load. I dropped hints in conversation, leaned conspicuously against the empty dishwasher, longed for some bit of acknowledgement. Even if I never revealed myself as the benefactor, I wanted them to notice that someone had given them a gift.

Next, I designed small acts of generosity for people outside my family. I tucked an envelope with some cash into the mailbox of a church member going through financial need. When the phone rang and it was a particularly needy acquaintance, I coached myself to give a generous amount of my time listening and supporting without jumping in to talk about my own problems.

Each well-intentioned act of love was exhilarating to plan as well as implement. But keeping it secret was a painful struggle. My selfish nature—the part of me that hungers for human approval—clamored for acknowledgement that I'd gone above and beyond. No wonder Jesus warned us of that tendency. If we feed that hunger, we become as obnoxious as a hypocrite announcing His donations with a trumpet.

I want to keep working on the "sleight of hand" that Jesus recommends: giving so naturally that I don't even notice myself doing it. Trusting Him to use the small gifts, so I don't have to go back and check whether people appreciated them. Receiving God's love and acceptance so fully, that He shrinks my craving for human approval and recognition.

FAITH STEP: *Plan and implement a secret act of kindness for someone.*

—Sharon Hinck

FEBRUARY 21

"In the same way, when God desired to show even more clearly to the heirs of the promise the unchangeable character of his purpose, he guaranteed it by an oath, so that through two unchangeable things, in which it is impossible that God would prove false, we who have taken refuge might be strongly encouraged to seize the hope that is set before us." Hebrews 6:17–18 (NRSV)

It overjoys me to read that passage because I am reminded that God's nature is unchangeable. What good news that is for us as sinners! He embodies all truth and cannot lie. For this reason, I can always be sure of His promises. He doesn't change his mind. If I come to God believing and asking that He will save my sins, He will do it! He promised He would accept the sincere seeker and He does.

Although people may disappoint me—even people whom I love and admire—He will never fail me. Never! What He said He would do, He will do.

In God there is no variation or shadow due to change. There are no discrepancies or inconsistencies in God. People are fickle, changeable and unpredictable, but God is exactly the opposite. He never changes or takes back His offer of grace and salvation. Difficult as it is to imagine this great generosity, we can hold it as true. God does not—cannot—renege on His promises. What a comfort that is. Our salvation does not depend on a fickle God but one whose promises endure forever.

FAITH STEP: *Memorize these verses from Hebrews and quote them to yourself when doubt enters your mind.*

— *Judy Baer*

FEBRUARY 22

"For we died and were buried with Christ by baptism. And just as Christ was raised from the dead by the glorious power of the Father, now we also may live new lives." Romans 6:4 (NLT)

*M*y neighbor's weeping willow slouches, with ominous melancholy, toward our back fence. Its branches do just that—weep—onto our yard: twigs and small, slender, tear-shaped leaves. It invades the airspace of my backyard, and has, on windy days, dropped large branches, oblivious to the nuisance and danger it creates. All right, it does provide shade for the house, which is sometimes appreciated. But as the weather cools and the leaves drop in earnest, I'm not so appreciative.

One branch in particular annoys me—completely dead, leafless, the gray pallor of its skeletal limbs, which are like finger bones reaching for the sky. It waits for the next storm to crash into my back deck, but until then does nothing, serves nothing. Provides no shade and disrupts the otherwise lovely view.

This morning, washing dishes, I looked out at the branch, my eye pulled by a flash of red against the gray. A woodpecker clung to the underside of the branch, its bright red-capped head drawing my attention. It pecked at the wood, apparently finding food within. Then a pair of cardinals flitted among the branches, stopping on the smooth, dead branch to offer a trilling song.

What appears useless or annoying is not always so. Sometimes the starkness allows a better view of the beauty we would otherwise miss.

Jesus let go of His privilege and power, and actually died for us, in order to bring us life. Following Jesus requires us to also let go of our ambitions and die to ourselves, so that we can live new lives.

FAITH STEP: *What annoying or useless thing in your life might actually serve a purpose, even if that purpose is to provide a backdrop to the beauty you might not otherwise see?*

—*Keri Wyatt Kent*

FEBRUARY 23

"Now a woman, having a flow of blood for twelve years, who had spent all her livelihood on physicians and could not be healed by any, came from behind and touched the border of His garment. And immediately her flow of blood stopped." Luke 8:43–44 (NKJV)

After many years of energetic activity, I was unexpectedly hit with a long-term illness that was not life-threatening, but completely life-altering. It gave me a new appreciation for the woman in Luke. She had tried everything, every remedy, every doctor, every treatment money could buy. Yet nothing was sufficient. "Chronic" is a painful word, full of the dread of unending struggle and daily disappointment.

In my own health challenges, I wanted to keep a hopeful attitude. I put my trust in scientists to research the disease and find answers. I also put hope in the government to fund studies and provide information. Each time I visited a new specialist, I hoped the doctors would suggest a treatment that would make a difference. I also optimistically tried all sorts of new nutritional choices.

But as months passed I realized research breakthroughs might not come, and certainly not as fast as I would prefer. As far as government funding, other needs took priority and little was being done to find answers. Doctors offered their best, but admitted there was no cure and few treatment options. Nutritional changes and other complementary medicine had minimal benefit.

When human answers disappoint us, that doesn't leave us without hope. Instead, we find there is only one safe place to put our hope. Like the woman in Luke 8, we can grab hold of Jesus. He has the power to heal with a touch. But He also has the power to give a different sort of miracle. He can give us grace to keep loving Him and praising Him each day, even while the illness lingers.

FAITH STEP: *Is there an illness or other problem you've been battling, where human solutions have disappointed you? Grab hold of Jesus today and ask for His help.*

—Sharon Hinck

FEBRUARY 24

"But Rehoboam rejected the advice the elders gave him and consulted the young men who had grown up with him and were serving him." 1 Kings 12:8 (NIV)

*K*ing Rehoboam made a terrible decision about whose advice to take, and it caused the ten northern tribes of Israel to split away from Judah and Benjamin. Rather than listening to the advice of the elders who had served his father King Solomon, he listened to the advice of his friends and spoke harshly and derisively to his people. The ten northern tribes rebelled and made Jeroboam their king.

At first, Rehoboam's decision seems like the brashness and immaturity of youth, but later the Bible says that Rehoboam was forty-one years old when he became king of Israel. A man of forty-one is definitely not an immature youth, and his friends would not be immature youths either.

How can we know whose counsel is wise? How can we know which advice our friends and family give to us is the best? In Luke 21, Jesus talks about how He will give us wisdom, but He's not exactly here in the flesh to go out for coffee with us and tell us what to do.

But He gave us His Spirit, and it's the same Spirit that gave Stephen the words to say to his accusers. The Spirit nudges us in ways we can't always understand or explain, but we know when the Spirit is leading us in Jesus' will, especially when the Spirit speaks to us as we're reading the Word of God.

FAITH STEP: *Spend more time in the Word this month. Let the Holy Spirit speak to you, make verses jump out at you, guide your thoughts and your heart. That's the best counsel you can have.*

—*Camy Tang*

FEBRUARY 25

*"They agreed that they were foreigners and nomads here on earth.
Obviously people who say such things are looking forward to a country
they can call their own. If they had longed for the country they came
from, they could have gone back. But they were looking for a better
place, a heavenly homeland." Hebrews 11:13–16 (NLT)*

*H*ome. I was really missing it as my SUV's odometer ticked the miles
farther away from my roots. After seven years living in a "new" place,
you'd think I'd feel at home there—but no.

Although I had spent my first three decades wishing for adventures
beyond the place of my steady suburban upbringing, I continued to be
surprised at how much I missed the familiarity of what I had left behind.

Now, as my own little family drove farther from my childhood family, I
chided myself again for feeling ungrateful: Look at all the dreams God has
answered! Stop complaining because you've been surprised by the locale.

To which my other self countered that I am very grateful; I'm just weary of trying to fit my square self into a round hole that still doesn't feel
quite right.

Blessedly, as I watched countless vehicles zoom by, the Holy Spirit whispered a precious reminder: "Let your roots grow down into me; build your
life on me. Then you will overflow with thankfulness." (See Colossians 2:7.)

Oh yeah. One more time I needed to refocus my roots. I suppose the
real tragedy would be to live blinded to the fact that the most desirable
place on earth is the pits compared to an eternity with Jesus. I will never
truly feel at home until I'm with Jesus.

FAITH STEP: *Purchase a small "Home Sweet Home" memento—a magnet,
plaque or wall hanging. Place it where you'll see it daily as a reminder of your
true home.*

—*Erin Keeley Marshall*

FEBRUARY 26

*"Greater love hath no man than this, that a man
lay down his life for his friends." John 15:13*

*A*ll throughout the Bible we see images of God as our Shepherd.

Psalm 23 says, "The Lord is my Shepherd, I shall not want." The New Testament describes Jesus as the Good Shepherd, and tells us that He lays down His life for His sheep. Jesus says, in John 10:3, that the sheep hear His voice.

I don't have sheep, but I have two goats named Vincent and Violet. When I speak to them, they know my voice. If I were a stranger they wouldn't listen, being very stubborn and ornery goats. But when I call Vincent he comes up to the fence for me to rub his head and scratch him between the horns. Violet eats acorns from my hand.

What a lovely thought that our Good Shepherd speaks to us. Here are just a few of the things He says in His Word: "Look to Me…I provide all of your needs. Cast your cares on me…for I care deeply for you. Rest in me…for my yoke is easy, and my burden is light. I will do the work for you. I will strengthen you, I will help you. I will guide you…follow me. I am always with you, I will never leave you. I will comfort you. My grace is sufficient. Don't be afraid, I will protect you. I go before you and I will bless you. You are precious and honored in my sight and I love you…."

FAITH STEP: *All that He is, He is for you. All that He speaks, He speaks to you. Do you hear your Shepherd's voice?*

—Gwen Ford Faulkenberry

FEBRUARY 27

"If we confess our sins, he is faithful and just and will forgive us our sins and purify us from all unrighteousness." 1 John 1:9 (NIV)

It's been a banner year for snowfall in our Midwestern hometown. Frequent storms dropped enough snow to measure in feet instead of inches. While blankets of white decorate the neighborhood and provide the fun of sledding and skiing, lots of snow also means lots of shoveling.

Our driveway isn't huge, but we have to clear it to get our car out to the street. This winter we've experienced the unique torments of various kinds of snow. Snow with an icy crust steals the traction and causes slipping and skidding as we work. Wet snow is heavy and backbreaking. Sleety snow stings our face as we work.

But by far the worst snow-shoveling experience is working while snow is still falling. Sometimes when the weather report warns of ten inches by morning, we have to make a start on it so it doesn't pile to unmanageable heights. Nothing is as disheartening as scraping and tossing for an hour, only to look back and see all the freshly cleared pavement covered again.

It reminds me of my efforts to clear sin out of life. I notice I've been griping too much, and resolve to change my attitude, but before an hour goes by, I've complained about something new. Or perhaps I manage to stifle the grumbling, and instead find that now I'm discouraged about a problem and not walking in trust and faith. I try and try to scrape away the messy motivations and selfish traits, but every time I turn around, there is more to deal with.

Last time we had a blizzard, our neighbor stopped by. "I just got a new snowplow. Want me to clean out your driveway for you?" What a gift!

That's just the way Jesus interrupts me in my crazy sin-shoveling efforts. "You can't do it yourself, remember? Confess and let me cleanse you." His forgiveness is complete, and then like salt melts away ice on the sidewalk, He sends the Holy Spirit to sanctify and prevent new sin from taking hold.

FAITH STEP: *Have you noticed a blizzard of thoughts, words, attitudes or actions you'd like to clear from your soul? Invite Jesus to do the work of sin-shoveling.*

—*Sharon Hinck*

FEBRUARY 28

"Be still before the Lord and wait patiently for him." Psalm 37:7 (NIV)

For years Saturdays were cleaning day. While my husband took our kids on an outing I'd clean the house from top to bottom. It was easier for me to clean—to work and see progress—than to sit at the park watching them play. I told myself that doing all the cleaning on one day gave me more time with them during the week, which was true, but the deeper truth is my inability to be still.

My "roll up your sleeves and have at it" attitude seemed noble as I homeschooled and started freelance writing. I didn't understand, though, why I felt so empty and unfulfilled by the end of the day. Even checking off a long to-do list didn't satisfy. That's when I came upon the message from this verse: Be still.

Something stirred inside as I read those words. I felt my Lord Jesus was talking to me, but I didn't want to accept the message. Soon I saw the verse everywhere. On a mug and journal I won as a door prize, and on the embroidered wall hanging made for me. Still? Is that what Jesus desired more than a clean house, well-educated kids, or my written Christian messages?

Still, I discovered, isn't simply lack of motion. The rest of the verse describes being before God and waiting for Him. It's more than just rest, although I need that too; it's being filled by the Lord's presence and hope. It's realizing that He can accomplish more with one whispered breath than I could with twenty years of labor. It's understanding you're not waiting for Him to do something. You're waiting for Him, because He is what you need.

FAITH STEP: *Put your to-do list down and instead spend five minutes in stillness before Jesus praising Him and asking Him to show up in your day.*

—Tricia Goyer

FEBRUARY 29

"When Solomon finished praying, fire came down from heaven and consumed the burnt offering and the sacrifices, and the glory of the Lord filled the temple. The priests could not enter the temple of the Lord because the glory of the Lord filled it." 2 Chronicles 7:1–2 (TNIV)

Have you ever wondered what exactly God's glory looks like? Smells like? Feels like?

Is it rolling clouds of smoke, acrid and harsh? Is it extreme heat or extreme cold? Is it blinding light? Is it like a sandstorm, whirling and strong?

Maybe it's all those things. But whatever it is, it was so intense, so strong, so awe-inspiring that the Levitical priests couldn't enter the temple.

Were they physically blocked from entering? Or were they so afraid they didn't dare enter?

In the Transfiguration, Jesus shone like the sun and became blindingly white. In Revelation, when the Apostle John saw Jesus, he passed out completely.

Jesus' glory is beyond human comprehension, so powerful, so frightening, so magnificent and so terrible at the same time, that the priests couldn't approach the temple, and John fell down as though dead.

This is the same Jesus who called us His friends, who loves us, who gives us grace. Sometimes we're so caught up in Jesus' kindness and humanity that we forget He is also God Almighty. He is both Kind Jesus and Awesome Jesus.

FAITH STEP: *Close your eyes and try to imagine how John might have felt. Try to imagine the awesomeness and awfulness of Jesus. This is the Jesus who is on your side. If God is for you, who can be against you?*

—Camy Tang

March

MARCH 1

"Yet the news about him spread all the more, so that crowds of people came to hear him and to be healed of their sicknesses. But Jesus often withdrew to lonely places and prayed." Luke 5:15–16 (NIV)

$\mathscr{I}$t's 9:20 pm, and I'm at the computer working. The phone rings. It's a friend, asking if I can watch her daughters tomorrow morning for an hour. She'll drop them off right after my daughter leaves for school.

The call waiting clicks, and I ask my friend to hold. "Keri, it's Annette. I'm here at the PTA nominating committee meeting, and your name came up," she begins. "We were wondering whether you'd consider an executive position on the board for next year."

Such opportunities raise a question: When should I say yes, and when should I say no? We sometimes think that the good Christian answer to any request is yes. But that's not what Jesus did. He often withdrew to lonely places, which means He occasionally had to say no. If He said it, we should too.

A wise friend of mine puts it this way: "I picture myself juggling a lot of balls. Sometimes I drop a ball. In most cases, that's not too big of a deal. But a few of the balls, like my husband and my kids, are glass balls. So I make sure I do whatever it takes not to shatter those balls. Some of the balls are rubber, and will bounce if we give them a little push now and then. Some are lead and weigh us down and we shouldn't be trying to juggle them in the first place."

Jesus did not juggle every ball that people asked Him to. We can serve and love people, but also ask for His help in determining which balls are glass, rubber or lead, and say yes and no accordingly.

FAITH STEP: *What balls are you juggling that you should simply let go of? What do you need to say no to, so you can follow Jesus to a lonely place?*

—Keri Wyatt Kent

MARCH 2

Then Jesus declared, "I am the bread of life. Whoever comes to me will never go hungry, and whoever believes in me will never be thirsty." John 6:35 (NIV)

$\mathcal{A}$ family pastime while we're driving is to look for wayside pulpits. Sometimes we come across a good one that seems tailored to a particular moment, a literal sign from God.

Other times we are not so fortunate. Last week on the way home from school we passed a church with a billboard that read: "Without the bread of life you are toast."

Reflective of her name, my ten-year-old daughter Grace commented, "That's not very encouraging."

Adelaide, three, cracked up.

Harper, who at eight possesses the makings of a modern-day prophet, observed, "It may not be tactful, but it's the truth."

Hackles rising, I tried to withhold my judgment. When my kids pressed me I blurted out, "I hate that sign and I think things like that turn people away from Jesus!"

They gaped at me wide-eyed.

Instantly, I felt a pang of conviction. Um, those are pretty strong words. The still small voice persisted: There are all kinds of people in the kingdom of God. Every church sign you read, just like every sermon you hear, doesn't have to be your cup of tea. Do you want your children to be critical thinkers, or do you want them harboring a critical spirit?

There's a fine line between those two things—and I had just stepped over it. Again. After confessing my weakness to God, I discussed it with my kids that night, and tried to explain the difference between thinking critically and being too critical. The inevitable question became, "How do we know which is which?"

I told them that (obviously) I don't always know, but I'm working on it. When it comes down to it, just like everything else in the Christian life, we have to rely on Jesus.

The next day I passed the sign again, and the irony hit me like a brick: without Him, I really am toast.

FAITH STEP: *Ask Jesus to help you discern the difference between critical thinking and having a critical spirit. His example shows us the way. Rely on Him today to help you walk the fine line that He did.*

—*Gwen Ford Faulkenberry*

MARCH 3

*"Lord, how often will my brother sin against me, and I forgive him?
As many as seven times? Jesus said to him, 'I do not say to you seven
times but seventy times seven.'" Matthew 18:21–22 (ESV)*

*C*hristians can be a topsy-turvy bunch. Sometimes we do things that the world has a hard time understanding. We do a lot of things others consider backward. When someone hurts us, we turn the other cheek, leaving ourselves vulnerable to even more hurt. We have to die to ourselves in order to live eternally. If someone needs our coat, we give him our shirt as well. Unlikely people take leadership roles in God's kingdom, like Moses, who stuttered. We look back to what Jesus said and did in the past to know our own futures. God chooses us not because we are ready to serve. He takes the reluctant servant, equips them and makes them ready.

We are in this world but not of it—and Jesus gives us the strength to persist when we are backward in the world's eyes.

FAITH STEP: *Do a backward thing today. Give more than you had planned to someone who needs it. Pay for a stranger's groceries. Take the lead in something that frightens you just because you know God wants you to do it.*

— Judy Baer

MARCH 4

"'What shall we say the kingdom of God is like, or what parable shall we use to describe it? It is like a mustard seed, which is the smallest of all seeds on earth. Yet when planted, it grows and becomes the largest of all garden plants, with such big branches that the birds can perch in its shade.'" Mark 4:30–32 (NIV)

*T*oday, on a cold day in late winter, I acted on faith by planting poppies. While it's way too early to plant anything else, this is prime planting time for poppies. The seeds are tiny—like the poppy seeds you'd find on a bakery roll. If I hadn't seen it happen every year, I'd find it hard to believe that by late June, those tiny seeds will become bright pink puffy flowers the size of my fist, blooming on stalks two feet tall or more.

I harvested these seeds last year from plants. I've done this for years, starting with some seeds given me by gardening mentors.

To plant poppies requires faith. And action. You simply scatter them on the soil (in some years, I've put them right on top of snow). The seeds need cold to germinate, so I'm hoping I haven't planted too late. Optimally, I should have planted them last month. But if I leave them in the plastic bag on the shelf, they'll never be flowers. They'll just be good intentions.

Jesus often used seeds as a picture of the kingdom of heaven. He was not talking about a someday, somewhere-else kingdom, but rather, a present reality.

Even when it's still winter, I trust spring will come. I trust God will provide, and help the seeds I'm planting to bloom. He'll take my small acts of faith, and grow them into something beautiful.

FAITH STEP: *What seeds do you need to plant today, even if you are skeptical that they will ever result in beauty or fruit?*

—*Keri Wyatt Kent*

MARCH 5

"Now there was a Pharisee, a man named Nicodemus who was a member of the Jewish ruling council. He came to Jesus at night and said, 'Rabbi, we know that you are a teacher who has come from God. For no one could perform the signs you are doing if God were not with him.'" John 3:1–2 (NIV)

*I*t doesn't surprise me that Nicodemus went to Jesus at night. The most obvious reason was that he did not want other members of the Jewish council to know about his visit. Another possibility is that his thoughts/worries/questions rose after dark, lifting and spreading like the glow of the moon. I've spent many a late hour lying in bed, thinking about the questions that are easy to brush aside during my busy day. Worried thoughts seem to multiply during the late-night hours.

Nicodemus didn't sit in the darkness alone and try to figure everything out. Instead he went to Jesus. We can do the same. Jesus didn't turn away Nicodemus' questions. Jesus never does. Nicodemus knew a lot, but Jesus had something special to share: "For God so loved the world that he gave his one and only Son, that whoever believes in him shall not perish but have eternal life" (John 3:16).

During his lifetime Nicodemus was pretty smart and highly respected, but when it came to trying to understanding Jesus' Words, His miracles, and the new thing God was doing, Nicodemus was clueless. I've learned if I want to understand the things of God, the best place to go is to Jesus Himself. I do this through morning quiet times…and through late-night seeking and prayers.

FAITH STEP: *What questions have you been brushing aside in the busyness of life? Take them to Jesus. He has good answers and will always have something special to share as you come to Him.*

—*Tricia Goyer*

MARCH 6

"Jesus said to them [the disciples], 'They need not go away; you give them something to eat.' They replied, 'We have nothing here but five loaves and two fish.' And he said, 'Bring them here to me.' Then he ordered the crowds to sit down on the grass. Taking the five loaves and the two fish, he looked up to heaven, and blessed and broke the loaves, and gave them to the disciples, and the disciples gave them to the crowds. And all ate and were filled; and they took up what was left over of the broken pieces, twelve baskets full. And those who ate were about five thousand men, besides women and children." Matthew 14:16–21 (NRSV)

A host or hostess' worst nightmare: five thousand hungry drop-ins to feed for lunch. Jesus, however, takes it in stride. He multiplies those meager loaves and fishes to feed them all and has baskets of food left over. The paltry loaves and fishes were totally insufficient to feed five thousand people. Yet, with Jesus in the mix, what was inadequate became sufficient.

He is able to do the same thing in our lives. What we bring to Him—our time, talent or wealth—is utterly insufficient, but He makes what we offer Him more than satisfactory. He uses and blesses and multiplies the gifts we bring. Be unafraid to offer Him your best even though you fear it isn't good enough. In His hands it will blossom and grow.

FAITH STEP: *What is it you do that you would like to offer to Jesus? Your singing voice? Your artistic ability? Your capability or willingness to work at whatever is assigned to you? Yourself? Offer Him that and know that He will turn it into a blessing for someone.*

– Judy Baer

MARCH 7

" 'The virgin will conceive and give birth to a son, and they will call him Immanuel' (which means, 'God with us')." Matthew 1:23 (NIV)

A while back my sister-in-law René had a miscarriage. Afterward, she suffered from severe depression and anxiety attacks and had to take medication to recover. It took her a year to gather her courage to try again for another baby, and when she did, she had another miscarriage. I will never forget her face—how it crumpled in pain—and the sobs that followed as the doctor confirmed that the baby in her womb was dead.

René and I often borrow from the line in Wuthering Heights when Cathy cries out, "I am Heathcliff!" Theirs is a crazed love affair rather than a friendship, but the principle remains that they are inseparable human beings. Cathy cannot discern where she ends and Heathcliff begins, and this is like René and me. As much as I could enter into her miscarriage experience, I did. We cried and prayed a lot together.

But human beings are limited. I could not be with her at every moment. I could not be inside her head. Even my brother Jim, who stood beside her and suffered with her, could not heal her heart.

At one of the lowest points in the aftermath, René told me she woke up in a cold sweat in the middle of the night. It was pitch-black, and Jim was beside her, asleep. She felt the darkness of her loss begin to suffocate her. All she could do was cry out to Jesus—and He answered. He spoke three words to her heart: I am here.

Immanuel—God with us—is a heady concept. However, even for God to be with us is not always what we want. It's definitely not all we would ask for, if we're honest. But it is enough to see us through—Jesus is enough.

FAITH STEP: *Jesus never leaves you nor forsakes you. Receive that truth down deep into your bones. His grace is sufficient, and you can trust that He will be enough for anything you face today.*

—Gwen Ford Faulkenberry

MARCH 8

"In your relationships with one another, have the same mindset as Christ Jesus: Who, being in very nature God, did not consider equality with God something to be used to his own advantage." Philippians 2:5–6 (NIV)

During a particularly rocky season in my twenty-year marriage, I found myself arguing with my husband frequently, which was counter-productive, to say the least. I cringe to tell you this, but one of the things we would argue about was who was better at arguing. "Don't challenge me to a battle of wits," I'd say, "because I'm smarter than you and I will win." Ugly, isn't it?

We all have God-given strengths. But the question is, can we use those strengths without hurting anyone? I obviously did not take this into consideration in my interactions with my husband. I was a clear and perfect example of how not to behave.

Jesus—who actually was the smartest person to ever live, who was fully God—willingly chose not to use those very real strengths to His advantage. The Bible calls us to live like Jesus did, to have the same mindset. When I repented of my pride and arrogance, things improved dramatically in my marriage. When I realized that Jesus provided not only an example but also real-time help via His spirit, the broken parts of my life began to heal.

The single Greek word that is translated "to be used to his own advantage" (or in some versions, "something to be grasped"), harpagmos, only occurs once in the New Testament. Scholar Craig Bloomberg points out that by becoming one of us, Jesus did not become any less God. He simply chose humility.

"The point then of the verse is not that Christ, in choosing to give up his position…gave up his deity or even his divine attributes," Bloomberg writes, "but that he didn't consider them as something to be used to his own personal advantage."

FAITH STEP: *Jesus was the perfect model of humility. Where, specifically, is He calling you to follow His example and let go of pride or advantage?*

—Keri Wyatt Kent

MARCH 9

"He who testifies to these things says, 'Yes, I am coming soon.' Amen. Come, Lord Jesus." Revelation 22:20 (NIV)

I like comings more than goings. This past fall, my husband and I sent our youngest off to college, and faced the emotional challenge of the empty nest. I paged through baby books and photo albums remembering the huge joy that accompanied the arrival of each of our children. We also rejoiced in their various milestones—graduation, marriage, moving to a new place, tackling a new career, busy lives full of their own unique callings. Yet those joys were tempered with the sadness of loss. Each event pulled them a bit further from us.

I also like comings more than goings when we have friends or family over to the house. In fact, whenever friends visit I find myself doing what we call the "Minnesota good-bye." At some point in conversation, a guest glances at her watch and says, "Well, we better get going." I agree and we stand up…and keep chatting.

Eventually we make our way toward the door, and the guests put on their coats. But then one of us thinks of a topic we meant to discuss and the conversation heads onto a new tangent as we stand in the foyer. We usually spend several minutes in the doorway, and often, my husband and I will walk out to the car with our guests…and talk some more.

We have a natural inclination to avoid separation and good-byes. We also love arrivals, whether through birth or a visit to our home. Perhaps that's why this verse fills me with so much joy. Jesus is returning—and He'll bring the end to painful good-byes. Amen. Come, Lord Jesus!

FAITH STEP: *Let's invite Jesus to come soon, but also to make Himself evident in our lives while we wait for His final coming.*

—Sharon Hinck

MARCH 10

"Therefore be imitators of God, as beloved children. And walk in love, as Christ loved us and gave himself up for us, a fragrant offering and sacrifice to God." Ephesians 5:1–2 (RSV)

*A*my Carmichael once said that a cup of sweet water cannot spill out bitterness, no matter how rudely it is overturned. Like many of her sayings, I find this truth to be terribly challenging.

Most of the time, if my cup gets spilled by accident—if I'm interrupted by an innocent person or otherwise affected by an innocent mistake—my water can be pretty sweet. But what about those other situations, the not-so-innocent ones? What about the person who knocks me down on purpose? Or perhaps worse, what about the person who has no regard for my cup whatsoever and just plows right over it, breaking it into pieces?

It's in those situations Carmichael's claim becomes most difficult. I'm sorry to say that many times I believe my cup to hold sweet water only to find, after it is rudely overturned, that it's full of hurt, anger or pride.

It's easy to think, when our cup spews out bitterness, that we're justified because the other person deserves it. We're under duress. They've pushed us to the point of hurt or anger, and we have no option but to respond as such. But, the truth is that we do have another option. We can choose to respond in love.

Responding to rudeness with love is not easy, and it is not something we can do in our own strength. But the offer comes to us to "be filled with the Spirit." (See Ephesians 5:18.) The Lord, who understands our nature, offers to empty us of our bitterness and fill us up with His love. It is when our cup is filled with Jesus that we'll spill out His love on others, no matter what.

FAITH STEP: *Ask Jesus to fill 'er up! Let Him pour Himself into you today, that you may pour out His goodness to others.*

—*Gwen Ford Faulkenberry*

MARCH 11

"A man was there by the name of Zacchaeus; he was a chief tax collector and was wealthy. He wanted to see who Jesus was, but because he was short he could not see over the crowd. So he ran ahead and climbed a sycamore-fig tree to see him, since Jesus was coming that way. When Jesus reached the spot, he looked up and said to him, 'Zacchaeus, come down immediately. I must stay at your house today.' So he came down at once and welcomed him gladly." Luke 19:2–6 (NIV)

The laughter of unchurched teen girls filled the room but as the leader of the teen-mom support group I could barely crack a smile. They were joking about their boyfriends and the latest movies they had watched, but all I could think about was their challenging circumstances and how much each one needed to hear about Jesus. If I spent every day meeting with a different, needy girl, trying to mentor her, it would fill up all my time. Yet how can I not do something? I felt helpless until God pointed out that I didn't need to reach out to everyone I met. Instead, I just needed to pray my heart would be tender to the right person at the right time. After all, that's what Jesus did.

Jesus no doubt had compassion when the crowds pressed around him. He knew their needs. He knew He could fill those needs. When Jesus saw a man up in a tree He knew that man was ready to hear the good news: That's someone who's not letting the crowds get in the way. That's someone who really wants to see Me.

Hundreds of curious people wandered home that night, but Jesus sat at the table of the one who was ready for the good news.

"Today salvation has come to this house, because this man, too, is a son of Abraham," Jesus exclaimed of Zacchaeus in Luke 19:9–10. "For the Son of Man came to seek and to save the lost" (NIV).

Jesus was a seeker of tender hearts. It encourages me that I need to have my eyes open and my heart ready to reach out to those who seem curious to get a better look at Jesus.

FAITH STEP: *Consider one person in your life today who seems ready and willing to listen. Go to that person and share a little about who Jesus is.*

—*Tricia Goyer*

MARCH 12

*"Everyone who hears these words of mine and acts on them will
be like a wise man who built his house on rock. The rain fell, the floods
came, and the winds blew and beat on that house, but it did not fall,
for it had been founded on rock." Matthew 7:24–25 (NRSV)*

ould you build your dream home in a swamp? On a sand dune? On a glacier? Of course not. The land beneath your house would sink or move or melt. It would be foolish to build a house without a soil survey to make sure there's not too much clay or sand. You'd want to find out how high the water table is before digging that hole in the ground.

Yet we are willing to build our lives around jobs, wealth, adventure, friends, family or pleasure. Is that any wiser than building a house on sand? What will remain if a flood of sorrow or the winds of trouble blow through your existence? What will be left? If the foundation on which you build your life is transitory, all will be swept away. But if you've built your life on the Rock, on Christ Jesus, you will survive.

The only reliable thing in this life is Jesus. Building our lives on any other foundation is foolishness.

FAITH STEP: *Think about your life. Where do you stand? What is your foundation? Ask Jesus to help you build your faith on Him, on the Rock that will withstand the winds of time.*

– Judy Baer

MARCH 13

"Don't pick on people, jump on their failures, criticize their faults—unless, of course, you want the same treatment. That critical spirit has a way of boomeranging. It's easy to see a smudge on your neighbor's face and be oblivious to the ugly sneer on your own." Matthew 7:1–5 (MSG)

As I drove past the church, the quote on the sign in front caught my attention: "Criticism is a subtle form of pride."

Yikes. The familiar itch of conviction made me shift in my seat. I'm not sure who came up with that saying, but they got it spot-on. I know this because I know both criticism and pride.

It's impossible to criticize with a heartwarming smile. A condemning spirit can't help but wear an ugly sneer, and that ugliness pushes people away instead of drawing them near.

Jesus is all about drawing us close so we can thrive in His soul-saving love. The ones He condemned were actually those with critical spirits, not those whom the criticizers were accusing. He called them a "brood of vipers" and warned others about them: "They tie up heavy, cumbersome loads and put them on other people's shoulders, but they themselves are not willing to lift a finger to move them…. Those who exalt themselves will be humbled, and those who humble themselves will be exalted" (Matthew 23:3–4, 12, NIV).

The entire chapter of Matthew 23 reads as uncomfortably as sitting on a tack. But at the end Jesus describes His own heart with simple, contrasting attractiveness that makes us crave His refreshment: "I have often wanted to gather your people, as a hen gathers her chicks under her wings."

I long for freedom from a critical, prideful spirit—my own and others'. Thankfully Jesus is the answer to both.

FAITH STEP: *Next time you find yourself thinking too critically about someone, take a private moment to look in the mirror. Do you see peace or strain in your features?*

—*Erin Keeley Marshall*

MARCH 14

"You have turned my mourning into joyful dancing. You have taken away my clothes of mourning and clothed me with joy, that I might sing praises to you and not be silent. O Lord my God, I will give you thanks forever!" Psalm 30:11–12 (NLT)

*I*f a piece of music has only loud, high notes, it is not beautiful. What makes music beautiful is the juxtaposition of high notes and low; of soft, quiet notes and strong, forte ones; of melody and harmony. To appreciate one, you must have the other. Variations in tone and volume and tempo make music that is beautiful or interesting. The music of our lives becomes flat when we take away the counterpoint.

So often, I find myself praying for Jesus to simply fix things, to take away any aches and pains in my life—be they physical, spiritual, emotional. I want life to be one long, high note.

But what kind of music is that? One of the strangest paradoxes of the Christian life is this: Jesus can change our circumstances, but sometimes, He does not. However, He always changes our perspective. He enables us to see the beauty, even in the midst of pain. That is how He turns our mourning into dancing. Our joy is sweeter and more satisfying because we have mourned. Jesus doesn't prevent our mourning but transforms it, in His perfect timing.

We set aside mourning and start dancing because of the fact that Jesus is in our lives—not because He's taken away the pain, but because He is right there in the midst of it with us. That presence in the midst of pain is what it means to be clothed with joy.

FAITH STEP: *What are you mourning right now? Write it down in a journal. Feel free to fully grieve whatever you need to grieve. Ask Jesus to meet you in the midst of that pain, so that He can transform it, in His timing, into joy.*

—*Keri Wyatt Kent*

MARCH 15

"Get away with me and you'll recover your life. I'll show you how to take a real rest. Walk with me and work with me—watch how I do it. Learn the unforced rhythms of grace." Matthew 11:28 (MSG)

GO, GO, GO! my spirit hollered.

Fortunately for my children, I stuffed those impatient words and led the way to our waiting vehicle. As my toddler and preschooler climbed ever so slowly into their car seats, I did some neck rolls to relieve tension. Could they move any slower?

I wanted to scoop them into their seats, but I knew they took pride in doing it themselves, so I avoided their tantrums and threw an inner one of my own.

As the minutes ticked—and ticked me off—we finally were buckled and ready to go. With a sigh, I shoved the gearshift into reverse, glanced in my rearview mirror…and saw my sweet kiddos waiting quietly, one sucking his thumb, the other sucking her first two fingers.

Oh, my hurried heart. How you stress out.

That hurried heart sank as it filled with compassion for my son and daughter. What on earth should a four-year-old and a two-year-old have to hurry so much for anyway?

I recalled a friend's comment over a similar situation with her kids. She said, "I don't know why I get stressed. It's just minutes." How wise!

Jesus' days contained the same number of minutes as ours, yet He always valued people over tasks. It's interesting that although His profession as a carpenter is mentioned, the Bible doesn't contain a single scene of Him doing that job. Instead, Scripture tells tale after tale of Him caring for people and offering refreshment wherever He went. The underlying message? He prioritized His primary ministry.

I felt His presence quiet me as I remembered the call I feel to make my family my first ministry.

FAITH STEP: *Commit this month to live unhurried. Even in busyness your spirit can be calm.*

—*Erin Keeley Marshall*

MARCH 16

"In the temple courts he found people selling cattle, sheep and doves, and others sitting at tables exchanging money. So he made a whip out of cords, and drove all from the temple courts, both sheep and cattle; he scattered the coins of the money changers and overturned their tables. To those who sold doves he said, 'Get these out of here! Stop turning my Father's house into a market!'" John 2:14–16 (NIV)

If I had one goal as a child it was to not get into trouble. As the oldest child and grandchild I tried to do what was right, always. My mom often told me I needed to set a good example for the younger ones in our family, but that wasn't the only reason. Seeing my stepdad's red face and lowered eyebrows scared me. I rarely got spanked or even grounded, but the angry look was enough to quicken my heart.

In Sunday school it confused me when I learned about Jesus getting angry and turning over the money changers' tables. The flannel-graph image of Jesus with a whip in His hand and His gaze narrowed in anger wasn't the Jesus I learned about the other fifty-one weeks of the year. After seeing that, I was pretty certain the Bible was wrong when it said Jesus never sinned. Since He'd gotten angry I was sure He had.

As I've gotten older I've learned godly anger and passion have their place. It's okay to be angry at those who abuse children or those who dishonor God and try to reap their own rewards from His grace, as the merchants in the marketplace were doing. In fact if we don't get angry about God being dishonored maybe there's a problem. Maybe we need to draw closer to Him and ask Him to help our hearts reflect His.

I still don't like angry people, but I appreciate when—like Jesus—they are angry for the right reason. When they want to make sure God receives the honor He should and His people are not taken advantage of.

FAITH STEP: *Can you think of someone who dishonors God and tries to take advantage of people and reap his or her own rewards? Mold your anger to pray for that person. Ask God to point out times you need to straighten up too.*

—Tricia Goyer

MARCH 17

"You came near and stood at the foot of the mountain while it blazed with fire to the very heavens, with black clouds and deep darkness. Then the Lord spoke to you out of the fire." Deuteronomy 4:11–12 (TNIV)

I grew up in church, so I heard all the stories about God and how He brought the Israelites out of Egypt, parting the Red Sea. I heard about the miracles Jesus performed, such as feeding the five thousand and healing the sick, and then about Him dying on the cross. After hearing the stories over and over again, they started to lose their impact.

I knew Jesus as my friend and my heavenly Father. I had visions of Him smiling down from heaven on me.

I didn't realize it, but I had made my vision of God too "safe" and familiar. I had boxed Him in so I only saw a fraction of His character. But God doesn't want me to only see a fraction, because that's not who He really is. I need to know all of Him, not just the beautiful and gentle parts of Him.

When God spoke to the Israelites from Mount Horeb, He was cloaked in darkness and clouds, and fire blazed from the mountain. Those words evoke a different view of God, don't they? At Mount Horeb, God was powerful and a little terrible, even. This is the same power that raised Jesus from the dead.

Reading about God in the Bible opens my eyes to more of who He really is. Jesus is still my friend and my heavenly Father, but He is also Almighty God.

FAITH STEP: *What is your view of God? Are you boxing Him in so you only see aspects of His character that you like or that feel safe? Make a commitment to read more of His Word every day so that God can show you all of Himself.*

—*Camy Tang*

MARCH 18

"Who then is the one who condemns? No one. Christ Jesus who died—more than that, who was raised to life—is at the right hand of God and is also interceding for us." Romans 8:34 (NIV)

"*I*'m praying for you."

Sometimes we use the words as a fallback when we feel helpless, as a last-resort way to offer comfort. But the promise can be a powerful act of love, especially if we follow through.

Recently, a woman e-mailed out of the blue to tell me that God had suddenly placed me on her heart and she was praying for me, although she didn't know why. I suspect she worried she would sound a bit silly, especially if there were no special needs in my life. What she didn't realize was that I was struggling with deep loneliness and confusion about some painful circumstances in my life. I had just asked God for reassurance and encouragement to keep me going. My friend had e-mailed me on a very crucial morning, and her words felt like a precious reminder directly from God to show He was aware of my need, loved me, and was working in the situation.

We can wait for someone to share a problem and then offer to pray, but we can also actively ask God to bring someone to mind that He wants us to support through our prayers. With or without their knowing, we can do kingdom work through our prayers.

After all, we have the example of Jesus. Along with all the other ways He shows us His love, He also prays for us. My spine tingles as I read that Jesus is interceding for me.

FAITH STEP: *Invite the Holy Spirit to bring a specific person to mind and pray for them. Consider texting, calling or e-mailing to tell that person, "I'm praying for you."*

—Sharon Hinck

MARCH 19

"But whatever were gains to me I now consider loss for the sake of Christ. What is more, I consider everything a loss because of the surpassing worth of knowing Christ Jesus my Lord, for whose sake I have lost all things. I consider them garbage, that I may gain Christ." Philippians 3:7–8 (TNIV)

This has always been a hard verse for me, because essentially Paul is putting my life in perspective. I have to put Christ first. Jesus has to be such a high priority that in comparison, everything else in my life is garbage. Dross. Trash. Worthless. Nothing.

That means my husband and my family. My job. My friends. My hobbies. My ministries. In comparison to my dedication and commitment to Jesus, they're nothing but garbage.

That's really hard for me. I'm sure it's hard for other people too. You don't want to consider your kids garbage, right?

But I think Paul is saying that the things and people in our lives that might seem important are actually not as important as our relationship with Jesus. When we put Jesus first, we enable Him to transform us. And when we become more like Him, we can love our family even more deeply and we can do our jobs with even more dedication and wisdom.

It's hard to put Jesus first in my life, because I want to be first in my life, and I want to put the things that I care about the most as the highest priorities. It's a daily struggle for me to seek Jesus' will above my own wants and desires, to act according to how He'd want me to act, to allow Him to daily mold me into a better person. Molding can be painful!

But I know it'll make me whole. It'll make my life beautiful.

FAITH STEP: *What in your life are you putting as a higher priority than Jesus? How can you put Jesus first in your life and practice "taking out the garbage" today?*

—Camy Tang

MARCH 20

"Our Father which art in heaven, Hallowed be thy name.
Thy kingdom come. Thy will be done in earth as it is in heaven.
Give us this day our daily bread. And forgive us our debts,
as we forgive our debtors." Matthew 6:9–12

God is our Father. We are kids of the King, princes and princesses because God adopted us. Our astounding sibling is Jesus. God's not a standoffish parent who rears us from afar, but a personal Father who desires to be involved in every part of our lives. He wants us to tell Him every little thing, the hurts and the joys, the trivial and the significant. He's interested in everything we do. Imagine! The Creator of the universe longs to be in conversation with us. Prayer is a time for Him to reveal Himself to us. It is a privilege and a gift we must take advantage of. He has even told us how to pray.

Dear Daddy, who lives in heaven, you are so awesome. Please come back and bring heaven with you. I want to do whatever you ask of me here on earth and then in heaven, forever and ever. Please give me food to eat and fill my needs because I can't do it without you. Forgive the bad things I've thought, said or done to others. And help me forgive the people who have hurt me. Don't let me be tempted by bad things but protect me from them…

FAITH STEP: *Today, talk to your Father in heaven as a child to a loving father.*
Use straightforward, uncomplicated words to express your heart.

— Judy Baer

MARCH 21

"Glory to God in the highest heaven, and on earth peace to those on whom his favor rests." Luke 2:14 (NIV)

I lived many years without peace in my heart. My attention was focused on unhealthy relationships. My desire was for the approval of others, no matter the cost. Yet the attention, affection and approval I received was never enough. I did what I knew I shouldn't to try to get what my heart felt was lacking. I had sex out of wedlock. I drank even though I was underage to get my friends' approval. I watched R-rated movies I didn't enjoy because I wanted to fit in. For every person who gave me approval, another refused. Even though I was trying to please others, my sins weighed me down.

Sin means missing the mark. It's choosing our ways above God's, and any way other than God's will always bring pain. But like the angels announced, Jesus made the way for peace. Not peace between nations, but peace deep in my soul—our souls.

Peace came first when I dedicated my life to Jesus. Peace comes daily when I turn to Him through all the challenges of life.

- When I'm worried, peace comes when I say, "Jesus, I trust you."
- When I'm tired, peace comes when I surrender, "Jesus, I need your strength."
- When I'm fearful, peace comes when I know Jesus is watching me, loving me always.

Because of Jesus, the peace sung about that night in Luke 2 is always available to me. All I need to do is ask. All you need to do is ask.

FAITH STEP: *What situation is taking away your peace? Imagine placing that problem on your open hands and stretching it up to Jesus. Realize He now has the situation in His grasp. Allow peace to come.*

—*Tricia Goyer*

MARCH 22

"Jumping out of the boat, Peter walked on the water to Jesus. But when he looked down at the waves churning beneath his feet, he lost his nerve and started to sink. He cried, 'Master, save me!' Jesus didn't hesitate. He reached down and grabbed his hand. Then he said, 'Faint-heart, what got into you?'" Matthew 14:29–31 (MSG)

*I*t is late March, yet winter still clings to the landscape. Tired of being cooped up, I take the dog for a walk in the deceitful sunshine: despite the clear, bright weather, the temperature is in the thirties, with a brisk wind.

As I walk against the wind, I think what a fitting metaphor that is for challenges, for those times in life when twice as much effort seems to yield half as much progress. When Peter tries surfing without a board, he's walking against the wind. Matthew 14:24 says, "The wind came up against them and they were battered by the waves" (NIV).

Walking or rowing against the wind is hard enough. Doing it on water, battered by the waves, seems impossible.

Sometimes Jesus asks us to do the impossible, with His help. In *If You Want to Walk on Water, You've Got to Get Out of the Boat*, John Ortberg writes: "Is there any challenge in your life right now that is large enough that you have no hope of doing it apart from God's help? If not, consider the possibility that you are seriously underchallenged. If you want to walk on the water, you have to be willing to get your feet wet first. Then you discover it is worth the risk."

Jesus calls us to walk on water. We want to accomplish great things. But when we face challenges, do we cower in the boat, or do we jump out expecting to do the impossible, with God's help?

FAITH STEP: *Spend some time journaling about the question, "Is there any challenge in your life right now that is large enough that you have no hope of doing it apart from God's help?"*

—Keri Wyatt Kent

MARCH 23

"We speak, not in words taught us by human wisdom but in words taught by the Spirit, explaining spiritual realities." 1 Corinthians 2:12–14 (NIV)

𝓘 love teaching literature, and when my students respond and learn to like reading and writing, and give me new ideas about things I've read a hundred times, I get really, really excited. It's just fun.

In my classes we read a lot of cool stuff that provokes deep thinking, like Kate Chopin on marriage, Tolstoy on faith, and Langston Hughes on race. We read poetry about growing up, isolation, love, and death. And we usually do a reader's theater with either a Shakespearean comedy or a Greek tragedy. I love digging into these works of art and mining the insights they offer.

I believe that knowledge is empowering in the natural sense. It's great when my students are able to carve out better lives for themselves and their families as a result of going to school. I get completely choked up when I see one of my students "make it," like a single mom on welfare who recently graduated and found a job that uses her talents and pays her bills. However, for all that's great about literature and knowledge, it will only take a person so far. Without Jesus, it's empty.

The deepest joy I have as a teacher is when I get to speak blessings of hope into the lives of my students and co-workers. I've found that all I have to do is show up and God will send someone by with a need. Yesterday it was a co-worker who was worried about her daughter. I was able to listen and offer a verse that the Lord brought to mind.

Other times I don't even have to show up. A student called me at home today and apologized for having to miss class. She asked for the assignment. But that really wasn't the only reason she called. Her partner, the father of her two children, had just been arrested for soliciting a prostitute, and she needed to talk to someone. Needed someone to pray.

I don't always know what to say in these situations; in fact, I seldom do. But when I find myself there, I also find the Spirit is with me to help me express truth and offer the blessing of hope.

FAITH STEP: *Who needs to receive a blessing of hope from you today?*

—*Gwen Ford Faulkenberry*

MARCH 24

"And when you fast, don't make it obvious, as the hypocrites do, for they try to look miserable and disheveled so people will admire them for their fasting. I tell you the truth, that is the only reward they will ever get. But when you fast, comb your hair and wash your face. Then no one will notice that you are fasting, except your Father, who knows what you do in private. And your Father, who sees everything, will reward you." Matthew 6:16–18 (NLT)

Fasting is not a popular spiritual discipline in our culture. When I was in my twenties, I tried fasting once a week—drinking only water and a bit of fruit juice on Wednesdays, in preparation for midweek prayer and worship service. This went all right until I fainted in church one Wednesday evening! I gave up on fasting for quite a while after that.

But it is possible—and sometimes harder—to fast from things other than food. For some, it might be an even greater sacrifice to fast from, say, Facebook or Fox News. Notice Jesus' word choice: He does not say, "if you fast," but "when you fast…"

Fasting—giving up something in order to focus on God—is a practice that Jesus engaged in. It can draw us closer to Him, but only if we can do it without bragging about it. Jesus warns us not to brag about this practice—or any spiritual practice, really.

What holds you in its grip? How would you finish the sentence, "Wow, I really need…"? A cup of coffee? A glass of wine? To veg out in front of the TV? In fasting, we discover the hidden need—for comfort, love, companionship, stimulation—that such surface "needs" attempt to meet. Could you, for a time, fast from that which masks your true needs, so that Jesus can step in and meet them?

FAITH STEP: *Today, try fasting. Rather than giving up all food, try giving up something that you consume mindlessly: soda, television, gossip. Don't tell anyone what you're doing.*

—*Keri Wyatt Kent*

MARCH 25

"Create in me a pure heart, O God, and renew a
steadfast spirit within me." Psalm 51:10 (NIV)

*M*y mom grew up in Pennsylvania Dutch country, with a deep tradition of spring cleaning. She passed along the habit to me, although I've never managed to emulate her degree of thoroughness. Each year, as soon as winter retreated enough to let us open the windows, she'd dive in to days of hard work. She'd pull everything from a room, scrub the walls and floors, and wash the windows. Then she polished the furniture and also used the time to sort through drawers and declutter, wash curtains and linens, and flip mattresses.

I groaned when she recruited me to dust endless bookshelves, or hand-buff the wood floors. But I have to admit that the scent of lemon polish and freshly washed curtains billowing in the crisp spring air was intoxicating.

Every time I read Psalm 51, I think of spring cleaning. Repentance is a time to fling wide the windows of my soul and invite the fresh wind of the Holy Spirit to enter. It's a time to invite Jesus to sort through the clutter I've accumulated and toss out the little pet sins that grow like dust bunnies.

He might push aside a larger dresser so I can see the dirt that's piled up behind it, or throw open a window shade so the light reveals where my spirit needs some polishing. He frequently uses Scripture to show me the actions, words or attitudes that He wants to clear out. Other times a friend might gently point out a blind spot, or I'll hear a sermon that convicts me. Sometimes He'll even show me the mess in my heart by letting me witness a similar problem in someone else. When I'm offended by someone's action, I've learned to take a peek into the rooms of my soul, because it's often a clue that I'm battling with that same root issue.

The wonderful part of inviting Jesus to spring-clean my heart is that I don't have to wait for spring. It can be a daily celebration of His forgiveness and the transformation He brings to my life.

FAITH STEP: *Invite Jesus to clean every nook and cranny of your heart.*

—Sharon Hinck

MARCH 26

"Let everyone be quick to listen, slow to speak." James 1:19 (NRSV)

*W*hy must I learn this lesson over and over? To dominate a conversation is to show a lack of respect for those I am with. To enjoy the sound of my words too much is self-centered. To talk over someone's words because I think mine are more important is egotistical. That's not the person I want to be.

We've always been a little "hard of hearing." Jesus spoke in parables because "seeing they do not perceive, and hearing they do not listen, nor do they understand" (Matthew 13:13, NRSV). We humans can be a little slow sometimes.

My desire is to hold my tongue and listen to others so that I can hear what their hearts are longing for. I can then hear that a man's wife is ill… that a mother is losing her apartment…that a young woman is being laid off at work…that a twentysomething man is battling drugs…that someone is going without food. If I genuinely hear people, I will truly know how to help them.

Christ is the Ultimate Listener. It is He who hears our cries and intercedes for us. I want to learn from His example.

FAITH STEP: *Can you think of times when you have diminished someone by not truly listening to them or enjoyed the sound of your own voice more than theirs? Listen first and speak second today.*

MARCH 27

"The apostles returned to Jesus from their ministry tour and told him all they had done and taught. Then Jesus said, 'Let's go off by ourselves to a quiet place and rest awhile.' He said this because there were so many people coming and going that Jesus and his apostles didn't even have time to eat." Mark 6:30–31 (NLT)

*W*omen often feel like we spend a lot of time pouring ourselves out, juggling a variety of responsibilities. Yesterday I got up early and wrote for a couple of hours. Then I worked at my part-time job for seven hours, came home and created something out of the nothing that was in the pantry for dinner, and then quizzed my daughter on "key terms" for an hour and a half to prep for a history test. By the time I fell into bed at about 10:00 pm, my neck hurt. Today was much the same.

It's important, in the midst of days like these, to find a way to replenish our reserves. Use whatever analogy works for you: put on your own oxygen mask first, prime the pump, fill your cup, whatever.

Jesus calls us not only to serve but also to rest. We must stop and let God fill us with His love and power, so that we can pour it into our families, our work, our ministry. Jesus invites us to come away, even while there are still many items on our to-do list. He invites us to come to a quiet place and rest. What would that look like in your life? You may think you can't afford to take some time for quiet reflection and prayer before starting a busy day, or to spend a bit of time with a friend for coffee and conversation, or to take a nap. But maybe you can't afford not to.

FAITH STEP: *Imagine Jesus is saying to you: "Let's go off by ourselves to a quiet place and rest awhile." How will you respond?*

—Keri Wyatt Kent

MARCH 28

"The gatekeeper opens the gate for him, and the sheep listen to his voice. He calls his own sheep by name and leads them out." John 10:3 (NIV)

I've been trying to walk regularly for exercise, and since I don't have a gym membership or a treadmill, I was out walking yesterday, in the rain.

The first time I walked in the rain, I was miserable. I had on a jacket, but it wasn't waterproof—it was only water-resistant. Very big difference, as I learned, when water began cascading down my back.

Also my hands were so cold, I couldn't feel my thumbs. I couldn't feel my ears either. And my jeans were soggy with water.

I reminded myself this was for my health, and then scurried home.

But the next time, I was better prepared. I borrowed my husband's waterproof jacket, I dug out some old ski pants that were waterproof, and I had on fingerless gloves and a knitted hat to keep my ears warm. And into the rain I went.

When I wasn't so uncomfortable, I realized how peaceful it was. No one except me, the crazy person, was out walking in the rain. I could smell the scent of rainwater, and it seemed to clear my sinuses and expand my lungs. The sound of dripping water was soothing and calming. And without all the noises that were normally around me in my house, I could hear my thoughts. I could hear my prayers.

That day, in the rain, in the quiet, I could suddenly hear Jesus so much clearer than before. It was like I had been in a big pen of noisy sheep, and Jesus was calling me. I hadn't been listening for Him, but when I heard Him, I recognized His voice, His touch in my spirit.

FAITH STEP: *Find a place where you can be comfortable and not distracted, where you can block out the normal noises of everyday life. Find a place like that so you can just listen to Jesus.*

—*Camy Tang*

MARCH 29

"He is able to save to the uttermost those who draw
near to God through him." Hebrews 7:25 (ESV)

I hate to admit it, but sometimes the story of Jesus dying on the cross and saving people from their sins gets a little familiar for me. It's not that it ever loses its power, or becomes boring or anything. It's just that it is so ingrained in me that I can almost take it for granted, like breathing.

The other day I was sitting in my Sunday-school class with Angie. She came to our church several years ago as a total vagabond, just showed up on the doorstep needing money for gas. She got that, but she also got Jesus. Her conversion and subsequent growth as a Christian was grand-scale miraculous. I was amazed by her—and Jesus in her—for a long time.

But that was years ago. I've gotten used to her being there now. We've been in Sunday-school class together; she's been to my house a lot; we're friends. I guess in a way I've started to take her for granted as time has gone by. She's become just normal Angie. One of the gang. Except that the other day I was reminded of what has happened in her life—the total transformation. And just like that, I was awestruck by Jesus again.

Our teacher was talking about how we never "arrive" as Christians, that we are always growing. It's like we arrive at one point and then realize there is so much further to go with the Lord; He never runs out of grace or tires of leading us onward and upward.

Angie made a little joke about arriving. She said she knew she'd arrived—at least to a significant place in her journey—when she got return-address labels in the mail and she could actually use them: "I never stayed in one place long enough before; I was always on the run."

In that moment the miracle of salvation welled up in me so strong I could have cried. It really still happens to people. Jesus still comes to those who receive Him and He still changes lives. It's a simple story—but, oh, so beautiful.

FAITH STEP: *How might He want to transform you? Invite Jesus to have His way with you—personally—today.*

—Gwen Ford Faulkenberry

MARCH 30

"He entered a certain village, where a woman named Martha welcomed him into her home. She had a sister named Mary, who sat at the Lord's feet and listened to what he was saying. But Martha was distracted by her many tasks; so she came to him and asked, 'Lord, do you not care that my sister has left me to do all the work by myself? Tell her then to help me.' But the Lord answered her, 'Martha, Martha, you are worried and distracted by many things; there is need of only one thing. Mary has chosen the better part, which will not be taken away from her.'" Luke 10:38–42 (NRSV)

$\mathcal{I}$ am such a Martha sometimes.

I think, "I'll just do a couple more chores and then I will have time for those things I really want to do." And a couple things turn into five. Then I start a load of laundry, mop a floor, pick up a few odds and ends and…I'm always of the mindset that if I get everything else done, then I can really concentrate on my prayer time. I have it so wrong!

I could work morning to night and never be done. Yet if I put God first like Mary did, the tasks still get done, the day unfolds as it should and I am carried through it in God's loving hand. There is always space for Jesus.

"Mary has chosen the better part, which will not be taken away from her." I need to remember that. Martha's work will have to be done again. There will be dishes to wash, rooms to clean, bills to pay, groceries to be purchased. But Mary's time at the Lord's feet will be with her forever. Imagine sitting at the feet of Jesus, listening to His words, hearing His voice. Nothing can replace that—for Mary or for us.

FAITH STEP: *Today, choose to "do" less and "be" more at the feet of Jesus.*

– Judy Baer

MARCH 31

*Then Moses summoned all the elders of Israel and said
to them, "Go at once and select the animals for your families
and slaughter the Passover lamb." Exodus 12:21 (TNIV)*

*W*e live in a society where the concepts of sin and debt don't mean the same as when Jesus was growing up. The Israelites knew that sin against God had to be taken care of. Sin created a debt that had to be paid.

Today, we don't sacrifice lambs or take a man's hand when he steals from us. People fudge what's considered a sin and don't always pay the consequences of their actions.

But the same principles of sin and debt still apply. If your enemy hurts you, you feel there's a sort of "debt" owed to you. Either your enemy pays that debt with some form of punishment, or you choose to forgive your enemy. If you forgive, then you are paying the debt for your enemy's actions.

When we sin against God, no matter how small, there's a debt that needs to be paid. Rather than us paying for our debt, Jesus has. He's the sacrificial lamb. At the Lord's Supper, which was the Passover meal, there wasn't a lamb on the table because Jesus was the Passover lamb. He's the sacrifice for all our sins.

Let that sink in. Jesus is the lamb that was killed to pay your debt. If we forget that, we take for granted what Jesus should mean in our lives.

FAITH STEP: *What can you write or draw on a card that will remind you to hold close your debt and how Jesus died to pay it? Take some time to create something that will help you remember not just during Easter, but all throughout the year.*

—Camy Tang

April

APRIL 1

"When Jesus entered Jerusalem, the whole city was stirred and asked, 'Who is this?' The crowds answered, 'This is Jesus, the prophet from Nazareth in Galilee.'" Matthew 21:10–11 (TNIV)

Jesus entered Jerusalem riding on a donkey. Crowds of people had gathered to welcome Him, praising Him and blessing Him, praising God for Him. They put their cloaks and palm branches on the ground before Him. They shouted "Hosanna!"—an expression of praise that also means "Save!"—because He was their King, come to save them.

People who didn't know who He was asked others in the crowd, who told them. They probably went to listen to Jesus that week as He taught in the temple. He proclaimed good news for the poor, freedom for the prisoners, sight for the blind—but not the way they expected. Most didn't believe Him. They would crucify Him in one week.

Our job as children of God is to prepare the way for Jesus. He'll proclaim freedom for the captives, and people will either believe Him or not. But it's not up to us to make them believe—we only need to pave the way.

Instead of throwing our cloaks in front of Him, we can give to the poor. Instead of shouting "Hosanna!" we can worship Him with our service in a foreign country. Instead of answering, "This is Jesus, the prophet from Nazareth," we can show Jesus' love to the people we interact with at work and school.

FAITH STEP: *How are you preparing the way for Jesus to reach others around you? Come up with a list of five things you can do this week.*

—Camy Tang

APRIL 2

"Sing to God a brand-new song, sing his praises all over the world! Let the sea and its fish give a round of applause, with all the far-flung islands joining in. Let the desert and its camps raise a tune, calling the Kedar nomads to join in. Let the villagers in Sela round up a choir and perform from the tops of the mountains. Make God's glory resound; echo his praises from coast to coast." Isaiah 42:10 (MSG)

Spring, spring, spring! Can you smell the fresh breeze through my open window? Ahhh!

I love the freshness of spring each year. I walk taller, feel healthier, enjoy more color in my face and a boost in my energy. Everything about spring breathes of life and newness. I love seeing green fields with baby calves reaching up for a drink from Mama. At home, I can't get enough of my own children running coatless around our yard, exploring each square foot as if it were brand-new. I can't help but lift my face to thank Jesus for the smile He gave me through His wonderful creation of springtime.

I guess that's why I love Isaiah 42:10, which draws a picture of a world reveling in the joy of praising God. I can almost hear it. It's amazing how God—the Ancient of Days, the Omega, the One Who Was and Is and Is to Come—is Lord not only of our past, but also of our future. He is Lord of all that will be new as He makes it beautiful in His time. (See Ecclesiastes 3:11.)

Imagine the newness experienced by people whose lives spanned the time before Jesus' birth until after His death. The handful of His people who believed in Him back then felt not only the longing for the Messiah but also the new joy that He arrived at last!

If springlike praise has faded in your heart, ask Jesus to plant in you fresh seeds of joy.

FAITH STEP: *Draw a picture of something you'd like Jesus to make new. Write on it a favorite verse or song of praise.*

—Erin Keeley Marshall

APRIL 3

"When the Son of Man returns, how many will he
find on the earth who have faith?" Luke 18:8 (NLT)

I smile at the light in my husband's eye as he measures sugar and pours it into the water-filled feeding tube. He gently stirs the mixture until it's the perfect blend. Then he secures the cap and goes outside to hang it on the hook by the window. It's that time of year again, and he is prepared to welcome back the hummingbirds to our deck feeder.

Before I met him I knew the basics of hummers: They're tiny and their wings beat quickly. But nothing in my world had been affected much by their flight patterns, their feeding habits, their personalities or even their beauty.

Now I enjoy watching our tiny friends return each spring almost as much as I enjoy my husband's delight in them. He loves how, when we're picnicking on the deck, they flit close by to let him know their sugar water is all gone. He's fascinated by how one bird assumes the alpha role and chases others from the feeder. There's a lot to hummingbirds, and he never fails to be prepared for them each spring.

Recently he said he likens that preparation to our trust in Jesus' promise to return. It's Easter season now, so those matters are particularly on our minds. Many people are surprised to see hummingbirds back already. Most people wait to prepare the sugar water until after they see one bird. He likes to be ready early, though, and acts in faith that the hummers will return. I love his insights. We have yet to see the first hummer this season, but we are prepared.

I believe God intended His creation to reveal clues to His love for us. I know those special birds will always remind me to keep trusting in Jesus' inevitable second coming.

And I can't help wonder if my moment-by-moment living reflects a solid faith and preparedness for that day.

FAITH STEP: *What do nature's details reveal about Jesus' love for you? How does your life show you're prepared for His arrival?*

—Erin Keeley Marshall

APRIL 4

" 'What shall I do, then, with Jesus who is called the Messiah?' Pilate asked." Matthew 27:22 (NIV)

*A*s the wife of a children's pastor I often find myself with a puppet on my hand or leading a group of children in their favorite Bible songs. I've also been known to act out a few Bible stories in my time. I love acting out Bible stories, unless I have to play a "bad" part, like the time I was a member of the crowd, crying out to Pilate to crucify Jesus. Tears filled my eyes as angry shouts escaped my lips, "Crucify him!"

It's easy to think of those "foolish people of Jesus' time" as the ones who really messed up. Jesus walked among them. They saw His miracles, and yet when they had to decide whether He should live or die, they chose death. How could they have done that to Him? we wonder. Couldn't they see who He really was?

The fact is, each of us must answer the same question daily: "What shall I do then, with Jesus who is called the Messiah?" Should I give Him access to my heart? Should I turn to Him for direction in my life? Should I allow His truths to matter more than my opinion? In quiet mornings it's easy to say yes to all these things, but following through is the hard part. Daily at work, through our friends and through popular culture, we get the message that Jesus doesn't matter. Voices around us cry out in independence and defiance, and too often we find our own voice joining in.

Sometimes I'm the foolish person who chooses to follow the crowd. But the closer I grow to Christ, the more I'm learning to consider what I am doing with Jesus this moment, this day.

FAITH STEP: *Consider the voices around you that cry out in defiance against Jesus. You may not shout the same angry words but your lack of submission to Jesus leads to the same result. What is one courageous step you can take to allow Jesus to be Lord of your life today?*

—*Tricia Goyer*

APRIL 5

*"After saying this, he spit on the ground, made some mud with
the saliva, and put it on the man's eyes. 'Go,' he told him, 'wash in
the Pool of Siloam' (this word means 'Sent'). So the man went
and washed, and came home seeing." John 9:6–7 (NIV)*

Every spring when I prepare my garden, I think about dirt. As I turn my
raised beds, rich, loamy compost feeds my soil. But there are many other
textures of dirt: heavy clay, grit that rubs between the toes, mud that clings
to everything.

You'd think the Holy God of the universe would like things sterile, pris-
tine. But He got His hands dirty when He formed Adam from the dust of
the ground. When the Pharisees were about to stone a woman, Jesus wrote
on the ground with His finger. He washed grit from His disciples' feet.
And He amazes me daily as He walks beside me in the muddy confusion
of my ordinary life.

One of the powerful messages of the incarnation—Jesus becoming
man—is that God doesn't hold Himself far away from us. He also uses the
real-life things at hand to do His miraculous work in our daily lives. He
could have healed the blind man with a touch, a word or even a thought.
It's so interesting to me that Jesus made some mud and used that as a tool
of healing.

This story makes me more alert to the ordinary and even messy aspects
of life that God can use: an unexpected phone call that interrupts our
agenda and steers us in a new direction, a broken window that gives us a
chance to teach a child about grace and forgiveness, a miserable cold that
reminds us to rely on God instead of our own strength, a bowl of soup that
creates a memory of love for our family, a friend's e-mail that suggests a
solution to a problem they didn't even know we had, a book we happen to
pick up on the precise day we need the message within, a new job, a birth,
a funeral and even a mud puddle. Jesus came down to earth and continues
to use the down-to-earth parts of our life to bring blessing.

FAITH STEP: *Invite Jesus to take the muddy struggles of your life and sculpt a
blessing from that humble clay.*

—Sharon Hinck

APRIL 6

"Lord, I have heard of your fame; I stand in awe
of your deeds, Lord." Habakkuk 3:2 (TNIV)

*S*ometimes, like if you've grown up in church, or if you've just heard about the crucifixion enough times, it starts to lose its hold on you.

"Yes, Jesus died for me."

"Yes, He took my sins on Him on the cross."

"Yes, He rose to give me new life."

On Good Friday, we remind ourselves of Jesus' sacrifice, but what about the rest of the year? Is Jesus' death for us so insignificant that we don't need to think about it for 365 days?

Paul stood firm in the face of persecution by carrying the death of Jesus with him. (See 2 Corinthians 4:10.) But we don't want to be reminded of Jesus' death only when we're in trouble or facing trials.

So take the time today, right now, to remind yourself of what exactly Jesus did for you. To let the enormity of His sacrifice sink in.

Habakkuk was in awe of the Lord's mighty deeds. Let's also be in awe of Jesus' one amazing deed, His taking our place, His taking away our sins. Be humbled. Be filled with wonder and amazement.

Give Jesus your reverence, your admiration, your praise, your fear. He is the lamb of our sacrifice, and He is also God.

FAITH STEP: *Give Him all of you—surrender yourself to Him in thanks for what He did. Be completely uninhibited in your love for Him, your gratitude, your worship. Stand up, right where you are, and be in awe of your Jesus.*

—Camy Tang

APRIL 7

*"I, the Lord your God, am a jealous God, punishing the children
for the sin of the parents to the third and fourth generation of those
who hate me, but showing love to a thousand generations of those
who love me and keep my commandments." Exodus 20:5–6 (NIV)*

We've heard it countless times, but it's such good news for us that it bears lingering over again. It's the synopsis of God's love story to us. Grab your favorite hot drink, sit awhile with me, and let's consider it all.

The Bible is the epic story of love that we scorned, which earned us damnation. Then because God wanted to spare us that horror, He created the legacy of grace through His Son, Jesus. Now all who accept His gift can enjoy unbroken relationship with Him.

Grace wins.

Okay, so the Old Testament age of wrath is over. Where does justice fit in now? It's still there, which is either wonderful or awful depending on whether a person's heart is for or against Jesus.

Because God is utterly holy, there's no overstating how much He despises our sin nature; that's the worst news we'll ever hear. But there's also no overstating how much He adores His grace. Best news!

Even during the era of wrath before Jesus came, God showed His gracious character to us. It's all there in Exodus 20:5–6. Even though we suffer the effects of our ancestors' sins for a few generations, He thrills to show His love to a thousand generations.

God must be just. Even so, He shows a strong preference for grace.

Amazing grace—how sweet that sounds!

FAITH STEP: *Think over your ancestry. Does your family tree appear to be rooted in Jesus' grace or suffering the effects of God's wrath? No family is immune to sin's curse, but you can be the generation that turns the tide toward Jesus. How are your life and faith affecting current and future generations?*

—Erin Keeley Marshall

APRIL 8

"Dogs surround me, a pack of villains encircles me; they pierce my hands and my feet. All my bones are on display; people stare and gloat over me. They divide my clothes among them and cast lots for my garment." Psalm 22:16–18 (TNIV)

*A*s a mom I learned very quickly not to let my children know when they were going to the doctor for immunizations. If I told them too early I'd hear about it for days. Most of the time I'd tell them when we arrived at the doctor's office, because knowing about the prick and the pain to come was as painful as the prick itself.

Realizing this makes me more in awe of Jesus' sacrifice; His death for our salvation was known. Hundreds and hundreds of years before Christ's death David wrote about it in the Psalms, down to specific details such as Jesus having His hands and feet pierced and lots cast for His clothes.

More than that, it was planned by His Father. Acts 2:23 reads, "This man was handed over to you by God's deliberate plan and foreknowledge; and you, with the help of wicked men, put Him to death by nailing Him to the cross" (TNIV).

Knowing Jesus faced pain and death for my sins causes my heart to ache. Realizing that God planned it from the beginning of time and He still created man makes it even more meaningful. My children being worried about immunizations for a few days pales to our Christ knowing of His death from creation, but Jesus setting His eyes on the cross long before He walked the earth makes me love Him even more.

FAITH STEP: *Take a moment to visualize Jesus' determination—set chin, fixed gaze—even at creation. Take extra time today to praise and thank Jesus for His sacrifice.*

—*Tricia Goyer*

APRIL 9

"No one lights a lamp and then covers it with a bowl or hides it under a bed. A lamp is placed on a stand, where its light can be seen by all who enter the house." Luke 8:16 (NLT)

There comes a time, when you're deeply aware of how much grace God has poured into your life, that you simply cannot hold it inside you anymore. It occurs to you that to hoard grace is an oxymoron, and that if you do so, that makes you, well, a moron.

You must release it, let it out. Share it. Jesus said that if you've been forgiven much, you'll love much. (See Luke 7.) He said, let your light shine. (See Matthew 5:16.)

Growing up, I was told shining your light was a metaphor for witnessing, which in the evangelical tradition I found myself a part of, meant giving a verbal witness: sharing the plan of salvation with people and dragging them, somehow, across "the line of faith."

I wonder, doesn't a life, radically changed by grace, shine brighter than an argument about the existence of God? Isn't grace lived out more compelling than grace theologically explained?

If we fully grasp the truth of grace, it would change how we live and especially how we love. We would shine. God's love and grace would flow through us—we'd become grace's conduit.

In many ways, grace—and the joy it brings—makes no sense. Which is precisely why it's such a gift. You can try to manufacture a positive attitude without experiencing grace. But it's going to be just that—manufactured. Or you can receive the grace of God, and then choose to let what is already inside simply shine out on everyone around you.

FAITH STEP: *Ask Jesus to make you aware of His grace today, and give you the courage to simply shine.*

—*Keri Wyatt Kent*

APRIL 10

"You ignore God's commandment while holding on to rules created by humans and handed down to you." Mark 7:8 (CEB)

During His earthly ministry, Jesus loved extravagantly, but confronted ruthlessly. Seemingly unconcerned with political correctness, He took on religious leaders who had gotten off track, pointing them back toward truth.

How often do we read their story and smugly look down our noses at the Pharisees in our lives, not realizing that by doing so we commit the same sins of pride and self-righteousness that Jesus was confronting in them?

What does it mean to follow Jesus, to love Him? So often, without realizing it, we live by a reductionist faith, trying to follow "the rules" while minimizing our risk. We try to be "good" by avoiding blatant sins like lying or cheating, and by reading our Bible and saying our prayers. But we secretly hope Jesus doesn't expect us to live as He lived—forgiving anyone who wronged Him, spending time with "sinners," loving the unlovely.

The college I attended had rules against drinking and dancing, among other things. Yet the Bible seems to indicate that Jesus drank wine and that King David danced with all his might as a form of worship. I'm not trying to make an argument for or against either activity, but only to point out this: Sometimes we hold on to rules created by humans and handed down—our traditions.

Now, those traditions are not necessarily bad—sometimes they are helpful. But sometimes, they pull us off track. We get caught up in arguing about styles of worship. We turn minor theological points into major ones. We say "this is the way it's always been done" without really looking at the full scope of history. Or we get puffed up with pride about how well we follow the rules.

Rules can be helpful, but they are not what we put our faith in.

FAITH STEP: *What are the "rules" you've learned about the way you practice your faith? Are those actually making you into a person who loves and lives like Jesus would?*

—Keri Wyatt Kent

APRIL 11

"I want to know Christ—yes, to know the power of his resurrection and participation in his sufferings, becoming like him in his death, and so, somehow, attaining to the resurrection from the dead." Philippians 3:10–11 (NIV)

What does it mean to "know Christ"? This is something I've struggled with a lot. Knowing Christ can't be knowing whether He prefers whole milk or skim milk, or if He likes a red tie more than a blue one, or if He's a "get up and go" type of guy or the sort to spend hours gelling His hair.

Even the phrase "to know Christ" seems to speak to a deeper part of me. To really know someone deeply, you have to know all of them—their hopes and fears, their weaknesses and strengths, the pretty parts and the ugly parts of them.

The great thing is that Christ is perfect! However, there are parts of Him that I don't always understand, like a lot of what is said about God in the Old Testament, and how Jesus is described in Revelation. Some of that seems so different from the Jesus in the Gospels.

But I think to truly know Christ, we have to try to fully understand all His extremes: How incredibly He loves us. How much He suffered for us. How desperately He wants us with Him. How He hurts when we turn away from Him.

When we try to understand all that, and begin to know Christ, it makes us want to respond to Him. We want to be transformed for Him. We are willing to suffer for Him. We are willing to be unselfish and giving, all for Him.

FAITH STEP: *Spend time with Jesus in prayer. Ask Him how you can truly know Him. Bare your heart to Him, and He'll bare His heart to you.*

—Camy Tang

APRIL 12

"I pray that you may be active in sharing your faith, so that you will have a full understanding of every good thing we have in Christ." Philemon 1:6 (NIV)

On a crisp fall day when I was in high school, I walked up to a strange door and rang the bell. My palms felt sweaty and my heart seemed stuck partway up my throat. As part of a youth evangelism team, I was walking through the neighborhood knocking on doors, sharing about Jesus with anyone interested, and inviting them to visit the local Christian church.

The team leaders had given us careful training on how to be prayerful, respectful and prepared to share the basics of our faith. Still, I wondered what I'd do if someone slammed a door in my face or pounded me with theological questions I didn't know how to answer.

A woman came to the door, eyes red-rimmed, face haggard. I politely explained I was from a local church and gave her information about our services. We chatted a bit and I asked if I could share a Bible verse with her. Inserting her name into John 3:16, I began to recite how God so loved her that He sent His Son.

Tears streamed down her face. She reached forward and hugged me. "I have to explain," she said through her tears. "My daughter ran away last week and it's been a terrible time. I needed to know God hadn't forgotten about me." I prayed with her, tingling with the awareness that God had sent me to that specific house on that specific day to share His love.

Whether with a friend or a stranger, sharing my faith is still often scary. But if I keep it to myself, I miss out on having a "full understanding of every good thing we have in Christ."

FAITH STEP: *Tell someone about Jesus' love for them today.*

—Sharon Hinck

APRIL 13

"Among those who belong to Christ, everything connected with getting our own way and mindlessly responding to what everyone else calls necessities is killed off for good—crucified." Galatians 5:24 (MSG)

*I*n my perennial garden this week, green tips push back the cold earth like a curtain, tremulously beginning to sprout. On a warm spring day, I get to work with my pruning shears.

Many of my flowers have tall beige spikes, dry and strawlike, towering above the tender shoots. The best way for me to help my perennials grow is to cut away those dead branches. The iris plants have wispy ash-blond ribbons curled around the new green shoots—last year's dead leaves. I gently pull them away and cast them on the compost pile.

No one would accuse me of hurting my plants with this pruning. What is dead must be removed, in order to make room for life. Similarly, what feels like life—getting my own way—will actually kill my spirit unless I submit to God's pruning, letting Him remove the sin in my life.

Our selfish ambitions, our mindless consumption and advertising-driven appetites—these are the dead stalks blocking new growth in our lives. The things we cling to are chaff—dry, useless and a hindrance. If we belong to Christ, if we really are beloved children, we must trust that Jesus has our best interest at heart when He takes away what we think we want. He's really simply creating space so we can grow, blossom and bear fruit.

FAITH STEP: *What "necessities" do you think Jesus wants to kill off or prune from your life? Where are you insisting on your own way, so much so that it hinders your growth?*

—*Keri Wyatt Kent*

APRIL 14

"If only you had paid attention to my commands, your peace would have been like a river, your well-being like the waves of the sea." Isaiah 48:18 (NIV)

"*I*f you had paid attention to God's commands…peace…your well-being—" The speaker's words from Isaiah caught my attention.

What did she say? Which commands? What about peace and well-being?

I sat up in the pew, alert and wondering what the connection was between paying attention—ironic, huh?—and peace and well-being. I was always on the lookout for ways to experience more peace.

I glanced down at my open Bible. There…Isaiah 48:18. It seemed once again God was reminding His people what they could have experienced had they stuck closer to Him. But that one verse didn't detail which of His commands. I stayed focused for the remainder of the Bible-study lecture.

Ever been amazed by a verse's simple depth? I began to wonder whether I was paying heed to all of God's commands—not just the Big Ten, but other ones tucked away here and there throughout Scripture.

For instance, how had my worrying been lately? Jesus tells me not to do it in Matthew 6:25. He also tells me repeatedly to trust Him, to not fear, and to love others. Do I exhibit all the qualities of love that 1 Corinthians 13 describes? Patience, kindness, humility, unselfishness, forgiveness, etc.? If not, I'm not really obeying the command to love.

I felt overwhelmed over how much work I had to do. My head swam and drowned any lingering threads of peace I had going for me.

But then I remembered Jesus' admonishment that living by His commands comes much easier when I focus on Him.

The next instant I felt something else: peace.

FAITH STEP: *Do your own study on Jesus' peace. Look up three verses about peace, and ask Jesus to help you stay focused on Him.*

—*Erin Keeley Marshall*

APRIL 15

"Now you are the body of Christ, and each one of you is a part of it." 1 Corinthians 12:27 (NIV)

I've been overeager since grade school. When the teacher asked a question, I'd wave my hand. Oooh. Oooh. Pick me! I was desperate to contribute. Even in pigtails and saddle shoes, I wanted to feel like my presence made a difference in some way—that I had something to offer to the discussion.

Impatient teachers rolled their eyes. Kind teachers found ways to be diplomatic as they said, "Sharon, let's give someone else a turn." Whether the message came with a frustrated or gentle tone, it was hard for me to grasp that by not being called on, I was giving a classmate his or her chance to contribute.

That's still a difficult concept for me. I love saying yes to new opportunities, but am not so good at laying down an activity when God asks me to. He often whispers to my heart, "If my purpose is for you to wait, will you trust I love you no less?" He also challenges me to celebrate the opportunities He gives to others to use their gifts, to be joyous as they get to contribute.

When the first snowstorm of the winter arrived recently, I set up a jig-saw puzzle. As I worked on it throughout the week, I glanced past the pieces that seemed dull and uninteresting. My eyes were drawn instead to the key red piece for the roof, or the vibrant blue bit over the treetops. I shoved aside a muddy brown piece and left it to wait at the side of the card table. But when the puzzle was complete, that last piece was vital. Each piece, each shape, each color, contributed to the finished work.

God hasn't called me to be every piece in the puzzle, or even to be the shiniest and brightest piece. He asks me to be the specific piece He made me to be.

FAITH STEP: *Has a life situation caused you to feel like you can't contribute as much as you'd like? Does it feel like all the other puzzle pieces are more important to the picture? Let's rejoice that God is giving others a turn, and trust that as we wait, we are also serving Him.*

—Sharon Hinck

APRIL 16

"For it is by grace you have been saved, through faith—and this is not from yourselves, it is the gift of God—not by works, so that no one can boast. For we are God's handiwork, created in Christ Jesus to do good works, which God prepared in advance for us to do." Ephesians 2:8–10 (NIV)

Outside my window, cold rain falls. The grass is greener than it was a few days ago, the trees have begun to bud—but today, the promise of spring remains just that, a promise. We've had a few warm days, but this is April in Chicago—definitely, as T. S. Eliot observed, the cruelest month. We can go from forty degrees to eighty and back again in a day or two. Today, it's forty-two and raining.

But still, the many bulbs that I planted a long-ago autumn come up. It happens every year. The crocus bloomed two weeks ago. Now the daffodils are up, and the scilla—delicate tiny lavender blooms, only a few inches tall—carpet the bed along the front walk.

A bulb is a nugget of potential. But only if you plant it. If you leave bulbs in the garden shed, which I've done, they dry out and turn to dust. They won't ever bloom unless you "save" them by putting them into the dirt.

All winter, the snow melted down through the earth to water them. The bulbs rest, bathed in grace—an essential prerequisite to blooming.

Paul's musings in Ephesians 2 can feel like a contradiction: We're not saved by works, but we're created to do good works? But Paul is describing a journey that begins with salvation. Being saved through faith is akin to being planted, and the good works we do are how we bloom.

FAITH STEP: *Spend some time with Jesus, thanking Him for the free gift of salvation by His grace. Then, ask Him to show you the works that you've been created in Him to do—and ask Him to give you the courage to bloom.*

—Keri Wyatt Kent

APRIL 17

"Don't be selfish; don't try to impress others. Be humble, thinking of others as better than yourselves. Don't look out only for your own interests, but take an interest in others, too. You must have the same attitude that Christ Jesus had." Philippians 2:3–5 (NLT)

*Y*esterday I thought I had my day planned. My goal was to tackle my to-do list and work on some freelance projects I was behind on. All that changed when I received a call from a teen mom who'd recently given birth. She had a doctor's appointment and needed a ride. Even though I had my plans, I felt nudged to lay down my interests for hers.

What started as one appointment turned into an all-day affair. The young mom asked to come to my house to use my computer to research some school reports. Then she asked if she could use my camera so she could get photos of her newborn. They were just simple things, really. How could I say no?

Sometimes I get overwhelmed with the needs of others, and it makes me consider how Jesus must have felt. He had crowds following Him, demanding His time. They wanted answers. They wanted to be healed. If Jesus—who was the Son of God—had an attitude of service and humility, should I do any less?

It's easy to complete a task; it's harder to impact a life. Marking another project off my to-do list won't matter for eternity. People matter most. When that young mom looks at those photos of her baby in years to come hopefully she'll remember our day and remember that there are those who love her with the love of Jesus.

FAITH STEP: *Has someone asked you for help recently? Put down your interests and reach out to help that person, asking God to help you take on the attitude of Jesus Christ.*

—*Tricia Goyer*

APRIL 18

*"I was hungry and you gave me something to eat, I was
thirsty and you gave me something to drink, I was a stranger
and you invited me in...." Matthew 25:35 (NIV)*

For years, my neighbor Bobbie and I drove to the west side of Chicago on the second Saturday of each month to serve breakfast at the homeless shelter.

One Saturday, after cooking three dozen jumbo eggs with plenty of cheese mixed in, hash browns, bacon and countless bagels and serving them to about twenty women, I visited with one of the guests. She told me excitedly that she was on the list to get a subsidized apartment within the next two weeks, and said God had been blessing her over and over lately.

She asked me how long we'd been volunteering there. I told her about two years, and she asked, "Why do you do it? What's in it for you?"

I pondered that one. The Bible says we should care for those in need, and that when we do, it's as if we did it to Him. "For me, to be here serving breakfast, it's worship," I told her. She nodded knowingly.

We talked about the value of living simply, whether you are in a shelter, a government-subsidized apartment or a suburban tract house. She told me about losing her job and her apartment, and ending up on the street, about how God had led her to this shelter.

Sitting at the shelter, listening to a homeless woman teach me about God's generosity, is like sitting at Jesus' feet. When we feed the hungry, it's as if we're tending to Jesus Himself. To have a conversation with women I would not otherwise cross paths with—and to be surprisingly blessed by that conversation—brings me into God's presence.

FAITH STEP: *How might you begin to practice what Jesus has asked of us: to feed the hungry, give water to the thirsty, or take in the stranger?*

—*Keri Wyatt Kent*

APRIL 19

"Also, if two lie down together, they will keep warm. But how can one keep warm alone? Though one may be overpowered, two can defend themselves. A cord of three strands is not quickly broken." Ecclesiastes 4:11–12 (TNIV)

When I was single, I struggled powerfully. Almost all my friends had significant others. They didn't make me feel unwanted, but I saw how close they were to their boyfriends, how those guys had become their best friends. While I had several friends, I couldn't say any of them were my best friend. I didn't have enough in common with them, and they didn't understand that deepest part of me. I thought a boyfriend, someone who loved me and who completed me, would be able to touch that part of me and make me feel accepted and whole.

I didn't realize how wrong I was, and I suffered for years, looking for the right person, asking God why He wouldn't send him to me. I finally realized He didn't send me a boyfriend because He wanted me to find that deep connection with Himself.

I was too caught up in finding a man to meet my needs, rather than relying on Jesus Himself. After all, that's the reason He died for me—to have that close connection with me, so that I would abide in Him and He in me. I needed to discover how to draw closer to Jesus, to allow Him to fill that God-shaped hole inside my heart.

And once that happened, Jesus led my future husband to me. And now the three of us are a cord of three strands.

FAITH STEP: *Are you struggling with singleness right now? My prayer for you is that you will draw ever closer and tighter to Jesus. If you're married, my prayer is that you will draw closer to both Jesus and your spouse so that you will be a cord of three strands.*

—Camy Tang

APRIL 20

"Early in the morning, well before sunrise, Jesus rose and went to a deserted place where he could be alone in prayer. Simon and those with him tracked him down. When they found him, they told him, 'Everyone's looking for you!' He replied, 'Let's head in the other direction, to the nearby villages, so that I can preach there too. That's why I've come.' He traveled throughout Galilee preaching in their synagogues and throwing out demons." Mark 1:35–39 (CEB)

*E*arly in the morning, my phone started ringing. By 9:00 am, I'd gotten five texts, two phone calls and three e-mails, just about the details of carpools and so on for activities at school and church for my fifteen-year-old. I love that my kids want to serve at church, that they play sports. But I seem to spend a lot of my time driving, or coordinating driving, for my kids' activities.

The rest of my day was full of writing projects, a meeting with a client (more driving), and more calls, e-mails and texts about other details of my life. I made some time for solitude by turning off the radio while driving, and by taking a walk late in the day.

Jesus didn't have to manage carpools while juggling work assignments, but He did have plenty of people who demanded much of Him. His life was full of interruptions—even His quiet time got interrupted! The Gospels, especially Mark's, read like a fast-paced novel, in which Jesus seems to keep a pretty busy schedule.

And yet, Jesus was never hurried. In the midst of other people's demands, He is unruffled. He always seems to have time for what matters. "Busy" is an external thing—our to-do list and responsibilities. "Hurry" is an internal state of agitation caused by how we choose to respond to our schedules.

FAITH STEP: *Read through Mark 1. Make up a list of the things Jesus does, the overall pace of His life. Journal about the hurry level of your life, and how you might be able to change that.*

—Keri Wyatt Kent

APRIL 21

*"Therefore, since we have so great a cloud of witnesses surrounding us,
let us also lay aside every encumbrance and the sin which so easily entangles us,
and let us run with endurance the race that is set before us, fixing our eyes on
Jesus, the author and perfecter of faith...." Hebrews 12:1–2 (NASB)*

As an author there is no better feeling than to get to the end of a book and write, "The End." I often sit back, thread my fingers behind my neck and breathe a sigh of relief. It is done.

Of course, "done" is a relative term. There is editing to do. Most of the time there is rewriting. There is talk of cover design and page layout. The "done" when I type "The End" is more like a "done-for-now."

Thankfully Jesus' "done" had more finality. "It is finished...." (John 19:30, NASB); "Father, into Your hands I commit My spirit" (Luke 23:45, NASB).

Jesus' story continued on, of course. We know of the resurrection, of Jesus' remaining days on earth and His ascent to heaven. Those who walk on earth today are even part of His story two thousand years later. Still, Jesus finished a chapter of life on earth we'll never return to again. The price for sin was paid. We can look back to that moment and accept it for ourselves.

Unlike the books I write, Jesus authored the plan and finished it through. Because of His Finish we can look forward to a life with Christ that never ends, and that's the best conclusion I can imagine!

FAITH STEP: *Have you thanked Jesus recently for His death and sacrifice? Take time to do that now. Also thank God for writing you into His story. And thank Him that your end on earth is only the beginning in heaven with Him.*

—Tricia Goyer

APRIL 22

"I pray that from his glorious, unlimited resources he will empower you with inner strength through his Spirit. Then Christ will make his home in your hearts as you trust in him." Ephesians 3:16–17 (NLT)

I wiggled my toes deeper under the soft blanket and inhaled the steam from my mug of tea. This is the life!

I love the rare evening when I can rest on the couch, cup of tea and good book in hand, knowing my kids are safe in bed and my husband is nearby. Those are the moments when the homey-ness of my home sinks through to my bones. I am content.

The Bible is filled with references to home, from God promising and leading His people to a new home in the Old Testament, to Jesus' words about creating a home for us to spend with Him throughout eternity. (See John 14:2–3.) God knows our need for a deep sense of home. Even He desires a home where He feels at home. In the Old Testament it was the tabernacle and then the temple.

Have you ever really considered the impact of our hearts being Jesus' home, as He spoke of in the New Testament? Think for a moment what that means: the Creator, Master, Lord and Savior of the Universe—the One who can't be contained—desires to make His home in you and me.

On those quiet evenings when I have time to reflect on the deep issues of life, I sometimes wonder if my heart is expanding to allow Him more breathing room in me. Does my heart, in the words of 2 Corinthians 3:18 (CEV), "show the bright glory of the Lord, as the Lord's Spirit makes [me] more and more like our glorious Lord"? Is my love overflowing more and more as I grow in knowledge and understanding of Him? (See Philippians 1:9.)

Come on in, Lord Jesus. Make Yourself at home.

FAITH STEP: *When do you feel most comfortable in your home? Do you think Jesus feels at home in your heart? Ask Him to be your Master Renovator.*

—*Erin Keeley Marshall*

APRIL 23

"Remain in me, as I also remain in you. No branch can bear fruit by itself; it must remain in the vine. Neither can you bear fruit unless you remain in me." John 15:4 (NIV)

As a child I worked hard to be good. In Sunday school I wanted to be the one who'd memorized the memory verse. In junior high I kept my locker perfectly clean and turned in my homework on time. Even today, as a grown woman, if I don't have my lesson finished I consider not going to my Bible study. A part of me would rather sit at home and miss seeing my friends than show up with blank answers on the page. How sad is that?

For many years I faced Christianity the same way. I wanted to be good. I wanted to be Jesus' star follower. I memorized the "fruit of the Spirit" in Galatians 5:22–23 and kept a mental list in my mind. "Loving, check. Joyful, check. Peaceful, got it."

The thing is, the fruit of the Spirit is exactly that—the growth that blooms out of an intimate, connected relationship with Jesus Christ. This fruit of love, joy, peace, forbearance, kindness, goodness, faithfulness, gentleness and self-control were never meant to be something I achieved from my own strength. As I spent mornings with Jesus, the fruit of the Spirit came as He bloomed in my life throughout the day.

FAITH STEP: *The fruit of the Spirit is a result of Jesus' Spirit flowing out of us in good times and challenging ones. In what aspect of your life have you tried to "be good"? What is one step you can take that will welcome Jesus into your life—your soul—each day so that fruit will start to blossom up out of you?*

—*Tricia Goyer*

APRIL 24

"The God who made the world…himself gives everyone life and breath and everything else…. God did this so that they would seek him and perhaps reach out for him and find him, though he is not far from any one of us. 'For in him we live and move and have our being.' As some of your own poets have said, 'We are his offspring.'" Acts 17:24–25, 27–28 (NIV)

One of my favorite hymns is "Great Is Thy Faithfulness." Despite my good intentions, despite the fact that I deeply love Jesus, I am not always faithful to Him. But "his compassions they fail not." He is faithful.

The Bible talks much more about the faithfulness of God than the faithfulness of people. God never gives up—He's always present, always seeking us out. This amazing truth is ironically the cause of our apathy, Mark Buchanan writes in *The Holy Wild*. Because "faithfulness is, by definition, the predictable, the habitual, the sturdy, the routine," it is easy to take it for granted.

So often, my prayers are asking Jesus to help me, to rescue me from the consequences of my unfaithfulness. I take His faithfulness for granted. His love is a constant in my life. Which presents a dilemma, Buchanan writes: "God's faithfulness is one divine characteristic that we rest in so completely that our rest has become apathy. 'In him,' Paul declares, 'we live and move and have our being.' So our dilemma: How do we rest in God's faithfulness, but never take it for granted?"

It is because of His faithfulness, not our own effort, that we are able to put our faith in Him.

FAITH STEP: *Go online and find an audio version of "Great Is Thy Faithfulness"—there are several good ones in a variety of styles on YouTube.com—and simply sit and listen. Let the words soak in, and let them lead you into a prayer of thankfulness for Jesus and His faithfulness.*

—Keri Wyatt Kent

APRIL 25

"We have sought the Lord our God; we sought him and he has given us rest." 2 Chronicles 14:7 (NIV)

*I*t happened again last night.

Sometime in the wee hours, I stirred from sleep to a dark house. On this particularly night, the dewy scent of spring nature wafted through the bedroom window and pulled me to attention.

God had gotten me alone again to listen for Him.

Have you ever woken with the sense that you needed to take a concern to Jesus? Maybe someone's face appeared in your sleepy thoughts, or possibly a nagging doubt presented itself again. Maybe a feeling of conviction over some sin kept you from quickly returning to peaceful slumber.

All of those reasons and more have claimed my sleep many times over. In fact, I think I wake up two-thirds of most nights with the conscious need to talk to Jesus. It's precious time, really. Often the quietest I have.

Last night's wake-up left me seeking Him about a hurting loved one whose nights are particularly difficult. When I hear God's middle-of-the-night call to present something or someone before His throne, I'm eager to do so, even though I know I may be sleepy later. Some things just take priority, you know?

After praying, my heart and mind felt restful, and I fell back to sleep. Then when I got about the day a few hours later, I sensed again that I needed to talk with Jesus, this time about a concern of my own. And again, only after releasing my burdened thoughts to Him did my spirit rest.

Jesus knew when He needed to talk to His heavenly Father (Luke 5:16), and He offers us a special kind of rest when we seek Him (Jeremiah 29:13; Matthew 11:28). What a gracious gift! But even more gracious is how He lets us know we need to seek Him when we're not conscious to recognize the need ourselves (Romans 8:26).

FAITH STEP: *Pay attention to Jesus' hints to seek Him today. What comes to mind? Pray it through, and enjoy His rest.*

—*Erin Keeley Marshall*

APRIL 26

"Then a cloud appeared and covered them, and a voice came from the cloud: 'This is my Son, whom I love. Listen to him!'" Mark 9:7 (NIV)

*W*e live in a culture marinated in words. The sheer amount of content on the Internet is staggering, and growing each day. In a world where so much information is flowing—through our computers, radio, television, cell phones—how do we know what to pay attention to? It could be that you are reading these words even now on an electronic reader. All this access to information might be helpful, if we could figure out how to wade through it all. How do we know what to listen to?

God said of Jesus, "Listen to Him!" I talk to Christians who wish they could have lived at the time Jesus walked the earth, so that they could listen to Him in person, see Him, let His warm embrace melt their doubts.

They forget that our culture has unprecedented access to Jesus. A generation or two ago, many Christian homes had only one Bible. Before the invention of the printing press around 1440, copies of the Bible stayed mostly in churches.

Today, as I write, I am looking up Bible verses on a website that offers me instant access to two dozen English translations as well as the Bible in Bulgarian, Arabic and Haitian Creole, to name a few. You can download the Bible on your BlackBerry. Bibles that look like magazines or even comic books exist.

As a result, we can listen to Jesus any time we want—if we'd only take the time to do so. When we sit down and read a portion of the Gospel, carefully reflecting on it, we can hear Jesus' voice. We can imagine ourselves in the story, and it is like spending time with Jesus. We can read His words, reflect on them, and truly listen.

FAITH STEP: *Today, read a short portion of one of the Gospels. Read slowly and thoughtfully, imagining yourself to be right there watching and listening to Jesus.*

—Keri Wyatt Kent

APRIL 27

"But seek first his kingdom and his righteousness, and all these things will be given to you as well." Matthew 6:33 (NIV)

Seeking first means before sleep, before vacation, before downtime.

Seeking first means before the husband, the kids and the in-laws.

Seeking first means before e-mail, Facebook and YouTube.

Seeking first means before housework and laundry.

Seeking first means before that cup of morning coffee or midday snack.

Seeking first means before that work project or budget meeting. (Believe it or not, God wants our attention and focus even more than our boss wants them.)

Seeking first means before chocolate.

First means first. It doesn't mean you have to get up and read the Bible before taking your shower; it's just making sure Jesus is not last on your to-do list and He is a priority during your day.

"First" is a heart attitude. He's the first on your mind during trouble. He's the first you thank during a celebration. First has Jesus on the forefront of your mind and looking at life through His point of view.

First doesn't mean not being who you are. It's going to Jesus and asking Him who He has planned for you to be—in your life, in your day.

Jesus asks for first, not because He wants to suck up all your time and energy, but rather He knows everything you set your mind and heart to works better with Him at your side.

FAITH STEP: *Go to your to-do list and write "Jesus" as the first thing on your list. Then take time—even if it's five minutes—to spend with Him and ask Him what "first" means for the rest of your day.*

—Tricia Goyer

APRIL 28

*"I know your works; you are neither cold nor hot. I wish that you
were either cold or hot. So, because you are lukewarm, and neither cold nor
hot, I am about to spit you out of my mouth." Revelation 3:15–16 (NRSV)*

Lukewarm coffee…tepid bathwater…blasé attitudes…half-hearted enthusiasm…barely warmed meals…lackadaisical participation…desultory contributions…disinterest…indifference. Not exactly the things you crave in your life, right? We send lukewarm food and beverages back to the kitchen to be heated, and we shy away from people who are indifferent.

God wants lukewarm Christians to "fire up," to become feverishly hot for His cause. In Revelation, He chastises the church in Laodicea for becoming lukewarm, indifferent and self-satisfied.

Apathy, complacency and self-sufficiency have no place in God's kingdom. He requires one's full heart. We get to read Scripture and talk to the Lord in prayer; we don't have to. Become an enthusiastic Christian through study of the Word, fellowship with other believers, and prayer.

FAITH STEP: *Pray, "Lord Jesus, pump me up with a spirit of joy! Let me not be blinded by the petty things of life. Let me live passionately for You."*

—Judy Baer

APRIL 29

"Jesus wept." John 11:35 (NIV)

*I*t's the shortest verse in the Bible, but its depth of meaning is significant. Jesus' dear friend Lazarus is dead. Lazarus' sisters are distraught. They'd seen the teacher heal so many. Why did this happen? Why couldn't—or didn't—Jesus heal Lazarus? Why didn't He come sooner? Doesn't He care?

When Jesus arrives, Lazarus has already been in the tomb for four days. Martha hears He's coming and heads out to meet Jesus. She wants answers. When Jesus was visiting last time, Martha donned an apron and headed to the kitchen. Knowing her personality, Jesus provides an answer: "Your brother will rise again." With Martha, Jesus got down to the bottom line.

Mary, on the other hand, is the tenderhearted sister. She was the one found sitting at Jesus' feet in Luke 10:39. When Mary approaches, she asks the same question, but Jesus' response isn't the same. Seeing her weeping He's deeply moved. He cries with her.

Two women, two personalities, yet a Lord who understands…who loves them just as they are.

Sometimes I'm like Martha. I want answers. I want an explanation for the hurt and pain. Through reading the Bible and praying, I find hope and comfort. Jesus never lays out the complete picture of how things will work, but He reminds me He's got the situation under control.

Other times I'm more like Mary. I don't need an answer; I simply need to feel Jesus' love. Just like Jesus asked for Mary, Jesus tells me to come, and in my coming I don't need to be ashamed of my tears. In fact, my heart finds a special peace knowing He's weeping with me.

FAITH STEP: *When is the last time you cried? Think back to that moment. Picture Jesus weeping with you. How does that change your view of that circumstance?*

—*Tricia Goyer*

APRIL 30

"Be still, and know that I am God." Psalm 46:10 (NRSV)

*G*ood morning, Lord.

As I sit in my cozy room looking out at what is left of the night sky as well as the peach-hued sunrise fringed by tall pines, I am reminded again of Your quiet but miraculous power. There is perfection in Your mornings, Lord, before the household is up and the lights come on, before the television news intrudes into the day and I pick up that rusty bucket of worries, cares and to-do lists that I tend to drag with me throughout my waking hours. When at night I close my eyes on the weariness, frustration and toil of the day, I turn my circumstances and my world over to You. I go to sleep on my messy situations and wake up to a clean palette of silence and beauty. You are the source of serenity and loveliness, Lord. You ask us to be still and know that You are God. You even give us beautiful morning hours—and moments of sanctuary throughout a busy day—if only we will notice and take advantage of them.

FAITH STEP: *Today, Lord, help me to see the beauty you have made, to find the pockets of time that I know are there. Help me to give thanks and praise and to be still so that I can hear Your voice and once again be assured that You are God.*

— Judy Baer

May

MAY 1

"Tell people who are rich…to do good, to be rich in the good things they do, to be generous, and to share with others. When they do these things, they will save a treasure for themselves that is a good foundation for the future. That way they can take hold of what is truly life." 1 Timothy 6:17–19 (CEB)

Last year, our family felt God leading us to give away our third car. With one teenager driving and the other less than a year from starting driver's ed, this might have been a foolish move. But we felt compelled, especially by the story of a young mom in need.

We gave the van to a single mom with five children who had recently lost her husband to cancer, who'd come into our lives through a strange set of "coincidences." She needed a car with five backseats (like our van) for her little ones—four of whom were in car seats. The van needed some major work, so several families from our church came together to pay for repairs to make it safe for this family to drive—repairs we actually didn't have the money to pay for by ourselves.

We ended up with three cars (an amazing blessing) because my ninety-two-year-old grandmother gave us her old car. (Yes, she drove it until my uncle insisted that she give it away!) We'd gotten rather used to the luxury of having an extra vehicle, but felt that living like Jesus meant being generous and sharing with those in need.

So giving away the van was an exercise in trust and obedience. It was also a reminder that we are indeed rich, compared to so many. We have no doubt that God will provide in the future.

Missionary Jim Elliott once said, "He is no fool who gives what he cannot keep to gain that which he cannot lose."

FAITH STEP: *How might Jesus be calling you to be generous and share with others?*

—Keri Wyatt Kent

MAY 2

"On hearing this, Jesus said, 'It is not the healthy who need a doctor, but the sick. But go and learn what this means: "I desire mercy, not sacrifice." For I have not come to call the righteous, but sinners.'" Matthew 9:12–13 (TNIV)

*A*fter I became a Christian, I spent a lot of time still stuck in my past. I hadn't been as wild a young woman as some other people I knew, but still, I wasn't proud of who I had been and what I had done. There were times I wasn't even sure I had changed all that much.

The guilt still gnawed at me, like a dog working on a bone. I spent too much time thinking about my past and worrying about reacting the same old way to new problems. My self-esteem took a hit right to the gut, because I didn't feel worthy of being a child of God, and I didn't understand how I could possibly please Jesus.

I spent a lot of time looking back when I should have spent my energy on looking forward.

Jesus didn't want me because I was perfect. He said Himself that He came for the sick, not the healthy. That also means He's ready to heal me and make me someone else. Someone new and better.

I closed the door on my guilt, my shame, my insecurities. I stepped out into a world where Jesus would mold me into someone He wanted me to be.

FAITH STEP: *Is there anything in your past that you're focusing on? Is there guilt or insecurity holding your back? Pray, believe in Jesus' forgiveness, and close the door on all those things. Jesus is more than capable of setting you free from your past.*

–Camy Tang

MAY 3

"Blessed be…the God of all comfort; Who comforteth us in all our tribulation, that we may be able to comfort them which are in any trouble, by the comfort wherewith we ourselves are comforted of God." 2 Corinthians 1:3-4

*M*y friend Misti miscarried her baby girl, Piper, shortly before she was to be born. In the years since the loss of Piper, Misti and her husband have suffered greatly. It is as though they've been walking through the valley of the shadow of death even as they experienced new joys and the birth of a healthy son, Griffin.

In conversations with Misti about faith, I have shared her search for meaning in the midst of her loss. It's difficult. Nobody but God really knows all of the answers. Something happened the other day, however, which redeems Misti's situation in a small way. It happened when she heard about a woman who lost her baby at full term.

"My heart just broke," Misti told me. "I knew God was telling me to go and talk to her."

Even though it was hard, she spoke to the woman. And by reaching out, she was able to help another person who suffered a loss similar to hers. The woman told her that no one else had understood the way Misti did. Misti was able to see into her heart and offer hope.

I'm not saying this is the reason God allowed Misti or this lady—or anyone else—to suffer. For most of us the pain still wouldn't be worth it even if that were true. I don't know all of the answers or the reasons He allows suffering. But I've seen through this situation that we can choose to trust Him and look for the good in anything—and it's a part of our own healing when we do.

FAITH STEP: *Elisabeth Elliot writes, "Repeatedly throughout our lives we encounter the roadblock of suffering. What do we do with it? Our answer will determine what we can say to another who needs comfort." Allow Jesus to comfort you today, so that you may extend His comfort to others.*

—Gwen Ford Faulkenberry

MAY 4

*"My sheep listen to my voice; I know them, and they follow me.
I give them eternal life, and they shall never perish; no one will
snatch them out of my hand." John 10:27–28 (NIV)*

"We'll talk again soon. I love you." I tried to infuse every ounce of support and compassion I could into my voice as the phone call ended. As I put the phone down, my hand shook and tears poured down my face. One of my adult children had just told me about a choice that I knew could lead in a bad direction. The feelings of helplessness were brutal.

When they were toddlers, if my children ran into the street, I could dash after them, swoop them up, and carry them to safety. These days, I sometimes feel that I'm standing at the curb while they play in traffic, spiritual dangers bearing down on them like semitrucks. I'm stuck on the curb, seeing the oncoming cars. I shout myself hoarse as that child smiles and waves and says, "I respect your opinion, but I'm fine right here."

After the recent tough phone call from one of my children, panic colored my prayers. But slowly, Jesus reminded me that my worry didn't glorify Him. Even those who are most precious to me—my children—are safe in His hands. The days of young children in the home—when I chose nutritious food for them, led them in devotions and held their hands when we crossed the street—are past. It hurts when they make worrisome choices. It is true that I can't physically whisk them to safety these days, but I continue to pray for them, listen, love, wait and trust. The Shepherd of our souls who began a good work in them will bring it to completion.

As I pray for my children each day, I thank God that I had the privilege of parenting them for so many years, and that He continues to guide their lives. I also ask Him to hold my hand tightly, and that if I wander off the curb, to pull me back to safety.

FAITH STEP: *Think of the people who matter most to you. Ask Jesus to guide them today.*

—*Sharon Hinck*

MAY 5

"There was nothing beautiful or majestic about his appearance, nothing to attract us to him. He was despised and rejected—a man of sorrows, acquainted with deepest grief. We turned our backs on him and looked the other way. He was despised, and we did not care." Isaiah 53:2–3 (NLT)

As I waited at the red light to exit the grocery parking lot, I found myself looking at a "least of these," as Jesus called them in Matthew 25:40.

Who are they? Jesus mentions them as the hungry, thirsty, lost, sick and imprisoned, categories that can broadly include anyone hungry for compassion, lost in loneliness or imprisoned by an unhealthy lifestyle.

While they may catch an awkward stare, they and their needs aren't really seen by many others. Sometimes they are abuse victims aching for someone to notice the bruise, the second glance that triggers the help they feel helpless to ask for. Sometimes they are wealthy and privileged, yet longing for love that doesn't demand perfection.

This particular "least of these" was a homeless man holding a cardboard sign requesting anything at all that anyone would spare him. Lately Jesus has been sensitizing my heart to look for behind-the-scenes pain, and I couldn't tear my gaze from this man. He, however, had lost so much dignity that he barely looked up.

Imagine the utter brokenness of not feeling valuable enough to even be seen. Invisible. Worthless. Instead of beautiful and priceless to Jesus.

When Jesus walked the earth, He saw people. Although He was not physically eye-catching by society's definition, His beautiful heart looked into people's souls, saw their desperation and cared enough to do something about it.

I gave the man some extras from my groceries and Sunday-school artwork personalized by my kids. Then I prayed that Jesus would nourish his spirit through our little bit.

Let's look and see today.

FAITH STEP: *Ask Jesus to coordinate encounters with His beloved "least of these." Then pay attention, because He will do it. He longs to love them through you.*

—*Erin Keeley Marshall*

MAY 6

"Whether you turn to the right or to the left your ears will hear a voice behind you saying, 'This is the way, walk in it.'" Isaiah 30:21 (NIV)

When my father-in-law Ralph was dying with cancer, my husband and I prayed that we would be a comfort to our family. It was such a terrible time of sadness, of never knowing really what to say or do. We just tried to be available when we were needed for practical things, as well as to listen, hug, pray for and love all of those involved—especially my husband's mother Barbara.

One evening after visiting them on a very difficult day, Stone and I were preparing to leave. We only lived a few miles away, so we rarely spent the night at their house. As we were gathering our coats, an amazing thing happened. In the same instant we both felt the Lord speak very clearly to our hearts and He said, "Stay." So we did.

That night we prayed beside Ralph's bed. Stone and I asked the Lord to send angels to minister peace and to release Ralph from his suffering. Then we kissed Barbara goodnight and went to our room on the other side of the house.

We had scarcely gotten into our pajamas when we heard her cry out. We met in the hall as she was running toward us, and together we walked back to their room. Ralph had peacefully passed from this world into eternity…and we had the privilege of being there, for him and for her.

FAITH STEP: *What is Jesus speaking to your heart today? Take a moment and listen for His still, small voice.*

—*Gwen Ford Faulkenberry*

MAY 7

"But seek first his kingdom and his righteousness, and all these things will be given to you as well. Therefore do not worry about tomorrow, for tomorrow will worry about itself. Each day has enough trouble of its own." Matthew 6:33–34 (NIV)

I ought to get a PhD in Worrying. I worry about things loooooong before they happen and loooooong after they're done. I worry about the right words to say to someone. I worry about waiting in line. I worry about getting lost. I worry about spending too much money. I worry about getting sick.

Lately I've been realizing how ungodly worry is—how worrying is actually not trusting God. I worry about the right words to say because I don't trust God to give me those words. I worry about waiting in line because I don't trust God to help me get everything done that day. I worry about getting lost because I don't trust God to be right there with me when I turn onto a random side street. I worry about spending too much money because I don't trust God to nudge my conscience before I pull out my wallet. I worry about getting sick because I don't trust God to heal me.

Rather than spending my energy on worrying, I need to focus on what God wants me to do. This could be something big like whether to move to a new state, or it could be something as small as to host a women's Bible study at my home one week.

If I "seek first His kingdom and His righteousness," if I focus on Jesus' will and my obedience to Him, He'll take care of the rest. "All these things will be given to you" means that Jesus will make sure everything turns out for the best.

FAITH STEP: *Take a few moments to pray and release your worry to Jesus. Even if you have to do this a hundred times a day, what matters is that each time you do it, you're telling Jesus, "I trust You."*

—Camy Tang

MAY 8

*"As a mother comforts her child, so will I comfort you;
and you will be comforted...." Isaiah 66:13 (NIV)*

We usually think of God in terms of a Father—and, of course, He is—and of Jesus as our friend and our brother. But this verse in Isaiah shows another side: A nurturer. A comforter. Someone who fusses over us and watches us grow with tenderness. A caretaker. Someone intimately acquainted with all of our ways.

The word mother conjures powerful images of childhood for me: I'm riding my bike too fast and hit a rock that sends me sailing. I'm running for home base and I fall down and skin my knee. I drop my double-decker ice-cream cone and the dog gets to eat it. I have a nightmare and cry out in the middle of the night. Who is there, in a flash, to comfort me? My mother. Her kisses could make things better. Her voice could calm my fears. Come to think of it, I still want my mother when times are tough.

I've been privileged to watch this principle operate in a friend of mine named Lori, with her baby, who is one. Lori and I can be at the far end of her house, deeply involved in some activity, and she can instinctively hear Johnathan waking up from his nap. Before he ever begins to cry she is already there to pick him up, soothe him and rock him.

God tells us He is like this. Before we even whimper He is there—to comfort, to heal, to restore us again.

FAITH STEP: *Are you in need of comfort today? Allow Jesus to put His arms around you and give you peace.*

—*Gwen Ford Faulkenberry*

MAY 9

"Blessed are the poor in spirit, for theirs is the kingdom of heaven." Matthew 5:3 (NIV)

One Sunday, our pastor challenged us to talk to God about what we would like to offer Him from our time, talents and resources. I squirmed in the back pew. For months, I'd been battered with health issues that had stripped away abilities and limited my relationships, work and activities.

While the choir sang, I picked up a pencil and scribbled on the back of my bulletin, pouring my heart out to God:

"Lord, what can I give you? I was weak before. Now I've become frail. I was empty. Now I'm beyond empty—a pocket turned inside out. I come to you without talent, ideas, energy or zest. But I come. The more vast my emptiness, the more abundant your grace is to fill it. Show me what I can offer you. But even when all I can do is touch Your cloak and tremble, thank You for turning Your gaze to me and calling me daughter. Amen."

I dried my tears and joined in singing the closing hymn, but continued to wrestle with the question during the week. What did I have for Jesus to use? I knew He loved the poor in spirit and could use my neediness to draw me closer to Himself. But I still wanted to offer Him something, wanted to give to Him and His people. Then one morning, He led me to 2 Corinthians 8:12: "For if the willingness is there, the gift is acceptable according to what one has, not according to what one does not have" (NIV).

Relief flooded me. He understood. My life had changed, and there were some things I couldn't offer anymore—activities that took strength, abilities or financial resources that I no longer had. These days my gift to Him might be a brief, quiet conversation of encouragement with a friend. Another day it might be all I could do to prepare a meal for my family. Some days, my offering might only be whispering "I love you" to God through my pain. But my gift was acceptable.

I'd rather be strong, rich in possibilities, vibrant with accomplishments. Instead He gave me the gift of His love and acceptance and showed me the blessing of being poor in spirit—aware of my needs, and relying on His love.

FAITH STEP: *Do you feel like you have nothing to offer Him? Tell Him where you are poor in spirit, and let Him reassure you of His acceptance.*

—Sharon Hinck

MAY 10

"The angel of the Lord encamps around those who fear him, and he delivers them." Psalm 34:7 (TNIV)

I once had a difficult work deadline to meet, and so I was up in my office very late at night. My husband had already gone to bed, but I was awake and working at my computer, fortified with some caffeinated tea and a box of chocolates.

We bring our dog into our bedroom each night when we go to bed. I like it because I feel as if she's there to protect us. Usually my husband takes our dog with him into the bedroom when he goes to bed before I do, so I closed my office door and kept working.

I finished in the wee hours of the morning, and I walked out of my office and tripped over something solid and furry. I flew headfirst into the carpet at the same time I heard a canine yelp.

Apparently our dog had lain down right outside my door, encamped outside my office, watching over me. I had rewarded her with a kick to the side, but she was okay. She got lots of love when I picked myself up from the carpet.

The Lord encamps around us just like my dog, guarding us. We may not even be aware of it, like I wasn't aware of my dog watching over me, but He's there, never sleeping, always protecting us. Jesus said it Himself: "And surely I am with you always, to the very end of the age."

FAITH STEP: *Are you entering into a difficult situation today? Remember that Jesus is encamped around you. Draw a picture on an index card of a ring of angels around you. Then put it in your purse so that you can look at it during the day. Pray for Him to help you to remember to rest and trust in Him to be watching over you.*

—Camy Tang

MAY 11

"You are the light of the world. A city built on a hill cannot be hid. No one after lighting a lamp puts it under the bushel basket, but on the lampstand, and it gives light to all in my house. In the same way, let your light shine before others, so that they may see your good works and give glory to your Father in heaven." Matthew 5:14–16 (NRSV)

*W*here's my light? Is it hidden in a closet, behind closed drapes, or tucked in a cupboard? Or is it out where others can see it—written on my face, energizing my behavior, enlivening my words and animating the best that is in me?

I cannot be a hidden Christian, silent when I should speak up or going along with the status quo when I know it's wrong. Neither can I go without explaining my light to others and putting it into action to serve the needs of others. The Bible tells us to be doers of the Word, not only hearers.

Why would anyone want to extinguish the light of a city or allow a lighthouse to go dim in the midst of a storm? Why would anyone live in a darkened house without switching on a lamp or drive at night without headlights? And why would I have the light of Christ in me and not want to share it?

FAITH STEP: *What are the ways you can let your light shine? Make a list of things you can do and act on one of them today.*

— *Judy Baer*

MAY 12

*"I will contend with those who contend with you, and your children
I will save…. Then all mankind will know that I, the Lord, am your
Savior, your Redeemer, the Mighty One of Jacob." Isaiah 49:25–26 (NIV)*

I reached for the remote and clicked off the television. Enough. I'd heard my fill of horrible news today. The world is so unsafe, it can be haunting.

I'm facing some of these fears as my husband and I have our home on the market. For months we've weighed pros and cons of various neighborhoods. We look at proximity to amenities and work, playmates for our kids, school districts, etc. At the top of the list is the desire for an area that feels safe.

On a recent visit to my parents' home, I sought their input, and our discussion wound around to the safety issues of children walking to school. More realities from the news flitted through my thoughts.

"The world just isn't the same as it was back when you were in school," my dad said. Funny, but I remember them saying the same thing when I was growing up—how the world was not the same as when they were kids.

Times may be a changin', but in a basic way they haven't changed all that much. No one has ever been immune to evil's dangers on earth.

So how do we live above fear?

Only by immersing ourselves in Jesus' promises and relying on Him to be God, our Protector and Healer. Second Timothy 1:7 says, "God has not given us a spirit of fear and timidity, but of power, love, and self-discipline" (NLT).

Repeatedly He urges us not to fear, so we need to let ourselves breathe in His care.

Jesus has our house hunt—and our family—in His care, just as He has you and yours. The evils of life can never outgrow Him.

FAITH STEP: *Write down your biggest fears. Pray through one each day this week, and write Jesus' name over that fear as a visible reminder that He is Master and Victor over all.*

—*Erin Keeley Marshall*

MAY 13

"The eyes of the Lord are on the righteous, and his ears are open to their cry." Psalm 34:15 (NRSV)

I want my life to be a prayer. I cannot save my prayers for an appointed hour or certain day. Instead, I must practice praying with each and everything I do.

Washing dishes? I can sing. At the gym? I will pray on the treadmill. Playing with my children? I can emulate the way Jesus loved the little children and called them to Himself. Talking with friends? I will allow only good, compassionate and generous words to come from my mouth. When dealing with strangers, I will be particularly kind and thoughtful, even though I will never see them again. When I'm feeling lonely, I will remind myself that I am never alone. I am always in Christ's presence.

I will keep this in mind when I am tempted not to return a neighbor's borrowed book or tell a white lie that I assume will not hurt anyone. It's the small things that need better housekeeping in my life. After all, nothing is small to the Lord, Who cares about it all.

He sees what I do in the dark as well as the light. He hears the thoughts I wouldn't dare utter. The sinful desires that pulse through me are clear to Him. I will pray that He helps me never to act on the sin that goads me. I do not want to grieve Him by doing something wrong—even when there are no other witnesses to my actions.

FAITH STEP: *Live today as if Jesus is physically beside you, hearing and seeing everything you do.*

— Judy Baer

MAY 14

I ask that Christ will live in your hearts through faith. As a result of having strong roots in love, I ask that you'll have the power to grasp love's width and length, height and depth, together with all believers. Ephesians 3:17–18 (CEB)

I have lived near Chicago most of my life, in various suburbs. I love spending time in the city, which is home to beautiful public gardens, great beaches along Lake Michigan and some world-class museums.

I dig museums. Chicago's Museum of Science and Industry, originally built as part of the 1893 World's Colombian Exhibition, has some incredible exhibits. One that I remember from my childhood is the model of the human heart, enlarged enough that people could walk through it.

When, as a child, I asked Jesus "into my heart," I thought of the heart at the museum, and imagined Jesus shrinking Himself so He could literally move in to my heart. Maybe hanging a few pictures and putting a comfy chair in the corner so He could hang out there.

What does it really mean, though, to have Christ living in our hearts? It does not mean He is camping in the left ventricle, but rather, that He influences all that we do and think. We will live in love, and act in love. I've heard it said that love is a verb.

Paul's prayer for the Ephesian church, and for us, is that Christ would live in and through us, through our faith. When His love is a part of our essential nature, when He's influencing our true self, we grow strong roots in love.

FAITH STEP: *Who can you pray this verse for? Are you mentoring or discipling someone? If not, pray that God would lead you to someone who needs your encouragement and prayer.*

—Keri Wyatt Kent

MAY 15

"I have come that they might have life, and have it to the full." John 10:10 (NIV)

A famous play by Eugene O'Neill called *Long Day's Journey into Night* portrays the worldview that life gets progressively more difficult, and then we die. Four members of a dysfunctional family gather in their living room as fog descends on the landscape and their conversation—reflective of their lives—becomes darker till finally it is night. The fact that so many people relate to this play is sad. However, it seems a lot of Christians hold the opposite worldview, which is just about as depressing.

We sing songs like "I'll Fly Away" and "When the Roll Is Called Up Yonder," which, I believe, were intended as celebrations of the fact that heaven is real. But a prevalent train of thought in mainstream Christianity seems to be that our lives on earth are a Long Night's Journey into Day. It's the idea that life is just drudgery, a constant battle with sin and evil, a place of suffering. But somehow when we die it will all be worth it, because "when we all get to heaven" that's when we'll finally live. We tend to lose our focus—or better, shift it to the afterlife, rather than recognizing the kingdom of heaven is here with us now. In this life too.

Jesus said in John 17:3 that eternal life is knowing Him. And the benefits of knowing Him start the moment we are saved. We can enjoy His presence, His peace and His victory over evil in the day-to-day. He died to give us no less! Sure, there are going to be difficulties, but the Christian life is the best life to live on earth as well as in heaven. In reality, it's a Short Day's Journey into More and More Day.

FAITH STEP: *Take a few minutes to meditate on Jesus, and all that He is to you here and now—as well as forevermore!*

—*Gwen Ford Faulkenberry*

MAY 16

*"Although most of the many people who came from Ephraim,
Manasseh, Issachar and Zebulun had not purified themselves, yet
they ate the Passover, contrary to what was written. But Hezekiah
prayed for them, saying, 'May the Lord, who is good, pardon everyone
who sets their heart on seeking God—the Lord, the God of their
ancestors—even if they are not clean according to the rules of the
sanctuary.' And the Lord heard Hezekiah and healed the people."*
2 Chronicles 30:18-20 (NIV)

*K*ing Hezekiah's Passover wasn't perfect. He was having his people celebrate the Passover for the first time in years, after they had been under a king who didn't follow the Lord. The correct Passover month had already passed, but Hezekiah decided to hold it anyway. Also, there were lots of people who didn't know the law; they had never been to the temple, and they weren't ceremonially clean.

But Hezekiah wanted to have this Passover celebration as a fresh start of obedience to God. Hezekiah knew that God would want them to celebrate the Passover even though they weren't perfect.

In our culture, we're often expected to be perfect. In high school, you're laughed at if you make social mistakes. In our workplace, we're reprimanded for errors. In the home, we feel we're a failure if our marriage is going through a rough patch. At church, if you don't have perfect faith, people worry you're falling away from God. But here, God is saying that we don't have to be perfect for Him to be pleased.

We forget that when Jesus called Peter, Andrew, James and John, they weren't the great men of faith we think of; they were just fishermen. And Jesus called them just as they were.

FAITH STEP: *Are you striving for perfection? Let it go. Jesus is calling you as you are.*

—*Camy Tang*

MAY 17

"Silver and gold have I none; but such as I have give I thee." Acts 3:6

*S*ometimes I am overwhelmed by the amount of need I see in the world. In my job as a university professor, I work with many students who are struggling to make it through school even as they balance jobs and families—many as single parents. It is important to me to be able to empower students with the blessing of an education. Most days, however, I am keenly aware that greater knowledge and a better paycheck are not enough to meet anyone's deepest needs.

For example, last week, I had a student burst into tears while contemplating an essay assignment. The question was, "What experience has caused you to grow?" When I asked her what was wrong, she opened the floodgates of a heart and home broken by a husband's betrayal.

Another student came into my office to explain why he had to miss class. Turns out his daughter was in prison, his wife was undergoing treatment for breast cancer in another city and his young grandkids had just moved in with him. Oh yeah, and he lost his job because of a layoff.

How I wish that I could fix these problems. I wish I had enough money to provide real relief. Something wise to say that would stop the tears, make everything better. Every once in a while I have a few extra dollars, or I am able to share a word that seems to shed some light. But the truth is that I have nothing in myself—really—to offer hurting people. Education won't do it. Money won't. Friendship, encouragement—these are good but not ends in themselves. In the end they, too, come up lacking.

The one thing you and I have to offer a hurting world—and the one person we need when we are hurting—is Jesus. He's the healer, the provider, the answer, the cure for everything that ails the world.

FAITH STEP: *How can you share Jesus today? Here are some ideas: listen with His ears, extend His hug, see with His eyes, pray with someone, speak what He has spoken to your heart.*

—*Gwen Ford Faulkenberry*

MAY 18

"In his distress he sought the favor of the Lord his God and humbled himself greatly before the God of his ancestors. And when he prayed to him, the Lord was moved by his entreaty and listened to his plea; so he brought him back to Jerusalem and to his kingdom. Then Manasseh knew that the Lord is God." 2 Chronicles 33:12–13 (NIV)

Manasseh was a terrible king. He worshipped idols and did all sorts of things to cause the people to turn away from the Lord. He went so far as to desecrate the temple. He was basically thumbing his nose at God.

But then Manasseh was captured and taken to Babylon. Very humiliating. Manasseh's experience made him finally turn to the Lord, humble himself and repent of his actions.

I can relate to Manasseh because God gave him a second chance, just like He gave me a second chance. Every sin we commit, no matter how small it might seem, hurts God, and yet He forgives us through Jesus Christ. Manasseh had led a horrible life, but God forgave him when he repented.

When the woman caught in adultery was brought to Jesus, she was supposed to be stoned to death for what she did. But Jesus spared her life and forgave her.

Jesus spared my life and forgave me. Jesus spared your life and forgave you.

FAITH STEP: *Thank Jesus today for what He did for you, and the grace He gives you every day. Is there some sin you haven't repented of ? Ask for forgiveness. The God of Second Chances is always ready to hear your prayers.*

—Camy Tang

MAY 19

*"God, the Master, The Holy of Israel, has this solemn counsel:
'Your salvation requires you to turn back to me and stop your
silly efforts to save yourselves. Your strength will come from
settling down in complete dependence on me—The very thing
you've been unwilling to do.'" Isaiah 30:15 (MSG)*

One of my clearest childhood memories is when I was five. My stepdad was running errands for my mom and dropped me off at a birthday party. The thing was, when I knocked at the door, a stranger opened it. My dad had gotten the location wrong. Not only that, I turned around to see he'd already driven away.

The people invited me in to call my mom, but I knew better than to go into a home with strangers. Thankfully, my aunt lived only one mile down the street. With present in hand, I walked to my aunt's house with the lady following me in her car, still offering to help me. I made it to my aunt's house and my mom picked me up, but from that point on I made a mental note that I had to take care of myself.

It's been a hard habit to break. When challenges come, I want to be strong. I strive to make things happen. My mind tries to figure out what I can do to control the situation. Jesus, of course, wants better for me. He knows I cannot help myself or save myself. His desire is for me to depend on Him. He is where my strength comes from, and He is where I'll find salvation.

Events from my childhood may cause me to try to figure out the answer alone, but remembering where my help comes from makes all the difference. Looking back, I wasn't walking by myself to my aunt's house. Jesus was by my side, protecting me and guiding me every step of the way. Jesus has never failed me, and He never will.

FAITH STEP: *Think back to an impacting moment that's caused you to be self-dependent. Write that down, and then write a prayer asking Jesus to help you depend on Him more.*

—*Tricia Goyer*

MAY 20

"Christ has set us free to live a free life. So take your stand! Never again let anyone put a harness of slavery on you." Galatians 5:1 (MSG)

"For the Lord is the Spirit, and wherever the Spirit of the Lord is, there is freedom." 2 Corinthians 3:17 (NLT)

One of my spiritual mentors used to regularly ask, "Where have you felt freedom lately?" Just as where the Spirit is, there is freedom, the converse is also true: where freedom is, the Spirit is. So if you are asking, "Where is the Lord in my life?" the place to look first is the place where you have felt great freedom.

In recent weeks, it became clear to me that I needed to make a move. I have been working part-time for a friend of mine, as an office manager and bookkeeper for her family's business. While the job provided much-needed income for a season, I had other opportunities that fit better with my gifts and long-term goals, work I was already doing the other thirty hours a week. It was time to give notice.

After prayer, talking with wise friends who knew me and feeling God's push to make this move, I quit the job. Immediately, I felt great freedom. I wasn't scared about the loss of income—I knew I had better opportunities elsewhere, that God was leading me.

Would you use the word freedom to describe any part of your life, especially your spiritual life? It's human nature to try to make our faith about rules. Galatians 5:1 is not about actual slavery or even a job that no longer fits. Paul is warning the early church—and us—against legalism, against thinking we can be saved by following the law.

You've been set free to live a free life. That doesn't mean you don't have any responsibilities, but that you are free to follow Jesus wherever He leads you.

FAITH STEP: *Where have you felt freedom lately? What if that's where God is?*

—*Keri Wyatt Kent*

MAY 21

"Then the disciples went out and preached everywhere,
and the Lord worked with them and confirmed his word by
the signs that accompanied it." Mark 16:20 (NIV)

One of the most challenging times of my life was when my family and I went on a mission trip to the Czech Republic. We taught English at a family camp to a group of people who either claimed to be atheists or had no apparent interest in Jesus. Our job was to get them to trust Christians and become curious about Jesus. We were halfway around the world in a strange culture, and it seemed like an impossible task. I knew Jesus was with us, but I wished I could see Him—see the confidence in His gaze that I lacked.

To me, the people who lived in Jesus' day were the luckiest people on earth. They got to see Jesus, peer into His face, hear His stories, see His miracles. Those closest to Him may have been the luckiest of all. When the disciples walked into a challenging situation, He was literally at their side.

How hard it must have been when Jesus was gone for good. How hard it must have been to leave that hill after Jesus' ascension. Maybe the disciples hung around awhile. Maybe they peered into the sky for a time, hoping for one last glimpse. I wonder when they realized He hadn't left them at all. As the words of the popular children's song goes, they discovered they had the "wonderful love of the blessed Redeemer way down in the depths of their hearts."

In the wonderful way Jesus works, the verse after He ascends speaks of the disciples heading off to spread the good news, but they were not alone. "And the Lord worked with them." Those six words make my heart sing.

The work Jesus asks me to do—to share His good news—is scary. Too often I feel like I'm stepping out alone. Yet even in the Czech Republic we witnessed God at work. He wasn't physically by our sides, but He was there—wooing, directing and guiding. He showed up when we stepped out. We didn't have to go alone.

FAITH STEP: *Look online for mission trips or ask someone at your church about opportunities. Seriously consider joining a team that's going out to spread the good news of Jesus.*

—*Tricia Goyer*

MAY 22

"It is absolutely clear that God has called you to a free life. Just make sure that you don't use this freedom as an excuse to do whatever you want to do and destroy your freedom. Rather, use your freedom to serve one another in love; that's how freedom grows." Galatians 5:13 (MSG)

I went to a Christian college, where I encountered wonderful professors, interesting students and a type of legalism I had, up to that point, not experienced. I grew up in a church that was truly a community—people conservative in their theology but fun to be with and intellectually stimulating.

My school had the intellectual part, the conservative-theology part and some fun people, but it also had rules that were strange to me. My parents had never objected to my going out dancing with friends, but for some reason I found myself at a college that didn't allow dancing (and a whole list of other things).

They preached God's unconditional love and grace, yet had rules that I chafed against—and some of which I did not keep. Perhaps I was trying to exercise some freedom, to test whether God really did love me unconditionally.

It took me a while to realize that true freedom means not living without rules, but living without regrets. Our culture tends to read this verse in Galatians and assume the "you" is singular. But the phrase "use your freedom to serve one another" points out that the "you" is plural. (A better rendering would be "y'all.") Paul assumes his words will be read in community.

When we abuse freedom, it is destroyed. And the community is destroyed along with it. When we serve one another, freedom flourishes. And community flourishes.

FAITH STEP: *Where are you most tempted to "do whatever you want"? What specific actions could you take to use your freedom to serve those in your community, your church or your family?*

—Keri Wyatt Kent

MAY 23

"When the apostles returned, they reported to Jesus what they had done. Then he took them with him and they withdrew by themselves to a town called Bethsaida, but the crowds learned about it and followed him. He welcomed them and spoke to them about the kingdom of God, and healed those who needed healing." Luke 9:10–11 (NIV)

I'm great at hospitality—when it's on my terms. When I pick the date and have time to prepare. When the casserole turns out perfectly. When everyone gets along and conversation flows.

We have friends with a large family, who have a different approach to hospitality. They often chat with another family at church on Sunday morning, and spur-of-the-moment invite them to lunch. No special preparations, just simple fare—even perhaps smaller portions because of the extra mouths to feed. No time to coach the kids to behave. No time to dust before guests arrive. Just pure welcome into their lives. They amaze and inspire me.

So does Jesus. In the account in Luke, He has taken His disciples aside. He needed time with them for the important work of teaching and training them. Perhaps this was also one of the times Jesus drew aside to spend time in prayer. At this point in His ministry, crowds begged for healing and miracles, and religious leaders badgered Him and set rhetorical traps. I can imagine that He was looking forward to some quiet conversation with friends in Bethsaida and a little rest.

Yet when the crowds figured out where He was and came clamoring, He welcomed them. Those words warm my heart. Jesus doesn't view me as a pest. He doesn't set terms for His hospitality. He opens His arms and welcomes me.

His example also challenges me. Will I focus on protecting my "me time" or will I respond openly and warmly when I'm interrupted? Will I focus on controlling the parameters of my hospitality, or will I adapt and change plans when a new opportunity pops up to serve others?

FAITH STEP: *When someone interrupts you today, welcome them warmly and invite Jesus to use you to bring comfort and healing.*

—Sharon Hinck

MAY 24

"What marvelous love the Father has extended to us! Just look at it—we're called children of God! That's who we really are." 1 John 3:1 (MSG)

 heard his footsteps before I saw him pajama-shuffle out to the living room. "What's up, Paxton-boy?"

"I'm dweaming of monsters again, Mom. You need to pway," he managed around his thumb.

Back in his room I tucked him in and then asked Jesus to help him feel safe and protected in his cozy bed. After a kiss and another whispered "I love you, buddy," Paxton was on his way to Dreamland.

That routine still amazes me, even after a dozen times. I marvel at my little boy's ability to take Jesus at His word. Just a prayer for protection, and all cares are set to rest.

I teach my children to trust Jesus, and they're born pros. So why do I still need so much practice believing Jesus will conquer life's monsters?

Because I've heard so much about the sorrows real-life monsters can cause.

Knowing well the realities of evil, Jesus still trusted his heavenly Father, and he urges us to have childlike faith. Perhaps we adults need a reminder of who our God is and what it means to be His child.

A child's ability to trust a parent depends on how well he knows that parent's love. As God's child, do I really know His love enough to trust Him with my concerns? Enough to rest during any moment, knowing He has potential pitfalls in hand? Do I really understand 2 Timothy 1:12 (NLT): "I know the one in whom I trust, and I am sure that he is able to guard what I have entrusted to him"?

Jesus is not surprised by life's monsters, and He still tells us to trust Him.

FAITH STEP: *Ask and trust Jesus to grow your childlike faith in the heavenly Father you share.*

—*Erin Keeley Marshall*

MAY 25

"'Be strong and courageous. Do not be afraid or discouraged because of the king of Assyria and the vast army with him, for there is a greater power with us than with him. With him is only the arm of flesh, but with us is the Lord our God to help us and to fight our battles.' And the people gained confidence from what Hezekiah the king of Judah said." 2 Chronicles 32:7–8 (TNIV)

*W*e live in a very self-sufficient society. You're expected to take care of yourself—as well as your family—and be independent and strong. You're considered weak if you have to ask for help. Society admires people who can accomplish things all on their own.

Independence isn't a bad thing. If we were too reliant on others to help us get our work done, we'd never finish our projects. Think about if we needed someone to help us cook dinner every night. Our family would starve if the help wasn't there one night.

But too often when we're facing trials and troubles and difficulties, we don't immediately ask God for help. When the disciples were in the boat and caught in the storm on the lake, they didn't wake Jesus up right away, even though they probably could have used the muscle power, at the very least, to help keep the boat afloat. I always wonder if they woke Him up because they needed Him to hold a rope or something like that, not necessarily thinking He'd do something miraculous.

But Jesus rebuked the storm and the disciples were in awe, despite the other miracles they'd seen Him do.

Aren't we like that, too? We finally call on Jesus to help us, and then we're amazed when He does something wonderful.

FAITH STEP: *Are you going through some troubles now? Are you working through something where you haven't yet prayed to ask Jesus for help? He'll be there to calm the storm for you, if you ask Him.*

—Camy Tang

MAY 26

"It is not by force nor by strength, but by my Spirit, says the Lord of Heaven's Armies." Zechariah 4:6 (NLT)

Two superheroes live in my home. I never know from hour to hour whether Spiderman, Batman, the Backyardigans or one of the Incredibles will come dashing down the hall to save me from vacuuming, loading the dishwasher or folding laundry. Their dad and I enjoy being whisked up in our kids' imaginative play.

While I love their innocence, I'm more of a superhero wannabe. Don't mock; you may be one too. Somewhere in crossing the line between the trusting days of childhood and the stresses of adulthood, most of us grown-ups adopted a messed-up hero mentality. We tend to live by the mistaken notion that it's up to us to come up with solutions to every problem, including the impossible ones that defy human ability to solve.

We read about relying on Jesus and how the Lord has proven faithful to every generation. We feel appropriate awe when we read of His miracles.

But those miracles are for other people, right? Our situations are different, right?

How exactly is Jesus enough for any problem or grief? He tells us, "Come to me, all you who are weary and burdened, and I will give you rest. Take my yoke upon you and learn from me, for I am gentle and humble in heart, and you will find rest for your souls" (Matthew 11:28–29, NIV).

Oftentimes Jesus doesn't remove our troubles. But He promises His strength, peace, joy and hope when we acknowledge Him as our hero instead of trying to assume that role. He offers those vitality-building qualities in unlimited measure. Our job is to stay the course with Him and trust that He will see us through to His goals, which may be different from our own.

Trust as a child, and be amazed at how Jesus will be your Superhero in His way and time.

FAITH STEP: *How can you "cease striving and know that [Jesus is] God" today (Psalm 46:10, NASB)?*

—Erin Keeley Marshall

MAY 27

"The tongue has the power of life and death." Proverbs 18:21 (NIV)

God's word compels me to season my own words, to say everything in love, to make sure whatever comes out of my mouth is not cursing, but blessing.

I'll admit I'm not too great at it. For example, I'm pretty sure speaking blessings of love doesn't include a lot of yelling, even if your little boy is terrorizing his big sister with a remote-control scorpion while your three-year-old dumps hot-pink fingernail polish on the hardwood floor. Something lovingly firm does need to be said—and done—in a situation like that. But I've been reminded lately that in other situations, limiting one's mouth to blessings of love may mean saying nothing at all.

My friend Hunter got a huge job promotion last year. When he took the promotion he was unaware there were any big problems with the firm. However, almost immediately he was bombarded with money issues that stemmed from his former boss's mismanagement. When he tightened the budget in order to deal with the problems, a lot of people got mad. Many employees complained to Hunter, and still others complained about Hunter, even suggesting he didn't know what he was doing, or that perhaps he was too young to do the job.

When people griped, it would have been easy for Hunter to place the blame where it was rightfully due instead of taking all of that heat. I never heard him do that. Every word I heard him say about his old boss was honoring. And when it came to questions about the budget, he just didn't say anything at all.

Hunter's silence had a huge impact on me. The old boss was able to retire with dignity, largely at Hunter's expense. And by not saying anything, Hunter spoke volumes for the cause of Jesus. To those few of us who knew what was happening, his silence said this: I choose blessing.

That's the principle of Jesus' love: My life for yours. And our tongues have the power to bestow that blessing or to take it away.

FAITH STEP: *Before you speak today, make sure your words pass the "blessing" test. And when in doubt, leave them out.*

—Gwen Ford Faulkenberry

MAY 28

"Very rarely will anyone die for a righteous person, though for a good person someone might possibly dare to die. But God demonstrates his own love for us in this: While we were still sinners, Christ died for us." Romans 5:7–8 (NIV)

*R*ecently a friend e-mailed me about some incredibly painful setbacks he was facing. Amid all the faith-rattling problems was an overwhelming financial mess. He also said that although he had prayed about it all, he felt hesitant seeking God's grace and help with the situation, because he had made some poor decisions that had brought about at least part of the problems.

As I struggled to find words of comfort and encouragement, I kept coming back to that line of his letter. I understood what he was saying, and often felt the same way about problems of my own making. If I got myself into a mess, was it fair to ask God to help me find solutions?

That concern has several flaws. First, it presumes that we can separate out "our fault" from various situations—that His grace is available to us only when we are completely innocent, when we've made flawless choices every step of the way. Yet when is that? When aren't our actions at least to a small degree influenced by motives corrupted by our sinful nature?

Second, with this approach we are left seeking answers in our own human abilities and strength—the same human limitations that got us into the problem.

Most important, the theory breaks down because of God's nature. I suspect God's grace is quite a bit bigger, more lavish, more kind, more merciful than we can grasp. The whole miracle of grace is that it's undeserved. Jesus was willing to die to save me from the tangle that sin has made of my soul. He is also willing to live in me to bring His wisdom, direction and power to the smaller tangles of my daily life.

FAITH STEP: *Is there a tangle that you've been hesitant to bring to God? Invite Jesus into the situation and ask for His help with it today.*

—Sharon Hinck

MAY 29

"Jesus looked at him and loved him." Mark 10:21 (TNIV)

A rich young man came to Jesus and asked how he could inherit eternal life. Jesus first challenged why the man had called him "good," to get the guy thinking about who he thought Jesus was. Then Jesus told him to follow the commandments, and the man insisted he was faithful.

Jesus had a very short conversation with him, and yet this phrase is here in Mark—Jesus loved him. He didn't know the man very well. The man had only just run up to Him and asked Him this question. He was a good Jewish boy, at least according to what he told Jesus. He was very wealthy, which Jesus might have somehow known, or He might have guessed it if the man was perhaps wearing the first-century version of Gucci or Prada apparel.

Yet Jesus just looked at him to love him. Isn't that pretty reckless and vulnerable? Isn't that being a bit hasty or unwise?

But isn't that how Jesus loves us? You might have hated Jesus for part of your life, or been indifferent to Him. You might have done things directly against what Jesus would want. You might have spent time trying to run away from Jesus.

Yet He chose to love us anyway, even when we weren't anything lovable. And if Jesus loved both us and this man in such a reckless, vulnerable way, shouldn't we try to love others like Him? To love people who may not be lovable?

FAITH STEP: *Spend some time in prayer to think of someone difficult for you to love. Ask Jesus to help you love that person with recklessness and vulnerability, just like Jesus loved the rich young man.*

—Camy Tang

MAY 30

"But the Master said to him, 'I know you Pharisees burnish the surface of your cups and plates so they sparkle in the sun, but I also know your insides are maggoty with greed and secret evil. Stupid Pharisees! Didn't the One who made the outside also make the inside? Turn both your pockets and your hearts inside out and give generously to the poor; then your lives will be clean, not just your dishes and your hands.'" Luke 11:39–41 (MSG)

Jesus criticized the Pharisees for being too focused on image management. If I'm honest, I'll admit that I, too, worry about appearances. But what is the antidote for superficiality? According to Jesus, it's self-examination and generosity—to turn our hearts and our pockets inside out.

Too often, we rewrite the Bible in our heads. What will make our lives clean? Avoiding watching certain television shows or movies? Sending our kids to private school? Voting a certain way? Only listening to Christian music? As the New Living Translation renders verse 41: "So clean the inside by giving gifts to the poor." We clean up our hearts by engaging in the spiritual practice of giving.

Giving breaks the strongholds of fear and worry. When we are generous, we wade into the abundant flow of God's grace. When we give without thought of what we'll receive in return, we reflect, with astonishing accuracy, divine generosity. We declare that our fear of scarcity will not rule our lives. We gain insight into how God feels giving to us. Is it possible that He delights in bestowing good gifts on His children?

Jesus asks us to give generously to the poor—that is, to give to people who cannot repay us. But I think Jesus knew that they could give us something worth far more. The poor have much to teach us about faith in the midst of suffering, about what it means to trust God.

FAITH STEP: *Today, give a generous gift to someone in need. Ask God to direct you in this.*

—*Keri Wyatt Kent*

MAY 31

"If you keep my commands, you will remain in my love, just as I have kept my Father's commands and remain in his love. I have told you this so that my joy may be in you and that your joy may be complete." John 15:10–11 (TNIV)

*I*n college, I had church leaders who opened their home and hearts to me. It meant a lot to me, and I wanted to do the same, so my husband and I started having a college Bible study at our house on Sunday around noon. We cook lunch and then have a Bible-study lesson. Right now, we're going through a video Bible study on sex and dating.

This past weekend, I was in the kitchen making more food when it hit me how happy I was to have boisterous college students eating teriyaki meatballs in my living room. Talking about history classes and quirky co-workers and YouTube videos. Coming into the kitchen asking for more food. Barreling through bags of chips and bottles of soda.

But it wasn't just a happy-happiness—it was a really deep-seated kind of joy that I felt deep down in my gut. A joy that had no logical explanation—it was just there. And it filled me entirely. David's words about cups overflowing came to mind.

I knew in that moment that this was what God wanted me to do, to open my home and my heart to these students. I wanted to chat with them about silly things like their favorite comedians and about serious things like sex. I wanted to help them grow in their relationships with Jesus. I was filled with joy and a desire to serve the Lord in this way, to be obedient to Him.

FAITH STEP: *Is there something Jesus wants you to do for Him? Have you hesitated in going through with it even though you know it's something God wants? Remember that with obedience comes love and joy.*

—Camy Tang

June

JUNE 1

"She was quick: 'You're right, Master, but beggar dogs do get scraps from the master's table.' Jesus gave in. 'Oh, woman, your faith is something else. What you want is what you get!' Right then her daughter became well." Matthew 15:27–28 (MSG)

*R*emember the old song "Que Sera, Sera"? Its fatalistic philosophy, disguised as a sort of happy-go-lucky acceptance, declared that "whatever will be, will be." If that's true, then what is the point of prayer?

What if the truth is, whatever will be, might not be? Is it possible that when we pray, we can change what will be? The Bible seems to indicate that it is possible to change what might be to something else. In other words, our prayers can change God's mind.

In Jesus' discussion with a Canaanite woman, He at first won't do what she asks. But she's clever and persistent and humble. She pleads, banters, bargains—and Jesus gives in. He changes His mind. This astounds me.

Similarly, the Old Testament is full of examples of God relenting from causing destruction, and of people bargaining with God. Think Nineveh. Think of Abraham trying to save Sodom and Gomorrah by asking if God will spare the cities if only fifty—no, wait, forty-five—no, forty, thirty… righteous people are found there. God lets Abraham bargain Him down to only ten righteous people being enough to spare the city—but even that many can't be found.

The fatalist in me wants to believe that what will be, will be. The Bible indicates otherwise: that we can banter and bargain with Jesus. It seems to be telling us that prayer can actually change things.

We must also be open to the truth that one thing that could be significantly changed by prayer is us. Prayer sometimes changes our circumstances, but it always changes our attitudes.

FAITH STEP: *Read the context of today's Scripture, Matthew 15:21–28. What outrageous request are you asking Jesus to change His mind about?*

—Keri Wyatt Kent

JUNE 2

*"You are precious in My sight…you are
honored and I love you." Isaiah 43:4 (NASB)*

While my husband's cousin Todd was under hospice care for cancer, Stone visited and prayed with Todd's young children and his wife Ginna.

He asked Ginna how she felt about the treatments Todd had undergone and their overall approach to fighting the cancer. As so often happens, it had been a grueling journey. Seeing someone die, regardless of the fight, you have to wonder whether all of the extra pain and suffering are worth it.

Ginna said that to Todd it was. She said he had to know he did everything he could to stay with his family—and he wanted them to know he fought for them. Stone asked her if she personally would do anything differently.

When he told me her answer, Stone started to cry. Ginna said her one regret was that they could have done another treatment a couple of weeks before, and they declined it because the end was inevitable. "But now," she told Stone, "I wish I could have a little more time with him."

The reason Stone was so touched by this was that she said it as Todd lay emaciated, unable to speak or move, the furthest thing in appearance from the strong Army Ranger he had once been. But he was still her Todd. With no thought as to the huge strain his illness placed on her personally, Ginna lamented she did not have more time to care for him, be with him and hold his hand.

This kind of love is so reflective of Jesus and His dedication to us. It is His love that sees through our human frailty to who we are inside—who we are to Him. To Him we are precious. He gave His life so that He could be with us forever.

FAITH STEP: *What a wonder that Jesus sees us as valuable. Today, pray that He will empower you to love others as He loves you.*

—Gwen Ford Faulkenberry

JUNE 3

"Therefore, I say to you, don't worry about your life, what you'll eat or what you'll drink, or about your body, what you'll wear. Isn't life more than food and the body more than clothes?" Matthew 6:25 (CEB)

Part of the reason we spend time with Jesus is to listen to what He says and then try to live as He would if He were in our place. We ask ourselves, What would Jesus do? We try to answer that question with our lives as best we can.

So these words of Jesus—read the full context in Matthew 6:19–34—seem to tell us that Jesus would not worry. If we want to experience His presence, and live as He would in our place, we need to find a way to let go of worry.

If you ask almost anyone to list biblical "sins," they'll likely offer you a list that includes adultery, lust, greed, murder, etc. Few, if any, would list "worry." Yet Jesus tells His followers, including you and me, not to worry. So if Jesus said don't do it, then doing it is a sin, right? But many of us seem to be expert worriers. We worry about what will happen if certain people get elected or don't, we worry about our kids, our money or our church. We watch the evening news and our faith flickers. Our faith is cloaked in fear.

When life is really hard, or challenges come your way, sometimes worry feels inevitable, impossible to avoid. But what if worry is a choice—and it's always the wrong choice? Why would Jesus say, "Don't worry," unless we actually had a choice to make?

FAITH STEP: *What are you worried about today? Write it down on a piece of paper. Then, deliberately choose not to worry about that thing. Choose instead to trust. Shred or burn the paper.*

—Keri Wyatt Kent

JUNE 4

"Greater love has no one than this, than to lay down one's life for His friends." John 15:13 (NKJV)

$\mathcal{I}$ have a good friend named Mr. Straley whose office is across the hall from mine. He teaches viticulture and enology, and I teach English. We are both busy when we're at work, trying to get everything done, but occasionally we'll just pop into one another's office and say hello. The other day I conned him into signing up for e-coupons my kids could use for chicken feed.

We both teach a night class, and agree that it creeps us out to be in the building alone after hours. Even though our campus is small, and in a small town, it's just not a great feeling to be here after everyone else goes home. We usually walk out together after night classes.

One day I knew I was going to have to come back down to my office and work after hours, because I had a writing deadline. I checked the campus cop's schedule, and it was not one of his late nights to work. It wasn't my normal night-class night, but I asked Mr. Straley if he happened to have class that night. He said yes, he did, but he was going off-site to visit a vineyard.

I guess he saw me frowning, because he asked me if I had to work in my office that night. I said I did, and it would probably be a late night. It might not have done me any good if there was a night class on campus; I would probably still be there long after it was done.

Mr. Straley offered something that touched me. He said, "Well, if you're scared you can call me at home and I'll come down here and walk you out."

I have a husband, dad and brother who would all do the same, and I would never ask such a thing of Mr. Straley. But the fact that he offered— well, I just appreciate that kind of friend. He's the real thing.

Jesus is a friend that sticks closer than anyone else—even our best friends and family. Whenever we have a need, we can count on Him to be there, no matter the hour.

FAITH STEP: *Jesus' love and loyalty surround you on all sides today. Take courage in Him!*

—Gwen Ford Faulkenberry

JUNE 5

"Wait and hope for and expect the Lord; be brave and of good courage and let your heart be stout and enduring. Yes, wait for and hope for and expect the Lord." Psalm 27:14 (AMP)

One of the hardest days of my life was moving two thousand miles away from two of my children. My husband had gotten a job in another state and we were moving with our youngest two children. My oldest son was planning a wedding and he wasn't about to move. Our oldest daughter was finishing up classes at the junior college and had no desire to move away from school and friends.

My husband's job was a ministry position, and we knew we were making the right choice. Still, I was lacking when it came to being brave and having courage. My heart felt like melted butter in my chest. My desire to be surrounded by my children was out the door. Then I remembered Jesus…

Jesus faced life on earth. He knew what it was like to be away from family. Once He started His ministry He was far from home. Not only that, He had a longing for His Father's kingdom. Remembering that Jesus understood my heartache helped me to turn to Him. I spent many mornings with my Bible and journal, looking to Him to show up in Spirit and guide me to the perfect passage that would carry me through my day. As He met me during those times, I came to expect Him more.

Six months after we moved, my daughter transferred to a college near us. Three months after that, my son and his new wife moved to live near us too. It's not something I expected, but I was thankful. I was also thankful that I learned to trust Jesus and hope in Him in new ways. I can't expect that things will always turn out how I desire, but I do know that when I turn to Jesus He will be there to see me through.

FAITH STEP: *Think of an impossible situation you're facing. Write down three things that are bothering you about the situation then cross them out and write this: EXPECT JESUS.*

—*Tricia Goyer*

JUNE 6

"When they landed, they saw a fire of burning coals there with fish on it, and some bread. Jesus said to them, 'Bring some of the fish you have just caught.' So Simon Peter climbed back into the boat and dragged the net ashore. It was full of large fish, 153, but even with so many the net was not torn. Jesus said to them, 'Come and have breakfast.' None of the disciples dared ask him, 'Who are you?' They knew it was the Lord. Jesus came, took the bread and gave it to them, and did the same with the fish." John 21:9–13 (NIV)

I love cooking-competition shows. Skilled chefs face various challenges to prove their creativity and ability under all sorts of difficult situations. Although my own culinary efforts focus on meat and potatoes tossed into the slow cooker, I enjoy vicarious cooking. I'm fascinated by the techniques I've never heard of, ingredients I've never tasted and the wild energy of high-tempo chopping.

My mind boggles as chefs describe an amuse-bouche of wagyu beef on a seared round of polenta, or their sous vide duck breast with a squid ceviche; and my mouth waters as they prepare crème brûlée or sculpt dark-chocolate delicacies. Watching the chefs at work has even inspired me to venture out of my comfort zone and I've had surprising success with a leek and shallot soup and some gluten-free carrot muffins.

As much fun as it would be to sample a meal by one of the skilled chefs on these cooking shows, I'd trade that in a second for the opportunity that the disciples had. How remarkable it must have been to come ashore and have Jesus serve up a fish fry on the beach. He fed them fish and bread, which probably stirred memories of the miraculous feeding of the five thousand. Jesus showed Himself to be attuned to human needs, and to be the generous provider.

I haven't sat along the shore enjoying roasted fish over coals with Jesus, but He is the provider of all that is good in my life, as He was for the disciples. When I pray, "Give us this day our daily bread," I often think of how Jesus called Himself the Bread of Life. I'm hungry for His presence—the daily bread that matters most to my survival.

FAITH STEP: *Savor your next meal as a reminder of God's provision.*

—Sharon Hinck

JUNE 7

"Go therefore and make disciples of all nations, baptizing them in the name of the Father and of the Son and of the Holy Spirit, and teaching them to obey everything that I have commanded you." Matthew 28:19–20 (NRSV)

Christ gave His disciples the Great Commission when He told His disciples to go out and "make disciples of all nations."

What does that have to do with me? I'm not one of the twelve disciples. I'm not particularly wise or fluent or bold. Shyness often overtakes me when I speak about spiritual things or about my faith. Surely there's nothing in these verses that applies to me! Yet if I know someone hasn't heard the good news of salvation and I say nothing, have I disobeyed God?

It terrifies me to think that because of my timidity or introversion, someone might not hear about Christ and His saving grace. I want to be noisy for Jesus. I want no one to miss His salvation because of my apprehension or lack of confidence.

There are endless opportunities to tell people about Christ's sacrifice and so many people who don't know Him. If I really accept as true that all unbelievers will spend eternity apart from God, why am I waiting? What holds me up? Laziness? Fear of criticism? Being pulled out of my comfort zone?

Is it because I don't want to give up those things that are important to my security and ease? Am I too busy hanging on to earthly things to do what God has asked of me? It's time to become uncomfortable with my inaction. He created me for a purpose—I must be available to God so He can use me as I'm meant to be.

If my mouth grows stiff and shy when I begin to talk about God, then I will begin by speaking with my life—my actions, my choices, my behavior—and ask that the Holy Spirit loosen my tongue and give me the words to converse for Him.

I don't want anyone to see anything in who I am or how I act that would hint that I'm not one of Christ's. I must speak not only with my life but also with my lips, and pray that what goes out from me—in any form—speaks blessings to someone else.

FAITH STEP: *Will you speak God's love and salvation today? How? To whom? Do it.*

— *Judy Baer*

JUNE 8

*"She answered God by name, praying to the God who spoke to
her, 'You're the God who sees me! Yes! He saw me; and then I saw him!'
That's how that desert spring got named 'God-Alive-Sees-Me Spring.'
That spring is still there, between Kadesh and Bered. Hagar gave Abram
a son. Abram named him Ishmael." Genesis 16:13–16 (MSG)*

As a mom of two preschoolers and a baby, I felt invisible. No, I wasn't the Disappearing Woman. It's just that the creative, witty, fun-to-hang-out-with woman was hidden under my baby-food-stained T-shirt and baggy sweats. I still had a reflection in the mirror, but the woman who picked up scattered toys and washed peanut-butter fingers was unrecognizable. Unlike Hagar, I wasn't in a desert, but there were times my sense of worth felt parched.

Just like God showed up in Hagar's time of need, He showed up in my life too. In a time when I felt unseen, God reminded me I was in His sights.

The angel of God found Hagar beside a spring in a desert, and God also led me to a spring of life: Jesus Christ. And through another story about a second woman at a spring—also unseen and unloved—God reaffirmed the only thing that could water my parched soul.

John 4:13–14 reads: "Jesus said, 'Everyone who drinks this water will get thirsty again and again. Anyone who drinks the water I give will never thirst—not ever. The water I give will be an artesian spring within, gushing fountains of endless life.'"

There are seasons in life when it seems no one understands or cares. Is the person in the mirror unrecognizable? Do you feel like no one is paying attention to you? That no one sees your needs or cares about the worries on your heart? It's during those times Jesus sees us and He gives us what we need most: Himself.

FAITH STEP: *Look in the mirror and write down what you see. When your list is complete, offer up your paper to Jesus and ask Him to fill you with Himself. Consider your reflection through Jesus' eyes.*

—*Tricia Goyer*

JUNE 9

"Whoever comes to me and does not hate father and mother, wife and children, brothers and sisters, yes, and even life itself, cannot be my disciple." Luke 14:26 (NRSV)

*W*hat is more important to me than Jesus? Nothing, I hurry to say—but is it true?

My family is important to me—my parents, siblings, husband and children. They mean the world to me! And my home—it's my sanctuary, really, my hiding place. It's the dream house my spouse and I built together as husband and wife. And my job! I have a very important job and I love it. It makes me feel proud to be the administrator over dozens of people. I'm good at what I do. Where would they be without me?

Then there is the business I built myself, from the bottom up. And, crazy as it may sound, there are my appetites—I love splurging on new clothes, expensive shoes and travel. I can't always resist these things even though they shouldn't be the priorities I sometimes make them. I justify my actions by telling myself that those little things don't matter, really, do they? There are so many things I wouldn't want to live without. I don't like hardship. I like a life of ease. And there's the rub.

Whatever stands in the way of Jesus, be it trivial or significant, is an idol. It becomes a pitiful, worldly deity that stands between me and the multiple blessings God has for me. By hanging on to these little gods for fear of losing them, I miss our God's greater, richer plan! In order to find out what that gracious plan might be, I must be willing to set aside what I treasure. Granted, it may come at a cost. But I submit it all to Him for the prize is too great to ignore: eternal life.

FAITH STEP: *Who comes first for you? Pray that Jesus gives you the strength and guidance to put Him first in everything.*

— Judy Baer

JUNE 10

"Some men came carrying a paralyzed man on a mat and tried to take him into the house to lay him before Jesus. When they could not find a way to do this because of the crowd, they went up on the roof and lowered him on his mat through the tiles into the middle of the crowd, right in front of Jesus. When Jesus saw their faith, he said, 'Friend, your sins are forgiven.'" Luke 5:18–20 (NIV)

*Y*ears ago I faced a big struggle. At a time when my husband and I were "satisfactorily" but not happily married—we'd fallen into a familiar rut—

a former boyfriend popped up on the Internet, stirring up old emotions that hadn't been there in a while. At first I was flattered, but worry quickly followed. I knew if my piqued emotions continued they could lead to wrong choices and broken promises.

When I felt weak, I turned to my friends. For a few weeks I felt like the paralyzed man on the mat. Because of my past ties, I felt too weak to go to Jesus myself. My friends knew this. Throughout the day I'd get e-mails with Scriptures or phone calls from those who wanted to pray for me. Their love and concern carried me to Jesus, but the best part came when I met Him in my weak state. Jesus, knowing my past choices and even my current, unhealthy emotions, forgave me. He wasn't concerned I hadn't gotten there all by myself. He was simply thankful I'd come.

I know now that when I'm facing a struggle I don't want anyone to know about, that's the time I need to seek support from the people God has brought into my life. It's hard to admit weakness, but true friends are those willing to carry us when we're too weak to take a first step.

FAITH STEP: *Think of a private struggle you haven't shared with your friends. Consider a way you can confess to them and ask them to help you find Jesus even in your weakness.*

—*Tricia Goyer*

JUNE 11

"While Jesus was still speaking, some people came from the house of Jairus, the synagogue leader. 'Your daughter is dead,' they said. 'Why bother the teacher anymore?' Overhearing what they said, Jesus told him, 'Don't be afraid; just believe.'" Mark 5:35–36 (NIV)

The most oft-repeated command in the Bible is simple and yet incredibly challenging: Do not be afraid.

Jesus says it at disconcerting times: in the midst of a squall that threatens to swamp a boat, when he's telling his disciples he's leaving, when a child dies. Jairus looks at Jesus when he hears this awful news, and the look on his face must have prompted Jesus to quickly tell him not to be scared, that everything would be okay.

What are you afraid of? Often our fears are focused not on what is actually happening, but what could possibly happen. When a child or spouse is late coming home, we are afraid they've been in an accident. When we're given a tough project at work, we're afraid we won't be able to do it. We don't confront, because we're afraid of conflict.

In Jesus' simple statement—"Don't be afraid; just believe"—we learn that the antidote for fear is faith. But where do we summon up faith like that?

John Ortberg writes in *Faith and Doubt* of his experience on a high ropes course at camp with his daughter. He thought he believed the ropes would hold him and he would be safe. And yet when he actually got up on the course, he said, "I found out my body did not believe I was safe."

Ortberg concludes: "Faith is coming to believe with my whole body what I say I believe with my mind."

When we are willing to take risks, to step out and believe the rope of God's love will hold us, we begin to really believe, and our faith pushes our fear aside.

FAITH STEP: *What are you afraid of? In which specific situation you're facing is Jesus telling you "do not be afraid"?*

—Keri Wyatt Kent

JUNE 12

"I Am Who I Am." Exodus 3:14 (NIV)

*W*ho does God think He is anyway?

I mean no disrespect with that question; it's one whose answer I review whenever my faith needs bolstering. Actually, it's a vital question we all need to have answered. Think about its impact: Our current lives and our eternity hinge on who God knows Himself to be. We all have ideas and preconceptions about who He is, but the only One whose answer matters is God Himself.

So really, who does God think He is?

Early on in the Bible, He reveals that He is a God who relates truthfully and with great deliberateness. For example, in this direct conversation with Moses, He said, "I am the Lord God. I am merciful and very patient with my people. I show great love, and I can be trusted" (Exodus 34:6, CEV). Of all the qualities He could have said first about Himself, He focused on the gracious ones. In Isaiah 43:3 (CEV), He says He is "the God who saves you," and then He showed Himself true in Matthew 1:20–22, when He sent His angel to proclaim that His Savior Son, Jesus, was on the way to us.

After spending thousands of years showing His awesome character, God the Father introduced His Son, Jesus, to the world. Jesus, in turn, proved that He is just like His Father—knowing exactly who He is and what He is about. He said He has the authority to forgive sins (Matthew 9:6), He would be in the grave for three days (Matthew 12:40), He commands angels (Matthew 13:41), He is the Messiah, the Son of God (Matthew 16:16–17), and He would rise from the dead (Luke 18:31–33).

Imagine if any Person of the Triune God—Father, Son and Holy Spirit—were not wholeheartedly confident of His identity. What kind of God would He be? Not one we could trust, that's for sure.

Today be confident that Jesus will continue to be Himself.

FAITH STEP: *Ask Jesus to help you be as confident in Him as He is.*

—*Erin Keeley Marshall*

JUNE 13

"When we've been there ten thousand years
Bright shining as the sun,
We've no less days to sing God's praise
Than when we'd first begun." ("Amazing Grace")

Those lyrics of "Amazing Grace" send chills through me. My lifetime is just a blink in eternity. How fearful and terrible it is to think of spending it apart from God!

But He promised me that Eternal life is mine in Jesus Christ. Jesus Christ accomplished it by going to the Cross for me. Praise Him!

This is good news. God cannot lie. It is not in His divine nature. God is truth. And despite my doubts, His truth is mine. I will go to heaven by His grace, not by anything of my own doing. Christ died on the Cross that I might be forgiven by God and receive the Holy Spirit Who renews me every single day. He save us, not because of any works of righteousness that we had done, but according to His mercy, through the water of rebirth and the renewal of the Holy Spirit.

What wonderful news! My weak and sinful self can't work its way to heaven—but Christ, through God, reaches out His hand and leads me there, dependent on Him to do for me what I cannot do for myself.

Our God is limited only by His own nature. Eternity is ours!

FAITH STEP: *Today give thanks for Jesus Who reaches into our helplessness and makes us whole.*

— *Judy Baer*

JUNE 14

*"After this, the word of the Lord came to Abram
in a vision: 'Do not be afraid, Abram. I am your shield,
your very great reward.'" Genesis 15:1 (NIV)*

When I first became a Christian at age seventeen I knew I'd made a great decision. I had made many bad decisions in my life, and accepting Jesus meant salvation for my soul. After I prayed the prayer of surrender, I also felt peace. Hope was another benefit—with Jesus in my life my future seemed much brighter.

It's only as the years have passed that I've realized that even more than the "benefits" a relationship with Jesus brings, He is the greatest gift—knowing Him, loving Him.

> Jesus before me.
> Jesus behind me.
> Jesus at my side.
> Jesus within.
> I can turn to Him.
> I can expect Him.
> He will never disappoint.
> He will never disappear.
> Jesus' arms around me.
> Jesus' smile upon me.
> Jesus wipes my tears.
> Jesus rejoices in my life.
> Jesus, my reward.

FAITH STEP: *It's easy to be thankful and excited for the benefits being in a relationship brings. Today make a list of all the ways Jesus Himself is your reward.*

—*Tricia Goyer*

JUNE 15

*"Let us throw off everything that hinders and the
sin that so easily entangles." Hebrews 12:1 (NIV)*

In northwest Arkansas, out in the boonies where we live, there is an evil plant species known as greenbriars. My mother says the only good thing she can think of that greenbriars do is to hide rabbits when they are running away from predators. Otherwise, they are ugly, razor-sharp, spread like the plague and are almost impossible to kill. Trust me. I can verify these things from personal experience.

Stone and I fought the battle of the briars when we cleared out a spot for our new chicken coop. As I fought through the labyrinth of horrible stickers I couldn't help but think of the verse about sin that easily entangles. I felt like I was in an animated movie. The briars seemed to reach out and grab me by the ankles, wrapping around my legs, stabbing into my T-shirt. It would have been so easy to fall if I hadn't been on my guard. I also had these wonderful clippers, sharp and strong, that enabled me to hack through. Then Stone—with thickly gloved hands—grabbed huge sections of briars and pulled them out to throw on a fire. It was actually fun for me to watch them burn.

The metaphor of the briars as "sin that entangles" will, I hope, be etched on my memory forever. Starting from the ground, these briars climbed trees, gaining strength as they climbed by killing out everything alive in their path. New briars mingled with last year's dead ones so that you couldn't tell where one ended and the other began. The insidious things took over a whole section of woods at the edge of our yard, and I could see that their intentions were further reaching. It almost—but not quite—overwhelmed us to try to get them out.

FAITH STEP: *Are you entangled in sin of any kind? Jesus cut the path through for us, that we might lay aside the sin that entangles. Trust Him for forgiveness and healing today.*

—Gwen Ford Faulkenberry

JUNE 16

*"When a Samaritan woman came to draw water, Jesus
said to her, 'Will you give me a drink?'" John 4:7 (TNIV)*

Sunday mornings always seem so busy for me. We rush to get to church on time, and after the service I usually need to talk to certain people about things related to ministries I'm involved in. The only time I'm relaxed is during the service, but I'm never really relaxed because I'm listening. Or I might be trying not to fall asleep—I have those days too.

Sunday mornings are sociable because I catch up with people I know, but I find I don't greet newcomers. I have people to see and since we have a Bible study at our house about an hour after service ends, we're usually hurrying to leave.

Also, I admit I'm not always sure who's a newcomer and who's been coming to church for a while. We don't have a huge church, but it's large enough that I don't know everyone's name, although their faces might look familiar.

Yet Jesus, in between turning water into wine and healing an officer's son, took the time to talk to a Samaritan, a "fallen woman." Jesus took the initiative and that moment changed the woman's life forever.

I doubt anyone's life will be so dramatically changed if I go up to talk to them at church, but you and I should be like Jesus here and take the initiative.

FAITH STEP: *Do you greet newcomers at church? Even if they're not newcomers, why not get to know a few new people this Sunday? Pray for God to guide you to people to greet.*

—Camy Tang

JUNE 17

*"When Jesus heard this, he marveled and said to those
who followed him, 'Truly, I tell you, with no one in Israel
have I found such faith.'" Matthew 8:10 (ESV)*

Have you ever heard someone gush about someone else—someone
else that you really don't like? Maybe your boss sings the praises of a co-
worker, and you know that co-worker doesn't deserve accolades. Or the
neighbors talk about the gal down the street who's such a good cook—but
you are pretty sure she buys premade meals at Costco and puts them in
her own dishes to look homemade. When we judge others, we often miss
out on what they have to teach us.

This verse is part of a story where a Roman centurion comes to Jesus
and asks him to heal one of his servants. We can easily skip over who it
is that is asking Jesus this favor: a soldier of the regime that oppresses
the Jews, a man who has the power to make their lives miserable. That
centurion, by law, could hand his heavy luggage over to any Jew in that
crowd and force him to carry it for a mile. (See Matthew 5:41.) That man
certainly didn't know God. The Jews would have despised him.

And yet Jesus talks to him! His followers, all Jewish, appear shocked
that Jesus, a good Jewish rabbi, would even answer this despicable character. But Jesus not only talks to him; He also offers to go to his house, which
in that culture, was significant—it meant friendship and acceptance. We
don't realize how scandalous this praise is, and how insulted and indig-
nant both the Pharisees and Jesus' followers would have felt.

The centurion humbly says that won't be necessary. Just say the word,
he says, and I know it will be taken care of. My servant will be healed,
because you have the authority to do it. And Jesus marvels at him. Then
He tells His followers that this despised Roman has more faith than they
do! Can we, like Jesus, extend scandalous grace that allows us to see the
good in all people?

FAITH STEP: *Does Jesus marvel at your faith? Or do you spend time being jealous of others you think don't deserve God's favor? The centurion believed that
Jesus' word was enough. Do you take Jesus at His word?*

—*Keri Wyatt Kent*

JUNE 18

"Then Jesus said to them, 'You foolish people! You find it so hard to believe all that the prophets wrote in the Scriptures. Wasn't it clearly predicted that the Messiah would have to suffer all these things before entering his glory?' Then Jesus took them through the writings of Moses and all the prophets, explaining from all the Scriptures the things concerning himself." Luke 24:25–27 (NLT)

As a newlywed, I had a chance to attend Bible-school courses through my church. The classes started with a test to see our overall understanding of the Bible. I failed miserably.

Even though I attended church for most of my childhood, I had little understanding of the Bible. Yes, I could tell you that David killed Goliath with a stone and a sling. Yes, I could name most of the Ten Commandments, but the big picture of God's plan and how the Old Testament related to the New Testament was beyond my grasp.

Once Bible classes started, our first assignment was to read every book of the Bible and write a one-page summary of what each book was about. We weren't supposed to use commentaries or study notes. Instead we were supposed to let God's Word speak for itself. Before reading, I'd pray and ask Jesus to give me insight, and He did.

Just like Jesus explained Himself to the men walking the road to Emmaus in Luke 24, He wants to explain Himself to each of us. The writings of Moses and all the prophets may seem overwhelming, but if we go to Jesus in prayer before we read He will show up and speak to our hearts.

The more I read the Bible and learn, the more I want to know. Not because I enjoy knowing things such as that Methuselah was the oldest man in the Bible at 969 years or that Noah used gopher wood to make the ark, but because it's a special moment when the Spirit of Jesus reveals truth to me in ways I hadn't known it before.

FAITH STEP: *Are there books in the Bible you've avoided reading because they seem complex and difficult? Sit with your Bible and read one or two chapters from that book. Ask Jesus to speak to you and show you Himself within those pages.*

—Tricia Goyer

JUNE 19

*"And God is able to bless you abundantly, so that in
all things at all times, having all that you need, you will
abound in every good work." 2 Corinthians 9:8 (TNIV)*

I remember to thank God for my food, or when He heals a friend, but I don't meditate on the abundant blessings He's given to me. "Abundant blessings" is certainly not a phrase I use every day, and I don't often see the things in my life as "blessings." I see them as their more mundane forms—car, house, friends, etc.

But a few months ago, I started a Thankfulness Journal. Each day, I listed five things that I was thankful for, and I tried not to repeat myself. It was amazing how many things I could list that I hadn't thought of before. It made me realize that God has truly blessed me abundantly. I have everything I need, whether it's material, spiritual or emotional.

I still have trials and struggles in my life. My life isn't perfect and problem-free, but I can stand back and see the abundant blessings God has given to me. I can also see that I don't thank Him enough for them.

Do you believe God has blessed you abundantly? What do those words mean to you? What are things or who are people in your life who are part of those abundant blessings?

FAITH STEP: *Start a Thankfulness Journal. Every day, list a few things you're thankful for. It'll keep you aware of the ways God blesses us, and how His blessings are richer than anything we could ask or imagine.*

—Camy Tang

JUNE 20

"Hezekiah received the envoys and showed them all that was in his storehouses—the silver, the gold, the spices and the fine oil—his armory and everything found among his treasures. There was nothing in his palace or in all his kingdom that Hezekiah did not show them." 2 Kings 20:13 (TNIV)

*H*ezekiah obeyed the Lord and led the people of Judah away from idolatry. God blessed him with great riches.

But that led to his pride in the things God had given to him. When envoys from Babylon came to Jerusalem, Hezekiah showed off his wealth. As a result, God told Hezekiah that Babylon would one day destroy the city.

God loves to bless us. Jesus talked about how God loves to give gifts to us, His children.

But Jesus also hates pride. He warned that those who exalt themselves will be humbled. Jesus is "gentle and humble in heart," and wants us to be like Him.

The problem is that when we are successful, the joy of success lifts us up. We're happy for ourselves, but that can make us prideful and inconsiderate of others. We do things that lift us up more, rather than lifting up Jesus or other people.

We boast about how our child got this award or our husband achieved those sales numbers. We announce a promotion or commendation. We say it in a way that makes it look like we're only inviting people to celebrate with us, but our inward attitude shows that we are bragging.

Success is not a bad thing, nor is it wrong to tell others about the good things God has given to us. But our attitude can be demeaning to people and neglectful of God. We have to watch out for that.

FAITH STEP: *Are you in a place of success right now? Take a hard look at your attitude. When you tell people, are you sure you don't have a little bit of pride in your heart? Thank God for you success, but also pray for God to help you to have a pure heart and motives.*

—Camy Tang

JUNE 21

*"But what happens when we live God's way? He brings gifts into our
lives, much the same way that fruit appears in an orchard—things like
affection for others, exuberance about life, serenity. We develop a willingness
to stick with things, a sense of compassion in the heart, and a conviction that
a basic holiness permeates things and people." Galatians 5:22 (MSG)*

*M*y family and I have lived in the same house for eleven years. We moved here from a house around the corner, where we lived for seven years. As a result, my kids have friends that they have known since preschool. I know my neighbors.

This is no small gift. I feel specifically called to live missionally in my suburban neighborhood, to live as Jesus would if He were in my place. I am always aware that my actions speak louder than words, and that Jesus has called me to truly love my neighbors by getting to know them.

This passage describes what "appears" in our lives when we are living God's way—that is, living as Jesus would if He were in our place. They provide a perfect description of Jesus Himself—affectionate, exuberant, serene.

These characteristics don't grow spontaneously. The Spirit plants and cultivates them in our hearts. My deep desire is to "develop...a conviction that a basic holiness permeates things and people." All people, all my neighbors, are made in the image of a God who loves them. He's asked that I be available so He can love them through me.

I can't force myself to bear fruit any more than an apple tree can try really hard to bear apples. It's simply what a tree does, what it was created to do.

FAITH STEP: *Read through today's Scripture. Do you see this type of fruit growing in your life? Rather than a to-do list, think of this as a description of what naturally grows when you live God's way. What barriers to growth do you need to remove from your heart?*

—Keri Wyatt Kent

JUNE 22

*"Your commands are always with me and make
me wiser than my enemies." Psalm 119:98 (TNIV)*

Satan has always been very deceptive. In the Garden of Eden, he clothed lies with truths to make it easier for Eve to believe him. He is a persuasive manipulator. He whispers softly so that you hardly even realize he's influencing you.

He also uses other people to do his work. Charismatic leaders can persuade you that everyone goes to heaven no matter what their religion is. A caring friend can tell you that premarital sex is okay if you love the other person. A family member can insist that it's more loving to keep the truth from your spouse.

Or maybe you yourself have been used by Satan to do his work in other people's lives.

When Jesus was tempted in the wilderness, He quoted Scripture at Satan. The Word was His sword in that fight. The Word can be our sword too, but that means we have to be familiar with it in order to use it. You wouldn't expect to win a sword fight if you hadn't been trained in swordplay, so you also have to train yourself in your understanding of God's Word before you can use it to fight the devil.

Delve more deeply into the Bible. When you know what Scripture says, you're more likely to hear alarm bells when someone is trying to deceive you about what's right or wrong, and you're better able to resist Satan when he tries to get you to influence someone else. The psalmist, King David, understood that the Word of God was what enabled him to fight his enemies. We can use the Word to fight our enemy too.

FAITH STEP: *Do you read the Bible consistently? Commit to reading a chapter a day this week, or finishing a book of the Old Testament, even if you don't entirely understand it. Take baby steps and slowly start to build upon your knowledge of the sword of the Word.*

—*Camy Tang*

JUNE 23

"However, God is rich in mercy. He brought us to life with Christ while we were dead as a result of those things that we did wrong. He did this because of the great love that he has for us. You are saved by God's grace!" Ephesians 2:4-5 (CEB)

I don't like the term "non-Christian." It not so subtly implies a "you're out and we're in" sort of thinking. The prefix sounds antagonistic, as if a person who doesn't know Jesus is somehow "anti-Christian." I like the label "seeker," which my church has used for years.

And yet, if you examine the Bible, the term "seeker" would accurately describe Jesus Himself, as well as those who are investigating a life of faith. Jesus said of Himself that He came "to seek and save the lost." (See Luke 19:10.) If we're dead, spiritually speaking, we can't seek truth until someone brings us to life—that's something only Jesus can do. So He seeks us out, because of His great love for us.

I love the concept of God being "rich in mercy." He's got overflowing coffers of mercy and grace, and pours them out abundantly on His children. We cannot save ourselves or earn His favor. He brought us to life, initiated love. In her book on grace, *Sin Boldly*, Cathleen Falsani writes, "I've heard it said that grace is God reaching God's hands into the world. And the Bible tells us that we are part of the body of Christ, that if we let the Spirit move through us, we can become the hands of Christ on earth. Hands that heal, bless, unite, and love."

So we've been saved by grace, not by our own efforts. And the appropriate response is to extend grace to others—not to label them, but like Jesus, to love them.

FAITH STEP: *Spend some time thanking Jesus for His life-giving love for you, for seeking you out. Ask Him for an opportunity to extend His grace to others.*

—Keri Wyatt Kent

JUNE 24

"Do not worry about anything, but in everything by prayer and supplication with thanksgiving let your requests be made known to God. And the peace of God, which surpasses all understanding, will guard your hearts and your minds in Christ Jesus." Philippians 4:6–7 (NRSV)

We are people with choice. We can choose to accept Christ or to reject Him. We can believe or mistrust. And we can worry—or we can pray.

The result of prayer is peace. It is the knowledge that our heavenly Father, the One Who created the world and everything in it, is in charge. Worry, care and fretfulness are not useful to Him. He doesn't need our help to make things run smoothly, only our trust and our permission.

By choosing to trust God and lay our worry aside, we are freed from anxiety and concern. Who better than the Creator is there to direct our steps? With Him in charge, we can spend our time in praise and thanksgiving instead of apprehension and unease. We can sleep at night knowing that He is awake and watching over us. He is on guard twenty-four hours a day directing not only our steps but also those of everyone around us.

FAITH STEP: *It is time to give up worrying and embrace the peace Jesus offers us. No longer start the morning by lying in bed concerned about the day ahead. Instead praise God and thank Him for being in charge of your waking hours.*

— *Judy Baer*

JUNE 25

"You will always have the poor among you, and you can help them whenever you want to. But you will not always have me." Mark 14:7 (NLT)

*O*nce a year, in December, the church I grew up in took a church bus down to a community center in the city, where we brought gifts for the poor kids. Although my church provided my only interaction with the poor, I didn't really think of caring for the poor as part of how I lived my faith.

In my religious context, I often heard Jesus' words about "the poor always with you" interpreted as a fatalistic pronouncement, saying that since they'd always be there, being poor, there wasn't much we could do. And so there wasn't anything we had to do.

In the last five years, I've been on a journey in which God has challenged the assumptions of my religious upbringing, and rocked my affluent white suburban worldview. I've taken classes, read books, served breakfast monthly at a homeless shelter, taken in foster kids.

When Jesus said, "You will always have the poor," He was using a common rabbinical technique of quoting a snippet of a Hebrew Scripture in order to refer to its context. He referenced a passage His listeners would have recognized: "Give generously to the poor, not grudgingly, for the Lord your God will bless you in everything you do. There will always be some in the land who are poor. That is why I am commanding you to share freely with the poor and with other Israelites in need" (Deuteronomy 15:10–11, NLT).

I believe following Jesus means looking not just at the words He said, but the words He read—and living my life accordingly. The Old Testament was the Bible Jesus read, and loved, and lived by. For me, part of loving Jesus is giving generously to the poor.

FAITH STEP: *Spend time reading and reflecting on Deuteronomy 15:1–10. Sometime this week, give to the poor not by writing a check, but by volunteering at a soup kitchen, food pantry or shelter.*

—Keri Wyatt Kent

JUNE 26

*"Where can I go from your Spirit? Where can I
flee from your presence?" Psalm 139:7 (NIV)*

Last summer my husband and I took our three kids to the beach for
two weeks. My brother and his wife came and joined us for the second
week, renting a house nearby with their two daughters, Madeline and Sophia. For seven beautiful days, our two families played in the waves, hunt-
ed for seashells, fished, built sand castles and ate fresh seafood together.

When we returned home, we all visited with my parents. Granny and
Pa asked the kids to each tell his or her favorite thing about the beach.
They experienced so many new things, and their thoughts were as varied
as their personalities. Harper loved catching different kinds of fish than
we have in Arkansas. Grace enjoyed sliding down sand dunes. Adelaide's
favorite thing was collecting shells, and Sophia had the most fun chasing
crabs. When it came to Madeline's turn, her answer surprised us all: "My
favorite thing about the beach was the Faulkenberrys!"

After she said that, we all had to agree with her—the best thing about
the vacation was being together. What's sort of funny, I suppose, is that
back home we are next-door neighbors. It's not as if the beach is the only
place we get to see each other. We have fun together just about every day.
But she was right. No matter where we go, it's who we're with that makes
the difference.

I thought about Madeline's statement—that her favorite thing at the
beach was us—and how it illustrates our relationship with Jesus. Certainly, circumstances change, and some places we go in life are better, easier,
more interesting, more exciting than others. But what really makes the
difference is Jesus' presence along the journey.

FAITH STEP: *Have you been looking for fulfillment in your circumstances?
Today, try looking to the One who is with you in all things and all places. His
presence can make all the difference in your journey, no matter where today's
circumstances take you.*

—*Gwen Ford Faulkenberry*

JUNE 27

"Then, because so many people were coming and going that they did not even have a chance to eat, he said to them, 'Come with me by yourselves to a quiet place and get some rest.'" Mark 6:31 (NIV)

$\mathscr{I}$ was a bundle of energy in my twenties. The world was full of opportunities and possibilities and I didn't want to miss any of them. Soon I was spread thin among my roles as a wife and mom, playing organ at church, teaching ballet, choreographing for local theater, speaking at churches and retreats, writing newsletters for our ministry. Part of the "I can do it all" generation, I tried to do it all—all at the same time.

Soon I found myself cranky and exhausted, and obeyed God's nudge to attend a silent retreat. On a crisp fall day, I restlessly fled the retreat center and strolled their hiking trails. "Lord, I know things in my life are out of balance, but there is so much to do," I said. "I can't slow down. Not now."

The trail led along a secluded pond. Green algae coated the water and a dank, heavy scent rose from the surrounding marshland. "You see, Lord. That's what I'm talking about. Still waters don't run deep. They are stagnant. I want to be a sparkling brook or a dynamic waterfall."

As I studied the pond, a lazy turtle pulled himself from the water to rest on a moss-coated log. A duck paddled in gentle patterns. Dragonflies danced over the lily pads. I realized that this quiet, still pond provided a lush home for all kinds of life. I headed back to the retreat center with a lighter step, ready to tackle the challenge of rest.

FAITH STEP: *Lord, teach me to find rest with You, so my heart can become a life-giving place during those times of stillness.*

—Sharon Hinck

JUNE 28

"So if the Son sets you free, you will be free indeed." John 8:36 (NIV)

*A*h, the weekend! For my family, summer weekends typically mean boat rides. That's when I watch my husband and children turn their faces upward to let the sun and wind blow away the cares of the week—just before I do the same.

Okay, so my kids are little and don't have too many stresses, but it still moves me to see them revel in this freedom. They take turns standing up front, and my husband and I always get a chuckle when they turn around—hair sticking straight up—to share their wide-eyed wonder with us. It's serious business.

What makes your heart soar, unhindered by weighty thoughts or pressures? Perhaps you feel free when you escape into a good book on a quiet afternoon. Or maybe you enjoy zooming past new sites on a road trip. Maybe freedom means lingering in a warm bath. Maybe it's hearing a good report from the doctor.

For all the feel-good nature of those freedoms, nothing compares to the soul freedom Jesus offers. Now that's the good stuff. He takes our freedom seriously, so seriously that He paid with His life to ensure we wouldn't have to miss out on an eternity of freedom with Him—freedom that includes constant fellowship with Him; no sorrow, pain or fear; and the endless opportunity to worship His glory.

But even while we're still on earth, Jesus offers us freedom. In Matthew 11:28, He tells us to rest from all that burdens us. And far from loading us down with have-to's, Galatians 5:1, 13 (CEV) says, "Christ has set us free!… Now hold on to your freedom…. My friends, you were chosen to be free. So don't use your freedom as an excuse to do anything you want. Use it as an opportunity to serve each other with love."

Do you take your freedom as seriously as Jesus does?

FAITH STEP: *Put hands and feet to your freedom in Christ by doing something kind for someone today.*

—*Erin Keeley Marshall*

JUNE 29

"And the Spirit of the Lord shall rest upon him, the Spirit of wisdom and understanding, the Spirit of counsel and might, the Spirit of knowledge and the fear of the Lord." Isaiah 11:2 (ESV)

Over the past year or two, I found myself praying the same prayer over and over: "Jesus, what should I do?" My husband's real-estate career was hitting some major bumps because of the economy. I wondered if, instead of writing books and doing freelance editing, I should venture into the corporate world—that mysterious place where writing was called "communications" and jobs came with that magical extra, "benefits."

For a few months, I applied for jobs that I didn't really want, hoping somehow my husband's career would turn around, or he'd find another job. I wondered how my working long hours in a corporate job would impact my kids, who still need me. I wondered, What is the best thing to do? Which way should I go?

Gradually, it dawned on me: I have access to Jesus, Who has wisdom, understanding, counsel, strength, knowledge. Rather than complain to Him about my situation, I needed to seek out that wisdom and counsel, which He'd made available to me. Jesus not only understood, but also had wise counsel to offer me.

When I prayed and asked Jesus to speak to me, and then got quiet enough to listen, He led me away from my search for a corporate job, at least for now. I continue to write books and edit, but He also provided two part-time jobs with very small companies, where I use my creativity and skills and have incredibly flexible hours. I'm working hard, helping to provide for my family, in a way that fits who I am.

FAITH STEP: *What situation are you facing today for which you need wisdom, counsel and knowledge? The Bible says Jesus has all those things. Today, ask for His help, and then listen and trust.*

—Keri Wyatt Kent

JUNE 30

"From his fullness we have all received, grace upon grace." John 1:16 (ESV)

Stone and I always knew we wanted to name a daughter Grace. We're so grateful for the grace the Lord has shown us in our individual lives and in our marriage we could never proclaim it enough. We also wanted to pass on the heritage we've received to our children.

When Grace was actually born, we looked for a verse to attach to her life, one we could pray over her. We came across this jewel in John 1, and I did a little word study with it. The image still blows me away.

It seems that the concept of "grace upon grace" in the original language is actually a word picture. The idea is compared to the ocean and the behavior of waves. When one crashes onto the shore and subsequently rolls back out to sea, another is already there to take its place. There is never any interruption. It is a constant flow.

This is the way the grace of God comes to us. Through Jesus, there is a constant flow. We cannot use up God's grace; it is there for each moment, and when that need is supplied, the next supply is already waiting—ready to rush in like a wave. It covers us, cleanses us, fills us. And then more comes, to cover and cleanse again, and to fill us even fuller.

FAITH STEP: *Are you in need of His grace today? It is already flowing toward you. Dive in—receive His fullness, one wave after another.*

—*Gwen Ford Faulkenberry*

July

JULY 1

"May you be strengthened with all power, according to his glorious might, for all endurance and patience with joy." Colossians 1:11 (ESV)

"Bye, Mommy! Daddy and I are goin' swimmin'!"

I watched my three-year-old son and my husband head down to the dock before I collapsed on the couch. As I thanked Jesus for my daughter's naptime, I marveled at how easily I could feel zapped of vitality.

An hour later my baby girl and I met our guys for some lake fun. The scene that greeted us still brings tears to my eyes.

"Look, Mom, I'm swimming!" Paxton hollered from the dock ladder. I reached him in time to see him push off and doggy-paddle to his dad.

He wasn't kidding! He was swimming! Okay, so he was wearing a life jacket, but this was still a huge milestone, because as much as he loves the water, he had yet to let go of us and venture off on his own. It was the cutest thing I ever saw, little legs pedaling furiously, little arms paddling the water like puppy paws. And the unrestrained joy that lit his entire body… oh, the precious ache of it all!

I clapped; I cheered; my heart soared with him in his exuberance.

And in that moment my weariness vanished, and I felt like I could swim across the lake with him just to share in his boundless joy.

Joy is powerful and wonderfully contagious. The Lord knew what He was talking about when He inspired the Scripture writers to connect strength and joy so frequently. (See Nehemiah 8:10 and Psalm 28:7.) And like my child's heart, Jesus' heart yearns to share His excitement for life and eternity with us. He doesn't need to share those gifts, but it brings Him pleasure to do so.

Thank you, Jesus, for speaking through my child's heart, so like your own. And thank you for the unexpected energy boost of shared joy.

FAITH STEP: *How can you share a joyous pick-me-up with someone today? Send a note, offer a smile or lend a hand.*

—Erin Keeley Marshall

JULY 2

"The Lord your God in your midst, The Mighty One, will save; He will rejoice over you with gladness, He will quiet you with His love, He will rejoice over you with singing." Zephaniah 3:17 (NKJV)

Growing up I never felt beautiful. We didn't have much money and all my clothes—except one new outfit every year—came from yard sales. A few times my mom tried to cut my hair herself and my long locks ended up at my ears, and after my baby teeth came in, my adult teeth came in crooked.

The worst year was sixth grade. I weighed more than my stick-thin friends and it was determined I needed glasses. I picked out Jordache frames—a popular brand at the time—but I still got made fun of when I showed up wearing them at school. "Hey, four eyes," I was greeted by Keith, the cutest boy in my class. I was horrified. After that the glasses stayed home. I'd have to walk to the front of the room to see the chalkboard, but at least I wouldn't have to face the trauma of being completely homely.

It's funny how we carry the feelings of low self-worth with us into adulthood. Even after I grew out of my ugly-duckling stage I still felt inadequate, unpopular. I carried this into my relationship with Jesus. I thought He loved me—because that's what Jesus is supposed to do—but I never felt truly beautiful in His eyes. Or at least I didn't feel that way until I stumbled upon Zephaniah 3:17.

I can still remember the rush of joy in my heart as I read those words. I imagined Jesus looking at me with complete infatuation. Like a groom singing a love song to His bride, I pictured complete love in His gaze. That type of love overwhelmed me.

I'm completely beautiful in His eyes. He doesn't just put up with me; He gave everything so I would be His.

FAITH STEP: *Read a few popular love poems, like "She Walks in Beauty" by Lord Byron, and try to grasp Jesus' immense love for you.*

—*Tricia Goyer*

JULY 3

"I have called you friends, because I have made known to you everything that I have heard from my Father. You did not choose me but I chose you." John 15:15–16 (NRSV)

I am honored when someone I admire reaches out to me and welcomes me into his or her inner circle. As children we all wanted to be part of the "popular" kids' group. And as teenagers it felt even more important to be part of the "in" crowd. But even as adults, there are people you know you'd have a lot in common with if only they got to know you. Unfortunately not all of them make that effort—or even realize you exist.

Yet, amazingly, Jesus Christ, Son of God, Lord of Lords and King of Kings, has invited us into His inner circle. He knows my name and likes what He sees. He not only wants to be my friend, but also chose me in particular! He's totally interested in being in conversation with me. And the best news of all? He chose each one of us with the same intention and love. We aren't worthy of His friendship. We can't earn it and we don't deserve it, yet He gives it to us freely, just for the taking.

He invites us into the ultimate Inner Circle—how can we say no?

Run toward Him, speed into His embrace!

FAITH STEP: *Today take your friend Jesus with you wherever you go. Think of Him as physically at your side in the coffee shop, at the library, at a meeting or anywhere you go.*

— *Judy Baer*

JULY 4

*"And this same God who takes care of me will supply
all your needs from his glorious riches, which have been
given to us in Christ Jesus." Philippians 4:19 (NLT)*

*A*fter mentoring teenage mothers for ten years in Montana, I thought I understood their needs for respect, for help, for education, for hope. When I moved to Little Rock, Arkansas, I realized some young moms need much more. Some have parents in prison—they need one person they can trust. Some are still young teens and live with their boyfriends who are also barely in high school—they need to be taught about purity and second chances. Some live without central heat or air-conditioning and don't have transportation or enough food. They need the basics of life. My heart aches when I see the many needs. I'm just one person. Thankfully, I know Someone to turn to.

Jesus loves these young women even more than I do. My heart aches because His did first, and when I turn to Him, Jesus reminds me I don't have to struggle to help alone. He already knows who He has to come alongside me. As I've shared the needs of these teen moms with others, mentors have stepped forward; food, clothing and diapers have been provided. And with all of these things that are passed out we tell the young moms that Jesus is the Supplier. Even when we aren't around they can turn to Him.

The message was sinking in. Yesterday when I was giving a young mom a ride she told me, "When good things enter my life I know they are from Jesus." I have faith that, since she now trusts Him as Supplier, she'll soon believe in Him as Savior. After all, that's the greatest need Jesus has provided for: the weight and burdens of our sin. And that's the most beautiful gift He gives us: salvation for our souls.

FAITH STEP: *Consider Jesus' bank account. Think of all He owns—in other words, everything. Let those thoughts of Him as Supplier build your faith. Once your faith is built, pray for others in your life who you know are in need.*

—Tricia Goyer

JULY 5

"Peace I leave with you; my peace I give you. I do not give to you as the world gives. Do not let your hearts be troubled and do not be afraid." John 14:27 (NIV)

"*H*oney, did you get a new purse?" My hubby called from the hallway.

"No. Why?"

"Whose white bag is hanging by the back door?"

"One of the gals forgot that after our Bible-study lunch today."

Beside it hung a potholder left behind by another friend. And in the closet rested a pair of shoes forgotten by one of the writers who came over for the monthly retreat day. Just a few inadvertent remnants from visits of the past week.

Then there are the intentional items. The gift of a puzzle, a book, a card, a plaque, a sweater. Everywhere I turn I'm reminded of the people who intersect my life.

But more than the tangible bits and pieces that are sometimes left in the wake of visits, friends have left other, larger things behind. Echoes of laughter. Memories of heartfelt conversations. Swirling creative efforts that filled each room. Scents of quiche in the oven and tea steeping in assorted mugs. A redolent spirit of prayer.

In every encounter we have with another person, we all leave something behind. I fear that I often leave behind self-important opinions, echoes of ugly whining or insistent striving to be understood. Instead, when I move on from a conversation, I want the thoughts, words, and spirit that linger to be filled with truth and grace. I want to leave what Jesus left with us— His peace. Reflections of Him.

FAITH STEP: *Thank Jesus for the peace He leaves with us, and think of something to leave behind to bless a friend you encounter today.*

—*Sharon Hinck*

JULY 6

*"I do not understand my own actions. For I do not do what
I want, but I do the very thing I hate. Now if I do what I do not
want, I agree that the law is good." Romans 7:15–16 (NRSV)*

Temptation is everywhere, pulling on me, tugging at my body and exhausting my mind. Paul said it: "I do not understand my own actions. For I do not do what I want, but I do the very thing I hate…. I can will what is right, but I cannot do it. For I do not do the good I want, but the evil I do not want is what I do" (Romans 7:15–16, 18–19, NRSV). That is my predicament. I am so weak without Christ.

Help me to resist temptation. I pray that He will teach me not to give into "I can't" thinking. I'm a Christian, a child of the King! I must avoid putting myself in places that tempt me to sin and surround myself with like-minded people who are a good influence for me and don't lure me into sinful behavior.

I can't depend on myself to fight this alone. I will throw myself on Christ's mercy and plead for help. I am so thankful that my Lord wants to help me through this, and that all I have to do is ask.

FAITH STEP: *Think of a temptation you've recently faced—to be rude, to eat too much, to gossip or something else. Whatever it might be, equip yourself through pray so that the next time you are tempted by something similar you are fortified and ready to fend it off.*

— Judy Baer

JULY 7

"But those who drink the water I give will never be thirsty again. It becomes a fresh, bubbling spring within them, giving them eternal life." John 4:14 (NLT)

*F*or the gazillionth time that hour I wiped sweat from the back of my neck. One hundred degrees. What a day for the zoo! Even the water buffalo looked dehydrated, though they lounged in shallow, stagnant ponds.

I reached for my water bottle once again, only to be disappointed that it was empty…again. Feeling desperate and utterly worn out, I scanned the map for the nearest snack station. All my present hopes focused on finding a way to quench my thirst and revive my spirit.

We certainly know what it's like to be thirsty without a drink handy. Living without water eventually results in death. We need it.

It's easy to understand our need for water, yet sometimes we don't understand how Jesus, the living water, provides far deeper satisfaction than mere H_2O. Not only does Jesus give us soul-saving satisfaction for eternity, but His kind of water creates life that bubbles over here on earth as well. Nothing stagnant about it.

Like a hundred-degree, steaming-hot day, our sinful world continually dehydrates our soul. Yet Jesus offers Himself as wonderful hydration for our spiritual thirst, filling us with peace, joy, hope and faith beyond what we've ever experienced. The refreshment of His presence is readily available to those who acknowledge their soul's thirst, as the woman at the well did.

Have you experienced Jesus' healing water?

FAITH STEP: *Buy yourself a new water bottle. Each time you drink, think of Jesus' offer to quench your eternal thirst.*

—*Erin Keeley Marshall*

JULY 8

"When Jesus was alone praying, his disciples came to him, and he asked them, 'What do people say about me?'" Luke 9:18 (CEV)

$\mathscr{I}$'m in the middle of writing this devotional, but hang on, someone's interrupting me again. Grrrrr.

How interruptible are you?

"Interruptability" is one lesson I know Jesus is training me in. Take an idealistic vision of a smooth day, add two children, several phone calls, a couple of broken toys, one overworked husband, work deadlines, a variety of spills, complaints and mistakes, and you've got my day in reality. It may remind you of yours!

Sometimes I think the quality of my love is exhibited by my reactions to people and events that derail my schedule. Sobering indeed. My heart hurts to think of numerous times I have failed to see what truly matters. Most often what truly matters involves being safe for someone else's heart.

I know Jesus is sensitizing me to my shortcomings in this area because my own heart really hurts when I remember the looks on my children's faces when I tell them I need to get something done—we'll play later. I had just given them the past twenty minutes of "my" time—wasn't that enough? Sometimes no, it isn't enough for their young, impressionable spirits. And how about making time to sit with my husband and listen to his needs?

Jesus was safe for people's hearts. Just look at His response to being interrupted in Luke 9:18. He didn't gripe or give His disciples a "smile" that registered dismay instead of a welcome. He lived the life God gave Him between many interruptions.

I can't help noticing His question to them and asking the same thing of myself. What do my responses to interruptions say about me? What feelings do those responses instill in others who come to me with real needs?

Above all, Lord, help me care for their hearts and trust You to care for mine.

FAITH STEP: *Priority one on the agenda today: Look for ways, within the interruptions, to care for someone's heart.*

—*Erin Keeley Marshall*

JULY 9

"I have told you all this so that you may have peace in me. Here on earth you will have many trials and sorrows. But take heart, because I have overcome the world." John 16:33 (NLT)

𝓘've had an extremely close relationship with my grandparents my whole life. My mom was a single mom, and we lived with my grandparents my first four years. After that I spent time with my grandparents many times a week. I looked forward to dinners around their table, watching old movies on the TV, and going on walks around the neighborhood. As my grandparents grew older I feared losing one of them. I knew it was inevitable, but I didn't think my heart could handle it.

When my grandpa was diagnosed with cancer I turned to the only place I knew to go—to Jesus. I asked Him to be with me each day as I helped my grandmother care for my grandfather. I asked Jesus to give my heart peace, and the amazing thing was, He did.

On the last day of my grandfather's life, I walked into the room and I saw him lifting his arms and praising Jesus. Later, through tears, Grandpa told me he saw Jesus with His arms outstretched. Jesus was welcoming Grandpa home. Not too long later my grandfather passed away.

All those years I had worried about what I was losing, but I had forgotten what my grandfather was gaining. Because Jesus had overcome the world, my grandfather was now with Him in eternity.

It's easy to find peace when everything in life is going smooth. But peace—Jesus our Peace—can also be found in painful times.

FAITH STEP: *Think about a friend who is facing the death of a loved one. Send him or her a note sharing your care. Also remind your friend that true peace can be found in Jesus.*

—*Tricia Goyer*

JULY 10

"As a deer gets thirsty for streams of water, I truly am thirsty for you, my God. In my heart, I am thirsty for you, the living God. When will I see your face?" Psalm 42:1–2 (CEV)

Nearly breathless, I tried to focus on the thrum of my running shoes against the scorching asphalt. Only another half mile.

Though it was still morning, the late-August sun burned my scalp, and my lungs begged for relief. Unrelenting rays targeted every uncovered inch of me, defying the sweatproof sunscreen I had lathered on less than thirty minutes earlier.

I was desperate but determined not to quit. No way would I negate the two-and-a-half-mile investment I'd already made in this workout. I would finish if it meant crawling the last few yards home!

Sometimes life feels like that run. Quite possibly you've felt desperate at some point in your story. Longing for a break, for relief, for peace, for contentment? Sometimes even blessings leave us feeling wound up and well…desperate. Stress is stress, even if it's good stress such as family commitments, much-loved career responsibilities or important ministry obligations.

Someone I care about has spent the last eight years in survival mode because of certain challenges her family is enduring. I'll never forget when she told me that she's partly afraid of things getting better—as much as she craves that rest—because she's terrified of returning to a lifestyle when she isn't desperate for Jesus' promises and presence to meet her minute-to-minute needs. That is an achingly beautiful place to be.

We may not think of struggles as gifts, but when we let our troubles draw us closer to Jesus, He amazes us with inexplicable peace and a new vision of where our strength comes from.

FAITH STEP: *Think of someone you know who is facing difficult circumstances. Ask Jesus to make their greatest desperation to be for Him. Pray John 4:14 for that person.*

—*Erin Keeley Marshall*

JULY 11

"The Lord has heard my cry for mercy; the
Lord accepts my prayer." Psalm 6:9 (NIV)

*M*y family and I went to a revival meeting once that nearly sent me into orbit. The subject was prayer, and the main points the speaker made were as follows: prayer is serious business, therefore we need to approach it properly; God doesn't hear your prayers until you are saved; we should pray about the spiritual side of things long before the physical; and prayer is best when we are wide awake—it's disrespectful to fall asleep when you pray.

The speaker was right about one thing, I suppose. Prayer is serious business. All throughout the Bible we're instructed to pray, and it's a privilege, a chance to commune with the living God. How does one approach it properly? It's a legitimate question, although when I talk to my Father, Brother and Counselor-Best Friend, I don't follow any formula. I just speak from the heart.

The Bible offers the Lord's Prayer as an example of what's appropriate. We are also given countless examples throughout the Old and New Testaments of God's people praying. From Abraham in Genesis to King David in the Psalms to Jesus in the Garden of Gethsemane, the patterns of prayer are as diverse as the personalities.

Stone and I had a talk with our kids after the so-called revival, a damage-control session. We emphasized praying from the heart. Don't let anyone tell you God can't hear a person's prayers, saved or not. Like Abraham, David and Jesus, lay your heart out there before Him. Don't hold back. He knows everything anyway. His will is going to be done, and our prayers are a way we participate in that. We're to come like little children before the throne of grace. We can ask anything in His name. The King hears us—inarticulate as we are—and He accepts our prayer.

FAITH STEP: *Today, when you pray, remember you are speaking to the One who gave His life for you. You don't have to impress Him; just speak from your heart.*

—*Gwen Ford Faulkenberry*

JULY 12

*"For the Son of Man came to seek and to
save what was lost." Luke 19:10 (TNIV)*

There's a word in that verse that I usually skip over—the word seek.

I know about how Jesus came to save all of us. And I know that I was lost before I came to know Jesus. What I don't always remember is that Jesus sought me.

There were numerous people in my life who slowly, carefully nudged me toward God. I may not have even been aware of what they were doing or how they influenced me. What I do know is the end result—my life given to Jesus, gladly and joyfully, and the rest of my life spent following Him.

But what about other people Jesus is seeking? I'm grateful to the people who helped me come to Christ, but what am I doing to be one of those people to someone else, someone lost?

Am I just sitting in my pew at church, content with my life, and not making the effort to seek out other people? If Jesus actively sought people, including myself, then shouldn't I also be actively seeking people?

I'm not the one doing the saving, obviously—that's Jesus' job—but I can be doing the legwork to seek out people, to make myself available for Jesus to use. He may want me to just smile at someone at the grocery store, or help a harried mom pick up some dropped toys, or respond with kindness when someone spews malice at me. Or He may want me to say something, whether to a stranger or a friend, that will help nudge that person closer to Him. Whatever it is, I need to be looking for these opportunities, looking for these people.

FAITH STEP: *Keep your eyes open today to seek people whom Jesus can touch through you. Be willing to be right there when He wants to use you.*

—Camy Tang

JULY 13

*"Rejoice always, pray constantly, give thanks in all
circumstances; for this is the will of God in Christ
Jesus for you." 1 Thessalonians 5:16–18 (NRSV)*

*F*amily, dogs, green grass, blue sky, friends, snow, sun, chirping birds, job, spouse, comfy shoes, a soft pillow, coffee, chocolate, smiles, music, art, books, evergreen trees, irises, fresh air, horses, friends…These are some of the things I'm grateful for, Lord, and Your creative hand provided them all.

Even though I may have money troubles, physical ailments, rebellious children or myriad other complaints, I still choose to give thanks to you. An attitude of gratitude is a decision I make each morning—even on the days when I have difficulty thinking of a single thing I'm thankful for. A baby's laugh, a purring kitten, a friendly hug…I look until I find. And I give thanks.

FAITH STEP: *Think of five things you are grateful for and concentrate on those today. Praise God for them.*

— Judy Baer

JULY 14

"When Jesus reached the spot, he looked up and said to him, 'Zacchaeus, come down immediately. I must stay at your house today.'" Luke 19:5 (TNIV)

Jesus was a pretty popular guy. He had crowds of people around Him who wanted to listen to Him, or perhaps test Him with tricky questions, or to get Him to heal someone. The disciples probably felt a bit like bodyguards most of the time.

Zacchaeus, being short, wanted to see Him but couldn't because of that large crowd, so he climbed a sycamore-fig tree. Zacchaeus may have chosen this tree because it has a sturdy trunk and wide, spreading branches, or he might have chosen it because it's an evergreen and almost never leafless, so it would be easy to conceal himself there. After all, he was a tax collector who had gotten rich cheating people, and maybe seeing Jesus made him ashamed of himself. He may not have wanted Jesus to know he was looking at Him.

But Jesus didn't keep His attention on the disciples next to Him, or the needy who wanted healing, or the clever Pharisees trying to trip Him up. He looked up—beyond the people directly around Him, outside of the circle pressing in on Him. He looked up to see Zacchaeus. To notice him.

How often do I look outside my circle of friends and family? How often do I notice people I don't know, who may be in need or who just want to be acknowledged by someone? Jesus had a lot of distractions around Him, but He took the time to look outside of Himself. So shouldn't you and I do the same?

FAITH STEP: *Today, make an effort to look outside of yourself, to greet one new person and show Jesus' love.*

—Camy Tang

JULY 15

"But he said to me, 'My grace is sufficient for you, for my power is made perfect in weakness.' Therefore I will boast all the more gladly about my weaknesses, so that Christ's power may rest on me." 2 Corinthians 12:9 (TNIV)

I have officially relinquished my sanity and have started running for exercise. It started off as more of a shuffle-for-thirty-seconds-and-then-walk-for-five-minutes as opposed to running. As my knees began to protest less and actually feel rather good, I built up slowly until I ran those thirty seconds and shortened the walking to thirty seconds, and that's where I still am today.

The first few times I exercised, I felt like my lungs were going to fly out of my mouth and my heart would follow in a sad heap on the sidewalk. My legs were jelly after only a few minutes, and I had to sit down to rest a couple times during my "run" so I wouldn't pass out in the middle of the street. My body had never felt so incredibly weak, and my soul had never felt so incredibly vulnerable.

It surprised me that when my body gave out on me, my soul felt tired and sick too. It was as if my entire being had no strength left.

When Jesus told Paul that His power is made perfect in weakness, I could believe it simply because I had absolutely nothing left. In that kind of weakness, I needed a jolt of something outside myself because I didn't have any energy, whether physical, mental or spiritual, to get me going again.

Jesus is so big, so powerful, so awesome, that His power can take me at my weakest and make me strong. I forget that sometimes, because in my daily life, I don't often reach that point of running on fumes.

FAITH STEP: *Is there something in your life that makes you feel weak and tired? Pray for God's grace. It's more than enough.*

—Camy Tang

JULY 16

"Because he himself was tested by what he suffered, he is able to help those who are being tested." Hebrews 2:18 (NRSV)

$\mathcal{I}$'m having a really bad day. Nothing has worked out the way I wanted it too. If I could go back to bed, wake up again and start over, I would. It's worse sometimes when I have such high expectations for success. But Jesus knows all about bad days too. In fact, He knows everything about them—the disappointments as well as the joys, the pain as well as the pleasure. He has experienced everyone's bad days!

Tempted? Hurting? Aching with loss? Riddled with guilt? Toxic with sin? Whatever it is that we suffer, Jesus knows. He is acquainted with pain; He personally felt not only my sins but also those of the whole world. He carried them to the cross. There is nothing hard, painful or evil that He doesn't understand. Christ is compassionate. He identifies with struggles because He felt them all.

FAITH STEP: *Start your day over. Go back to bed if you have to. Then begin it with prayer.*

— *Judy Baer*

JULY 17

"Later when Jesus was eating supper at Matthew's house with his close followers, a lot of disreputable characters came and joined them. When the Pharisees saw him keeping this kind of company, they had a fit, and lit into Jesus' followers. 'What kind of example is this from your Teacher, acting cozy with crooks and riffraff?' Jesus, overhearing, shot back, 'Who needs a doctor: the healthy or the sick? Go figure out what this Scripture means: "I'm after mercy, not religion." I'm here to invite outsiders, not coddle insiders.'" Matthew 9:10–13 (MSG)

I was talking to a couple of other women at the health club, and in the course of conversation, one of the women said that her family has taken in one of her son's friends: a teenager whose family life is so bad that he needed to escape it. She didn't mention any religious motivation for doing this.

I don't know if this woman is a Christian, but she sure was acting like one, at least in this area of her life. That's no small sacrifice, to take in a troubled teenager.

I have Christian friends, on the other hand, who avoid hanging out with the other moms from the PTA or the neighborhood who are not believers. They don't like how those moms drink beer or swear or forward dirty jokes on e-mail.

If we claim to follow Jesus, it does not mean we simply believe that the things He taught are true. It does not mean that our only mission is to convince others they are true—although that may be part of it. To follow anyone means to go where they go, to do as they do. So we have to ask ourselves—do we, in our twenty-first-century lives, ever eat with sinners?

Jesus didn't just think loving thoughts toward sinners. He spent time with them. He extended amazing grace that changed lives and hearts. How can we do the same?

FAITH STEP: *Who is someone you consider an "outsider" that perhaps Jesus is asking you to reach out to?*

—Keri Wyatt Kent

JULY 18

" 'We have here only five loaves of bread and two fish,' they answered. 'Bring them here to me,' he [Jesus] said." Matthew 14:17–18 (NIV)

*W*riting is usually lonely work. I sit in my little office, sighing over my two small fish and rather dry loaves of barley bread, feeling the futility of the offering in the face of the world's needs. I suspect people in other careers struggle with the same discouragement. Most of the time we do the work in front of us, love the people around us, stay alert for tiny ways to help someone, sing an off-key melody of praise…and wonder if we are making a difference.

Often God doesn't let us see the results of our work. All the better. We walk by faith. Called to serve—not necessary to succeed. God is producing fruit, fruit that will last but is often growing in secret. It's not for us to tally.

I like to imagine there will be a time in heaven when God will page through a scrapbook with us, and He will trace the impact of some of the simple acts of love we offered, remind us of the hours of closet prayer we weren't sure He heard, and show us the second act of the story. I would love to hear how He breathed power and life into a word, a prayer, a gift—and multiplied it until baskets were needed for the leftovers.

God can make a difference through our lives. Not because of our greatness—relying on our own resources would lead to stinky fish and moldy bread—but because of His ability to multiply. He imbues our simple lives with His grace so that we can tear off a piece of barley loaf and pass it to a friend. And they can break the bread and hand it to another. And somehow it doesn't run out.

FAITH STEP: *Can you sing Him a chorus of praise today, even if your throat is hoarse from tears? Can you listen to a friend, even if you can't solve her problem? Can you pray one more time over a need, even when it seems your prayers bounce off the ceiling? Can you do the simple act of love that no one sees and no one appreciates? Bring what you have to Jesus, no matter how inadequate it seems. Jesus may be planning a miracle.*

—Sharon Hinck

JULY 19

"He drew me up from the pit of destruction, out of the miry bog, and set my feet upon a rock, making my steps secure." Psalm 40:2 (ESV)

Like many kids raised in the church, I spent my late teens and early twenties questioning my faith, pushing back against the rules, rebelling as best a good Christian girl could. Mine was a rebellion that was, by the world's standards, quite unremarkable. Still, my behavior, which I thought was an exercise of freedom, was actually self-destructive.

Thankfully, I had a moment when I turned around, that is to say, repented. Jesus came running to meet me. He pulled me from the miry clay and we began again.

Perhaps you have a similar story—you once were lost, but now you're found. Perhaps you didn't grow up in a family of faith, so you didn't so much rebel as simply stayed lost, until Jesus pulled you out of the pit. Maybe your self-destruction was more spectacular than mine.

Here's the thing: even if we can point to a time when Jesus rescued us from ourselves and our bad choices, even if we repented and changed and began anew, we still are in need of daily rescue. We may not be living a wild lifestyle, but we can still be tempted—perhaps to sins like pride or gossip or jealousy.

Every day, we need Jesus to set our feet on the rock of His love, to walk beside us to keep our steps secure. We need to remember we've been pulled from the pit, and have mercy on those who are still stuck in the mud.

FAITH STEP: *Today, ask Jesus to set your feet on solid ground, to walk beside you. Then ask Him to show you someone who needs to be encouraged, or even helped out of the mire.*

—*Keri Wyatt Kent*

JULY 20

"O God, from your sacred home you take care.... You find families for those who are lonely.... You set your people free." Psalm 68:5–7 (CEV)

I met Rhonda when she started coming to the same Sunday-school class I attend with several other ladies. It was evident to me early on that she was smart, a hard worker, deeply committed to her two teenage daughters and loads of fun. What was not so evident was the pain and loneliness she'd experienced as a young mother, divorced and estranged from much of her family.

Earlier this year, Rhonda married Craig, a guy who also goes to our church, and our class celebrated with her. Not long after that, we celebrated the news that she and Craig were expecting. The months since then have been like a science experiment as we've watched Rhonda's tummy expanding and monitored the baby's growth from week to week. We just had a big shower and will soon join Craig and Rhonda as they welcome little Sacia into the world.

Something so precious to me about this story is being able to watch Rhonda's happiness unfold in the context of our Sunday-school class. As we've all talked and studied Scripture together, she has shared aspects of her past, and how her faith has grown through seeing God bring her to the point she is at now. Instead of having to go it alone, Craig's mother and sister have embraced her—and she them—in a circle of love. She also has our Sunday-school class and church. Rhonda's gratefulness for these simple blessings has been beautiful for me to witness, a reminder that God really does make dreams come true.

FAITH STEP: *Is there a desire of your heart that you long to see fulfilled? Trust Jesus with it today. He is the Author and Finisher of our faith, and He makes all things beautiful in His time, His way.*

—Gwen Ford Faulkenberry

JULY 21

"But he was pierced for our rebellion, crushed for our sins. He was beaten so we could be whole. He was whipped so we could be healed." Isaiah 53:5 (NLT)

There comes a moment of clarity in your life: it often occurs around the time you make your first rent payment out of money you actually earned yourself. You realize that everything has a cost. There was a cost to your parents or whoever raised you. Whether they paid only for a roof over your head or spoiled you extravagantly with far more than you needed, they paid your way.

You realize that if your childhood was carefree in any way, it was because someone else footed the bill—they provided you with food, shelter, clothing and probably a lot more than that.

This should not incite us to guilt, but gratitude. And hopefully it enables us to be transformed slowly from takers to givers—to provide for our own children, or perhaps, to turn around and provide for our parents if they need our care. Even to extend generosity to strangers.

Perhaps your vision is clouded by memories of scarcity or lack, blocked by visions of pain inflicted rather than gifts given. But it is possible to grieve what was missing and simultaneously be grateful for what was given.

And that clarity should make us wonder—where else has someone paid my way, without my being fully aware of it? Jesus has paid a debt on our behalf that we could never have paid. He took the punishment for our sins. He stood in our stead so that we could be in relationship with Him.

We need not wallow in guilt, and it would be senseless to try to repay this debt with anything but gratitude. Perhaps appreciating Jesus' gift to us can help us to be grateful as well for imperfect gifts given by our families.

FAITH STEP: *Take a moment to reflect on the good things you have been given in this life, both from your family and from Jesus. Thank Him for those things.*

—*Keri Wyatt Kent*

JULY 22

"And the boat was already a considerable distance from land, buffeted by the waves because the wind was against it. Shortly before dawn Jesus went out to them, walking on the lake. When the disciples saw him walking on the lake, they were terrified. 'It's a ghost,' they said, and cried out in fear. But Jesus immediately said to them: 'Take courage! It is I. Don't be afraid.'" Matthew 14:24–27 (NIV)

*A*s Jesus approached the storm-tossed boat, the disciples saw Him, but didn't recognize Him. In fact, at first His presence added to their terror. They thought they were seeing a ghost.

Reading their first reaction made me think of the fear-inducing situations I've faced. How often has Christ been present in my storm, but I haven't recognized Him? Was He wearing the face of a person I don't like all that much? Did He come from a direction I didn't expect? Perhaps I was so weary from rowing against the wind, I expected nothing but more bad news.

When Christ speaks, He seems to ignore the immediate problem, saying, "Take courage! It is I."

If I were the disciples, I think I would have liked to hear, "It's okay, I'll tell the storm to stop now," or "I'll get in and help you row from here." Perhaps I'd even appreciate a six-step plan for getting safely to shore.

Instead Jesus offers one key thing: the truth that He is present.

I want God to respond to my trials with explanations for their existence, clear step-by-step plans for solving them and even a few promises about the value of enduring them. Yet here Jesus gives the disciples the answer He often gives me: "I'm here."

Sufficient. The answer I need. The answer powerful enough to propel me from the boat and onto the water, as Peter discovered as the scene continued.

Jesus doesn't provide a weather report, a new sailing technique or an empty pep talk. He gives me first what matters most: Himself.

FAITH STEP: *Think of the worst storm buffeting you today, and hear Jesus tell you, "Take courage! It is I."*

—Sharon Hinck

JULY 23

"The Lord looks at the heart." 1 Samuel 16:7 (NASB)

I'm a part of a group of women who meet monthly, kind of like a very laid-back sorority in which everyone is welcome and there are no membership requirements. We call ourselves the Small Town Sisterhood. In my estimation the sisters are all lovely, smart and extremely "together." Especially LuAnn. It was her turn to host this month, and to give you an idea of what she is like, she offered to cook the whole meal herself instead of delegating parts of it to others. Think Martha Stewart and you get the general gist of what it's like to visit her home.

I had spent the previous night on a campout with my three kids out in the Ozark National Forest with a bunch of back-to-nature types. It was fun, and also a bit hilarious. When I called my children in from the woods they came running, alongside their new friends, who had names like River, Rainbow and Wren. I corrupted a few of those kids with Doritos while their mothers tried to get mine to eat things like boiled amaranth and flaxseed.

As usual, I was flying in from camping about the time the STS was gathering at LuAnn's. When I dropped off the kids at home, and headed back out the door, Stone gave me a look that said, Surely you're not going like that. My hair was matted and I had on a T-shirt with sweatpants that were grass-stained from hiking. No makeup, of course; I wouldn't have dared wear it camping with the granola gang even if I wanted to.

When I arrived at LuAnn's beautiful house, with its perfect landscaping and shimmering lights along the walk, I admit I did wonder at the wisdom of my decision. But that was only for a second before LuAnn flung open the door and pulled my stinky self in with a hug.

Isn't that a perfect picture of Jesus' love? To all of our pretensions, our hopes for grandeur and our failures both outward and inward, He says, "I love you. Come to Me—just as you are."

FAITH STEP: *He knows your heart. Why not pour it out before Him today and let Him love on you a bit?*

—Gwen Ford Faulkenberry

JULY 24

"Yes, the Sovereign Lord is coming in power. He will rule with a mighty arm. See, he brings his reward with him as he comes. He will feed his flock like a shepherd. He will carry the lambs in his arms, holding them close to his heart. He will gently lead the mother sheep with their young." Isaiah 40:10–11 (NLT)

Sometimes it's hard to feel special to God when there are six billion other people on this planet. As a mom of young kids I knew I could turn to God for the big stuff—like when my husband and I considered moving two thousand miles, or for my husband's new job. But did God really care about the little stuff? Did He care that my son spilled Kool-Aid on the carpet and I couldn't get the stain up no matter how I tried? Did God care that I often felt like Play-Doh—smooshed and smashed and stretched—in my role as a mom? These things were hard for me to believe until I found Isaiah 40:11 during one morning of Bible reading: "He will gently lead the mother sheep with their young."

The previous verses speak of God's power and rule mixed with His tenderness and care. God can do anything. He is all-powerful. And what does He choose? He chooses to carry His lambs—His children. He chooses to gently lead mothers who have young.

Jesus said, "I am the Good Shepherd" (John 10:11).

Jesus doesn't have to lead us and guide us. He chooses to. I don't have to turn to Him for the big and small stuff, but my days are 100 percent better when I do. Yes, there are six billion people on this planet, but I've discovered when I've turned to Jesus in the dailyness of life He is there. To be led, I need to look to the One I'm following. The more I do that, the more I realize He's closer than I think.

FAITH STEP: *Find a 3x5 card and write out the Scripture, "He will gently lead those who have young." Post it in places you spend time such as near the kitchen sink or in the bathroom. If you have young children, use it as a reminder to ask for Jesus' leading in that moment. If you don't have young children, use it as a reminder to pray for friends and family members who do—and who often get overwhelmed by the challenges of daily life.*

—Tricia Goyer

JULY 25

"Now all glory to God, who is able, through his mighty power at work within us, to accomplish infinitely more than we might ask or think." Ephesians 3:20 (NLT)

For many years I wanted to write a novel. As someone who grew up loving to read I thought there could be nothing cooler than getting published. There was a huge obstacle, though: I have no degree in literature or creative writing. Instead, I read books on the writing process and attended writers conferences. Once I realized how hard getting a book published would be I focused on writing magazine articles. The publication of a book eluded me for many years.

Over time some of my friends I met at conferences started to get their books published, and I felt the same as I had in fourth-grade kickball…I'll always be the last one picked. For a long season, my prayer times were more like whining sessions. Other times I'd just pout. Didn't God realize that if I was published I could point many people to Him through my words?

My thinking of this changed after one writers' meeting I attended. The speaker shared how God launched her career only after she relinquished her writing desires to God. That sounded like a great idea to me, so the next morning I got on my knees. The only problem was even as I prayed words that sounded good, I knew they didn't come from my heart. If I was going to do this, I had to give Jesus everything—my hopes, my dreams, my longings.

Ephesians 3:20 speaks of God "who is able, through his mighty power at work within us." It wasn't about me and what I could accomplish. It was about what Jesus could work within me as I let Him.

Jesus wasn't concerned about me being a great writer. What He desired (and still desires) is that He has access to every part of my life. The more of myself I surrendered to Jesus over the years, the more He's done the work. And through Him I've accomplished more than I could ask or even think. Today I have enough books to fill a bookshelf, but more important I walk through life depending not on my own strength, but on Jesus who is at work within me.

FAITH STEP: *What is one dream you desire to accomplish? Say a prayer of relinquishment to God. Tell Him you're tired of trying to accomplish your dreams in your own strength, and ask Him to work within you, for His glory.*

—Tricia Goyer

JULY 26

"The seed that fell among the thorns represents others who hear God's word, but all too quickly the message is crowded out by the worries of this life, the lure of wealth, and the desire for other things, so no fruit is produced." Mark 4:18–19 (NLT)

I love to garden. Weeding—not so much. However, weeding is an essential part of gardening. Weeds grow right next to my tomatoes or flowers, and if left alone, will eventually cause destruction. Weeds hinder the growth of what is good in a garden. Unchecked, they'll keep a garden from being fruitful.

Jesus said that the seeds of truth He plants in our hearts get crowded out by worries, as well as by our desire for wealth or our desire for more stuff. I can say I don't desire wealth, but the fact is, I wish we had a little more. Not a lot, you understand. Just a bit more.

Further, in a random hour of almost any day, I probably have a dozen worries flit through my brain. I don't consciously decide to worry; in fact, I try not to. But still, the cares of this life march right on through: How will we manage to pay for college? Will my husband find a new job? Are my kids on the right track? Did I say the wrong thing to a friend? Will I meet the deadline for this project?

Jesus is the only one who can give me the fruitful life I long for. I cannot get it by trying harder, but rather by opening my life to Him, letting Him eradicate the weeds of worry and covetousness, while cultivating contentment and trust. Ironically, the way to cultivate contentment is to simply stop trying so hard. Trust grows when we surrender to Jesus.

FAITH STEP: *What unhealthy worries and desires for stuff or wealth are crowding out growth in your life? Are you willing to let God pull those weeds from your life?*

—*Keri Wyatt Kent*

JULY 27

"But if I say, 'I will not mention his word or speak anymore in his name,' his word is in my heart like a fire, a fire shut up in my bones. I am weary of holding it in; indeed, I cannot." Jeremiah 20:9 (TNIV)

I am soft-spoken, but I am also a loudmouth. I know that sounds strange, but it's true. In general, I am content to listen to conversation going on in front of me, but when I do have something to say, I say it. Sometimes rather forcefully.

And sometimes, after the words come out of my mouth, my foot goes in. I'm sure some of you can relate.

But sometimes, I feel like the words are burning inside me, like the other day at the college Bible study at my house. I wanted the students to know a biblical truth related to dating relationships, and I spoke to them passionately about it because I care about them.

Jeremiah talked about how the Word of the Lord was so strong within him that he couldn't keep it in even if he tried. It was a fire inside him, raging to come out.

When Jesus was entering Jerusalem and the disciples were praising Him, the Pharisees told Jesus to stop them. He answered that if they stopped, the stones would cry out in their place.

When God wants to say something, it gets said. Like with Jeremiah, it will burn inside you until it has to come out. It's a powerful thing, and it can be a little scary, but it can also be awesome, like the disciples praising Jesus. We just have to be willing to be used by God—we have to be willing to be those stones crying out.

FAITH STEP: *Pray for Jesus to show you who to speak to today and to give you the words to say to that person.*

—*Camy Tang*

JULY 28

"Ask, and you will receive. Search, and you will find. Knock, and the door will be opened to you. For everyone who asks, receives. Whoever seeks, finds. And to everyone who knocks, the door is opened." Matthew 7:7–8 (CEB)

"Those who find their lives will lose them, and those who lose their lives because of me will find them." Matthew 10:39 (CEB)

These two verses, just a few pages apart in the New Testament, seem to represent a paradox: whoever seeks, finds. But whoever finds, loses.

This seeming contradiction is resolved by asking what is being sought. In Matthew 7, Jesus is talking about seeking God. Seeking the Way, the Truth, the Life. If you seek Jesus, you'll find Him. If you seek truth, you'll find Jesus, who is the Truth. And when we seek Jesus, we let go of our own agenda. And discover the other truth: Whoever loses, finds—but only if they "lose" because of Jesus.

If you seek your own agenda—your life—you lose. I know, because I've chased my own ambition and desires. You may not experience physical death at that moment, but you won't be fully alive. To seek Jesus is to let go of the grip you have on your own priorities. And when you open your hands to release those things, Jesus fills them abundantly. In surrender, there is freedom. When you let go of your life, you experience real Life.

As a way to rationalize selfish behavior, some people will abandon responsibility, family and more, saying that they need to "find themselves." That sort of selfish seeking usually backfires. But when we actually seek meaning, when we seek Life and not just our own lives, we will find it. The question we must grapple with is, how do we lose our lives for Jesus' sake?

FAITH STEP: *If someone were to observe your daily life, what would they say your priorities are? If they examined your calendar and your checkbook, what would they conclude that you are seeking?*

—*Keri Wyatt Kent*

JULY 29

"...According to the eternal purpose which He accomplished in Christ Jesus our Lord, in whom we have boldness and access with confidence through faith in Him." Ephesians 3:11–12 (NKJV)

I'm not much of a thrill-seeker, but I know that new experiences are valuable. So at a family reunion in Colorado one summer, I decided to push my limits and climb a thirty-foot pole to a zip-line descent.

The climb was easier than I expected. Pure panic helped me find the necessary handholds and clamber up. When I reached the platform, I hugged the pole, hyperventilating. I told myself that I was breathing hard from the climb and the lack of oxygen at high altitudes. But the swaying of the pole and the sight of treetops beneath me were the real causes. The poor camp counselor had a tough time hooking in the new carabiner for the zip line and unhooking me from the climbing belay, because I kept my nose pressed against the pole.

"Nice climb. Okay, now turn around and step off," he said cheerfully.

Um, I don't think so. I managed to turn on the tiny platform. "Can I hold the rope here?" Discussing the finer points of harnesses and ropes seemed like a good plan. Anything to stall.

"Hold them together. That's right. Now, when you're ready," he said.

How about the twelfth of never?

But that morning, when I'd thought about the wonderful soaring ride into space, I'd said, "Lord, let my jump be a prayer. Let it yell to the heavens that I trust You—that I'll climb when it's scary, and step out of comfortable places and fly with You."

So I counted to three and stepped into space. The harness caught my weight, and I flew through the glorious Colorado sunshine.

No wonder camps have found these sorts of challenge activities so worthwhile. It's a chance to enact a little parable—one that I'll carry in my muscle memory. Life is full of leg-quivering risks. But God provides boldness and faith through Jesus Christ, and enables us to do things we would have bet we could never do.

FAITH STEP: *Is God nudging you to a step of faith?*

—*Sharon Hinck*

JULY 30

"A father of the fatherless and a judge and protector of the widows is God in His holy habitation." Psalm 68:5 (AMP)

*Y*ears ago I thought the way to please God was to live the best Christian life I could. In life, there were so many things that I strove for and I longed to do. I gave hours each day to cleaning and maintaining a home. I focused on my career, my family and my church, yet was it enough? After striving to be perfect, I wore myself out. Yet, the more I walked with Jesus, and grew closer to Him in everyday life, the more I asked Him to give me His ear. As I read the Bible, I started to realize that there were other things that mattered to God that I wasn't giving time and attention to. Two of those things were orphans and widows.

God speaks numerous times in the Bible of caring for these two groups of people: children who, through no choice of their own, don't have one or both parents in their lives and widows who, through no choice of their own, poured their lives into a spouse only to lose him to death. My heart became tender, and when the opportunity to care for my grandmother came after my grandfather's death, we opened our home. Even as we cared for her, my husband and I also decided to open our home and our hearts through adoption. Now we have a sweet baby girl who has joined our three biological children.

Of course, just because we've taken these drastic steps doesn't mean that's God's desire for you. Maybe you're called to help in other ways—to take a meal to a widow and spend time with her or to take a fatherless boy to a baseball game or a motherless girl shopping. Each of our walks with Jesus goes down a different path. Yet though our journeys vary, Jesus' heart is the same. Ask Him to show you how your heart can match His. You may not have the perfect house or a stellar career, but your gift to those in need will make Jesus smile.

FAITH STEP: *Write a list of widows and orphans you know. Pray over the list and ask God to show you who to reach out to today and in what way.*

—Tricia Goyer

JULY 31

"He said to the man with the withered hand, 'Step up where people can see you.' Then he said to them, 'Is it legal on the Sabbath to do good or to do evil, to save life or to kill?' But they said nothing. Looking around at them with anger, deeply grieved at their unyielding hearts, he said to the man, 'Stretch out your hand.' So he did, and his hand was made healthy." Mark 3:1–5 (CEB)

If you really study the life of Jesus, you'll see that He was not afraid of confrontation. Imagine the scene: Jesus is in the synagogue, and His detractors are watching Him, trying to catch Him in the act of healing on Sabbath.

The man with the withered hand didn't ask for a healing. He wasn't looking to stir up trouble. But Jesus puts him front and center, to make a point. To teach. The Pharisees had gotten so caught up in the external aspects of God's law that they seem oblivious to the heart of God. Jesus is deeply grieved by their attitude.

As followers of Jesus, we are called to love, to show mercy and so on. But we often inaccurately assume that to be like Him, we should avoid confrontation. This text shows us that at certain times, confrontation is necessary. It calls us to follow Jesus to the difficult place of standing up for truth. This text also reminds us how easy it is to get caught up in legalism, to elevate tradition above the Word of God.

FAITH STEP: *Where is Jesus asking you to confront wrong thinking or legalism? Second, is there an area of your life where you have an unyielding heart? Where you are grieving Jesus?*

—*Keri Wyatt Kent*

August

AUGUST 1

"As the deer pants for streams of water, so my soul pants for you, my God. My soul thirsts for God, for the living God. When can I go and meet with God?" Psalm 42:1–2 (TNIV)

$\mathscr{I}$'ve sung this song in church, but the words have always been hard for me to grasp. What is it like to "pant" for God? To "thirst" for God? What does that really mean?

The Bible tells us crowds followed Jesus even when He tried to get away from them. They wanted to hear Him. It was as if they needed to hear Him. As if they were thirsting for Him.

When I first became a Christian, something inside me suddenly clicked into place. There was relief and a feeling of freedom. And there was also a sense of homecoming, of being where I belonged.

A part of us longs for Christ. That's why the crowds followed Him. That's why I felt that sense of belonging. A piece of me resonates with Jesus Christ, because I was created by Him. Being one with Him makes me whole again.

The psalmist understood this longing in us for God. It's not just a mental or emotional desire for God—it's a yearning deep in our souls.

But then life happens. We become busy; our lives become cluttered. The yearning loses intensity. We shove Jesus to the side because there's not enough room for Him to be front and center in our lives.

Let's recapture that yearning in our hearts for Jesus. Let's dredge up that desire for more of Christ. Let's lift our souls and reach for Him, worshipping Him with all that we are.

FAITH STEP: *Pray for Jesus to teach you to pant for Him, to thirst for Him. Pray for help to make Jesus your heart's desire.*

—*Camy Tang*

AUGUST 2

"And the seed that fell on good soil represents those who hear and accept God's word and produce a harvest of thirty, sixty, or even a hundred times as much as had been planted!" Mark 4:20 (NLT)

So often, reading this parable or hearing it taught as I grew up in the church, the focus was on the harvest. This verse is rightfully linked with Jesus' words in John 4:35, which says the fields are ripe for harvest.

In the church I grew up in, this harvest, ripe for the picking, has to do with winning converts to the faith. Since it came after Jesus' conversation with the Samaritan woman and the subsequent conversion of many in her town, that makes sense. But so often we think, What do I have to do to get busy harvesting? Yet Jesus is not saying the good seed represents a farmer who does the harvesting. It represents the soil. Good soil, in which seeds can grow.

And how does soil become good? As a gardener, I can tell you: the soil can't become good on its own. In fact, the Gardener has to work with it. It has to be broken apart so that is softened. It has to have rocks and weeds pulled from it. Good soil has organic matter in it: nutrients produced by the decay of dead leaves or manure. Circumstances in my life that, at the time, felt like "manure" have often been used by God to help me grow.

So if Jesus is telling us to be "good soil" so that our hearts can be fertile ground for His Word, perhaps we will have to submit to Him, allowing Him to break us, to pull the weeds of materialism and worry and perhaps even "fertilize" us with what feels like dying to self.

FAITH STEP: *How is Jesus trying to work the soil of your heart? Are you resisting Him because it feels difficult? Ask Him to help you see the purpose of the struggles in your life.*

—Keri Wyatt Kent

AUGUST 3

"Do not grieve the Holy Spirit of God…. Be kind to one another, tenderhearted, forgiving one another, as God in Christ has forgiven you." Ephesians 4:30–32 (NRSV)

Lord, I am troubled. I ache for this world, this time, this place. I'm not doing enough. I want to bear fruit for you. I see people needing jobs, homes, food, basic necessities—and what am I doing? Too little! But I'm not sure how to do more. I open myself to You and ask that You show me where I am needed most. Is my time best spent in prayer? In action? If it is in action, then help me to discern where my talents fit and where I can serve you best. A homeless shelter? A food shelf? Offering a listening ear? Visiting shut-ins? Put me where I need to be. I'm flailing around, wanting to help but hesitant to act. Make me bold in service of You! Help me to love people, no matter who they are, just because I know You love them too.

FAITH STEP: *Make a list of places you might make a difference—a nursing home, with an ill friend, a project at church—then volunteer. If it is where God wants you, He will show you. If not, try something else. You will know when you find that place that needs you.*

— *Judy Baer*

AUGUST 4

"Then he told the people to sit down on the grass. Jesus took the five loaves and two fish, looked up toward heaven, and blessed them. Then, breaking the loaves into pieces, he gave the bread to the disciples, who distributed it to the people." Matthew 14:19 (NLT)

I love this story because Jesus doesn't produce a meal for more than five thousand people out of thin air. He tells the disciples, who want to send the crowd away, "You give them something to eat" (Matthew 14:16). The disciples protest that they don't have enough. Jesus takes their small provision and blesses it, but then gives it to the disciples to distribute. He forces them to not just give, but get involved.

My friend Shayne Moore, author of the book *Global Soccer Mom*, describes herself as just a stay-at-home mom of three who also happens to be a social activist. In between loads of laundry or driving the carpool, she'll fire off an e-mail to her congressman or call the White House to voice concern for the poor.

She's taken her loaves and fishes, and given them to Jesus. He has blessed them, handed them back to her, and asked her to distribute them to the people. And she's taken that assignment seriously. She's had the opportunity to visit ministries in Africa, where she saw women who had medicine to treat their HIV.

When she asked how the women had access to those meds, she found out that they got them because of an aid package that Shayne had lobbied her congressman to approve. "I realized, I was that woman's high-powered lobbyist," she writes.

You may think you don't have enough—just a few loaves and fish. But when you give what you have—a few hours of time, a small amount of effort—Jesus can bless and multiply it.

FAITH STEP: *What bread and what fish are Jesus giving back to you, to distribute to those who need it? Where is He asking you to not merely give, but get involved?*

—Keri Wyatt Kent

AUGUST 5

*"I keep my eyes always on the Lord. With him at my right hand,
I will not be shaken. Therefore my heart is glad and my tongue
rejoices; my body also will rest secure." Psalm 16:8–9 (TNIV)*

These days, doesn't everything seem very unstable? The economy, the international political climate, gas prices, jobs. Even the earth itself is rocking with earthquakes, tsunamis, tornadoes, hurricanes. We read in the Psalms about how God is our rock, but how can we feel secure when everything around us is crumbling?

I think the answer comes from the disciple Peter and the psalmist David. In Matthew 14, Peter gets out of the boat and walks on the water toward Jesus. Peter did fine until he took his eyes off Jesus and saw the stormy winds, and then he became afraid and started to sink.

If we deliberately channel all our energy into keeping our focus only on Jesus and not on the upheaval around us, then we won't be afraid. We'll be stable. We'll be at rest.

When we look at other things and don't focus on Jesus—His will for us, His power, His sovereignty—then suddenly we'll be as unstable as everything else.

In this psalm, David keeps his eyes on God, and then he isn't shaken by the things around him. He had enemies on every side, enemies within his palace, and his own sin to contend with, but he trusted in God to help him and save him. That focus on God brought him unshakeable rest.

FAITH STEP: *Take some time to ignore everything around you and focus on Jesus. Keep your eyes on Him and rest secure.*

—*Camy Tang*

AUGUST 6

"For the eyes of the Lord range throughout the earth to strengthen those whose hearts are fully committed to him." 2 Chronicles 16:9 (NIV)

On the day I married my husband, the word commitment took on a new meaning. Commitment meant not flirting with other guys. It meant listening to my husband and loving him. Commitment meant I'd put his desires above my own.

From the day my first son was born I understood commitment at yet another level. It meant staying attentive to my son's needs. It meant sacrificing my time, my energy and my desires for another.

Every time I sign a contract for a new work project I'm committing I'll get the job done. I commit that I will do good work and deliver it on time. There are other places we're committed to—our homes, our communities, our church. In each of these areas our dedication and our commitment is seen and appreciated by others.

I don't know why "committing to Jesus" is a concept that's hard to grasp. So many times we want our pastor or church leaders to tell us the dos and the don'ts of our Christian walk: "Just tell me what to do to be a good Christian and I'll do it. Give me a list to follow and I'll check off each box."

That wouldn't work for our other relationships, so why do we think it'll work with Jesus? Instead we need to show our dedication just like we do to our spouses, children and friends. It means putting Jesus first, listening and loving Him. It's putting His desires above our own. It's also staying attentive and sacrificing our time, our energy and our desires. It means connecting with Him in ways that are meaningful to you—through music, journaling, praying, fasting or studying with other believers. When I feel He's called me to a task, it's diving in and working with all my heart.

The best part is that Jesus takes notice of our commitment. There may be times when our friends, spouses and especially our children don't appreciate our effort, but our dedication to Jesus will never go unnoticed.

FAITH STEP: *Share your commitment to Jesus with someone this week—not with your words, but with your actions.*

—Tricia Goyer

AUGUST 7

"So the Lord God sent them out of the Garden of Eden, where they would have to work the ground from which the man had been made. Then God put winged creatures at the entrance to the garden and a flaming, flashing sword to guard the way to the life-giving tree." Genesis 3:23–24 (CEV)

Have you ever wondered what the Garden of Eden was like during pre-Fall days? What did Adam and Eve do all day? Did nature's colors look more vibrant? What was it like to pet a lion's head without fear?

Perhaps no two people ever lived with greater regrets and if-onlys than the first two people God created.

Consider the level of grief they experienced after God sealed off His idyllic Garden from them. They are the only people who have truly known what we all lost with that first sin. They walked and talked with God Himself…until they no longer could.

Suddenly they knew loneliness and the crippling bite of shame. They felt strife not only between themselves and God, but also with each other, the animals (some of which became threats), and an unruly earth. Their digestive systems had to adjust to eating meat. They had to wear clothes. They faced pain and dissatisfaction in their work. Eve experienced pain in childbirth. And if those things weren't enough, one of their sons killed his brother; surely they battled bitterness, confusion, unspeakable grief and fear after that.

Now consider what it would have been like to walk with Jesus while He was on earth. I've often wondered if I would've had an easier or more difficult time believing in Him if I had been there to witness His ministry. Was it His grace that timed my life for here and now, to hear "His story" as "history" and read His Word instead of relying on verbal accounts? One day I will hear His answer.

Rejoice that He timed your life as He did. He knew best back at your conception, and He still knows best for today and your future.

FAITH STEP: *How does "His story" comfort you about your "history" and your future?*

—*Erin Keeley Marshall*

AUGUST 8

When He saw the throngs, He was moved with pity and sympathy for them, because they were bewildered (harassed and distressed and dejected and helpless), like sheep without a shepherd. Then He said to His disciples, 'The harvest is indeed plentiful, but the laborers are few. So pray to the Lord of the harvest to force out and thrust laborers into His harvest.'" Matthew 9:36–38 (AMP)

What do you do when you get overwhelmed with all the people who need help, guidance, love? I wish I could say that I turn all my thoughts toward Jesus and lay my concerns at His feet. I do that often, but only after I've worried, schemed and stayed up half the night trying to figure out how to help the most amount of people with my limited time and resources. I wish during these moments Jesus was bigger in my view than my problems.

Last year I prepared to launch a program for needy teens in the inner city. The number of teens who needed help overwhelmed me, yet I knew I couldn't help them on my own. I also knew that if my heart was breaking, Jesus' heart was too.

"Dear Lord, you are the Lord of the harvest," I prayed. "Jesus, You care more than I do. I pray for laborers for Your harvest."

One by one I met up with people willing to help. One lady read about the group from an e-mail posting. Another woman was a foster mother to a teen in need and wanted to assist us. I also spoke to a group of moms, and four of the women there stepped forward to help. In the end, ten women and men joined me as leaders. They were loving, dedicated and passionate about Jesus. If I had interviewed people for years I couldn't have stumbled upon such a committed group, yet Jesus brought them to me. He knew my heart, He knew theirs and He joined our efforts to reach more teens for His glory.

I'm learning that I don't have to try to figure everything out. Instead I simply need to turn to Jesus, who already has the answer.

FAITH STEP: *If you could start a program to reach out to the harassed, distressed, dejected and helpless, what type of program would it be? Ask Jesus to show you what the first step in starting that program would look like.*

—Tricia Goyer

AUGUST 9

"The fruit of the Spirit is love, joy, peace, patience, kindness, generosity, faithfulness, gentleness and self-control." Galatians 5:22–23 (NRSV)

"For I fear that when I come, I may find you not as I wish, and that you may find me not as you wish: I fear that there may perhaps be quarrelling, jealousy, anger, selfishness, slander, gossip, conceit, and disorder." 2 Corinthians 12:20 (NRSV)

*W*hat a contrast there is between these two verses! One is the work of the Holy Spirit in us; the other, Satan's handiwork. The fruits of the Spirit are the qualities Christ Himself embodied. By unifying oneself with the Holy Spirit, these gifts will blossom and grow in us. Without being tapped into this Ultimate Power Source, those efforts will wither and fade on the vine.

I want to love with abandon, feel and show joy without restraint. I desire Christ's peace in my heart and that my watchwords become forbearance, mercy and patience. I will show kindness, goodness and gentleness toward others and faithfulness toward the Lord. All these things are impossible without Christ, but tapped into His vine means I will be fed by His Spirit.

FAITH STEP: *Think of the fruits of the Spirit and strive to embody one of them today. Consciously show that trait to everyone you meet.*

— Judy Baer

AUGUST 10

"When the perishable has been clothed with the imperishable, and the mortal with immortality, then the saying that is written will come true: 'Death has been swallowed up in victory.'" 1 Corinthians 15:54 (TNIV)

*T*here are days I get so tired of all the things I have to deal with. The Mount Everest of laundry to be washed. The Mount Fuji of dirty dishes. The endless fires I need to put out at home and at work. I feel exhausted and despairing.

I know that this world is not my home, that the Kingdom of God is coming. Jesus said so in Revelation: "I am making everything new!" But when facing a week of jury duty or a busy Saturday of youth group activities, it's hard to think about the new heaven and the new earth. I just want to go somewhere to sleep.

But I have come to realize that I'm focusing my energy on things that are dying. This world is dying. Yes, there are things I need to do—such as filing taxes and paying the mortgage—but I am focusing so hard on all the other things that take up my day that they seem endless. I begin to tell myself that these things on my to-do list are the whole of my world. That this is all there is.

But it's not. I need a larger perspective—to see that these things will pass away. They take up my time, but they shouldn't become my entire world or consume me. I have a new world waiting for me someday.

FAITH STEP: *We can still tackle the mountain of laundry and the pile of dirty dishes, but we can distance ourselves and get control of our stress levels, remembering that this is not all there is. One day, death will be destroyed and we will be made new. That makes the laundry seem not so important anymore.*

—*Camy Tang*

AUGUST 11

"I was angry, good and angry, because of Israel's sins. I struck him hard and turned away in anger, while he kept at his stubborn, willful ways. When I looked again and saw what he was doing, I decided to heal him, lead him, and comfort him." Isaiah 57:17–18 (MSG)

𝓛ord, please help me grasp what you're trying to teach me…and Jesus, please help me be a quick learner. How many times have I breathed that prayer? Countless, I think. I'm not too fond of pain, but I also know my hardheaded streak. As a result, I lean on Jesus' mercy and trust that He won't use any more drastic measures than necessary to get my attention.

Reading through much of the Old Testament, it seems God had to let His people learn their lessons the hard way, and oh my, those lessons often hurt terribly. However, as Isaiah 57:17–18 shows, God is so very merciful. He really does allow us to suffer for our wrongs only as much as necessary to get our attention and draw us back on track with Him.

Sometimes His discipline may feel unmerciful, but consider the alternatives. Imagine how we'd hurt—or how we'd hurt others—if we continued on a sinful path. It's easy to forget, especially when temptation hits, just how serious sin is. Just one act of disobedience sent Jesus to a horrible death; that one disobedience was "only" taking a bite of forbidden fruit.

When Jesus lived on earth, He spoke often about turning from sin to follow Him. Even in our stubbornness He shows mercy, desiring above all to heal us rather than let us suffer the consequences of our wrong choices. (See Matthew 13:15 and Mark 3:5.) He is too compassionate to allow us to remain as is.

Sin always leads to pain, and obedience always leads to blessing—here or for eternity. Let Him get your attention, and spare yourself a world of hurt.

FAITH STEP: *How has Jesus gotten your attention? Thank Him for knowing just what it takes to help you stay close to Him.*

—*Erin Keeley Marshall*

AUGUST 12

"Give us this day our daily bread." Matthew 6:11

*S*ometimes things loom up before us that seem impossible. Facing a big surgery, or the death of a loved one, or a lost job, or even a pile of unending laundry can feel like facing Mount Everest. We know that with God all things are possible, and we know He gives us the grace we need. But will it be enough? Fear closes in. Weakness. Uncertainty. How will we ever have enough strength to handle it?

I was thinking about this one day when I was baking bread. It smelled so good coming out of the oven. The dark gold color of the outside signaled perfect crispness. Like my Granny used to do, I rubbed butter over it, allowing it to melt into the fluffy interior. Before the bread could even cool, my family devoured a whole loaf.

This was fun, but it's not typical of our bread-eating behavior. We buy most of our bread at the store, and it comes pre-sliced. On Monday I use two slices for my husband's sandwich, and on Tuesday he gets two more. It's the same for my kids. Two slices each, lathered in peanut butter and jelly. Then two slices the next day. Not the whole loaf at once.

Our bread-eating habits are the perfect metaphor for how God's grace works—and His strength, His mercy, His power. When we're contemplating Mount Everest we may want the whole loaf, but God knows what is good for us. He knows what we really need. He slices off enough for the first step. Then, when it's time for the next one, another slice is there. And another and another and another till the journey is done. The whole loaf is ours—but God gives it as needed. Never too little, always just the right amount to fit our need.

FAITH STEP: *What is your deepest need today? Trust Jesus for it. He is Your manna from heaven.*

—*Gwen Ford Faulkenberry*

AUGUST 13

"The Lord looked and was displeased that there was no justice. He saw that there was no one, he was appalled that there was no one to intervene; so his own arm achieved salvation for him, and his own righteousness sustained him." Isaiah 59:15–16 (NIV)

*I*f you want something done right, do it yourself. Never has that catchphrase been more profound and true than when Jesus achieved salvation for us.

Often when we utter those words, it's with a sarcastic tone. We're aggravated that no one can get it right and—let's face it—probably a little cocky thinking we're more capable. However, when I read Isaiah 59:15–16, Jesus' attitude shows compassion, not arrogance. The fact that "He was appalled that there was no one to intervene" on our behalf shows deep love for us; He simply could not bear to let us destroy ourselves and each other.

Actually, Jesus has every right to be arrogant and cocky; there's no besting him. But given the opportunity, he humbled himself to ensure justice. (See Philippians 2:8.) And through His just actions, we thrive in His grace.

That's worth more than a passing glance: Through His accomplishment of justice, we thrive in His grace.

We deserve His justice, but He offers His grace instead when we acknowledge our humble position and surrender to His loving ways on our behalf. Many people fight Him on that, but what we need to understand above all is how He fights for us.

The more we realize how much Jesus gave for us—and still gives us—the more we feel appalled that we cost Him so much. May that deepening understanding of His sacrifice ever increase our sense of awe at being loved so greatly.

FAITH STEP: *Does anything shock you anymore? While we might witness and hear of shocking behavior in the news, ask Jesus to shock you more today with His abundant love for you.*

—Erin Keeley Marshall

AUGUST 14

"I know what it is to be in need, and I know what it is to have plenty. I have learned the secret of being content in any and every situation, whether well fed or hungry, whether living in plenty or in want. I can do all this through him who gives me strength." Philippians 4:12–13 (NIV)

I always thought of myself as fairly content. Sure, I'm occasionally curious about what it would be like to have someone else's level of beauty, talent, wealth or success, but it doesn't tug me too persistently.

Yet recently sourness has invaded my thoughts in another way. Instead of coveting what someone else has, I dwell on what I once had, once could do, once was, and I contrast that with my new realities and limitations. Self-pity lurks in the space between the things I long for and the reality I live.

It's hard to stay content when we see others enjoying things that we long for. But perhaps it's even more difficult to combat the longing for things we did once enjoy and no longer can. Loss is an inevitable part of life. We may face loss of loved ones, loss of jobs, loss of health and abilities. Living in contentment is a daily battle, whether we're tempted to compare to others, an ideal, or our past circumstances.

During times of significant losses, as I've laid down things that were precious to me, I've found comfort in remembering that Jesus understands loss. He set aside the glories of heaven to come to earth. Earlier in Philippians we read a description of how He "did not consider equality with God something to be used to his own advantage; rather, he made himself nothing by taking the very nature of a servant" (Philippians 2:6–7, NIV).

Contentment sounds like such a deceptively mellow, easygoing word. But some days it takes fierce, stubborn courage to walk in it. For any of us facing a painful loss—job, relationship, ability, health, plans, purpose, circumstances—I pray for God to breathe the courage of gratitude into our hearts and keep nudging our focus back to Him.

FAITH STEP: *What tends to make contentment difficult for you? What helps you beat off the temptation of self-pity?*

—Sharon Hinck

AUGUST 15

"You are the Christ, the Son of the Living God." Matthew 16:16 (NKJV)

ooking through an old photo album, I found a cute—and hilarious—picture of my younger brother, Jim. He's about five years old, standing in front of the fireplace in our childhood home, and his arms are raised in the air as though he's about to take off in flight. Around his neck is tied a red cape that flows out behind him in the back. He's wearing Underoos—a blue T-shirt with an S emblazoned across the chest, and matching briefs. Superman.

It seems that at one time or another, Superman is every little boy's hero. My dad loves to tell the story of the time—around the same time as the picture was taken—he and my brother were walking together in the near dark. As they walked back toward the house from the barn, my brother held a flashlight, shining it on the path in front of their feet. My mischievous dad said to my brother, "Jim, did you know that I am really Superman?"

"You are not."

"I am too, really."

About that time my dad gave a whoosh sound and started running. Jim jerked the flashlight up in the air, searching the sky, and yelled, "Dad? Dad!"

My dad circled back to him and scooped him up, laughing.

We all like that story because it's funny, but I think my dad likes it so much because it demonstrates my brother's precious heart toward him. He was a smart kid, but when it came down to it, he really believed my dad could be Superman. The proof of his faith was in where he shined the light.

I believe we bring delight to the heart of God when we have that kind of faith in Jesus—the kind that says, "I believe You are the Christ, the Son of the Living God, the Savior." In spite of what anyone else may believe about Jesus, I want to be the one shining my light up to the sky, looking with the eyes of a child for His salvation.

FAITH STEP: *Is there an area Jesus is asking you to step out in faith? Shine your light up to the sky!*

—*Gwen Ford Faulkenberry*

AUGUST 16

*"If you, then, though you are evil, know how to give good gifts
to your children, how much more will your Father in heaven give
good gifts to those who ask him!" Matthew 7:11 (TNIV)*

*M*y husband and I have something we laugh about between us. He is Mr. Doom and Gloom while I'm Miss Blissfully Unaware.

When driving to his parents' house for Christmas, he said things like, "Let's hope the pass isn't snowed in," and "Let's hope our car doesn't break down," and "Let's hope we don't get lost."

I got annoyed with him because while the weather report talked about snow, it didn't say anything about a blizzard. We had a rental car, so even if it did break down, we'd get towed and the car would be replaced pretty quickly. And aside from the fact we had a GPS unit, it wasn't like we were going somewhere completely new, so it was unlikely we'd get lost.

Being the not-so-tactful wife, I teased him: "Are you trying to create bad luck?"

We shouldn't be heedless and blithely disregard danger, but we also shouldn't be expecting God to slam us with problems left and right. God is good. It's repeated over and over throughout the Bible. Even when trials come, God is with us because God is good.

Jesus made a point of challenging a rich young man to think about why he'd called Jesus a "good" teacher. Jesus reminded him, "No one is good except God alone." He won't make our lives problem-free, but He will bless us and give us good things. His blessings give us more than we could ever have wanted, because He loves us and He is good.

FAITH STEP: *Are you worrying and expecting pitfalls in your life? Stop right there and remind yourself that God is good.*

—Camy Tang

AUGUST 17

"If I only touch his cloak, I will be made well." Matthew 9:21 (NRSV)

That's the strength of the Lord's power. If I reach out in faith, He will respond. I'm not worthy of the gift of eternal life He has given me through His death and Resurrection. Yet because of Christ's graciousness and mercy, when He feels me desperate and reaching out to the one person who can save me, He responds. When I clumsily fumble about for the fringe of His cloak, extending my desperate hand and my heart to Him, Christ takes action. It doesn't matter how we get to Christ, but only that we do.

I imagine my lowly self touching the hem of His garment, of being felt and seen and picked up and cradled in Christ's arms. He wants to hold me, if only I will reach out my arms to Him. And I am in such desperate need of my Lord and my Savior.

FAITH STEP: *Reach out to Jesus today and trust that He feels your need and rescues you.*

— *Judy Baer*

AUGUST 18

"But they that wait upon the Lord shall renew their strength; they shall mount up with wings as eagles; they shall run, and not be weary; and they shall walk, and not faint." Isaiah 40:31

I hate waiting. I think of waiting rooms, where you sit, leafing through a two-year-old copy of *People* magazine, with a quiet, half-formed dread, thinking of all the things you are not getting done.

The word wait, although it's a verb, seems inactive, passive. In English, in our culture, waiting has that connotation. Sitting around and tapping our feet. Not really doing anything. Wasting time.

But the Hebrew word in the original text, qavah, was full of energy and faith. *Strong's Exhaustive Concordance* notes: "The word stresses the straining of the mind in a certain direction with an expectant attitude…a forward look with assurance." Its more ancient meaning is to collect or bind together—active words.

To wait upon the Lord is not the same thing as to wait upon a bus or to wait upon the dentist. Waiting on the Lord is active, engaged, expectant. Do we have the strength to wait on Jesus?

We don't just wait for God to do something, we wait upon Him. Our faith has a focus, an object: Jesus. We rest in Him, allowing Him to renew our strength, to help us so that we can run and not be weary. We turn our lives over to Him and trust Him.

So often, we waste energy trying to impress Jesus—see how many committees we serve on, how much we do! But when we run ahead of Him, we end up weary. Sometimes we need to wait: listening, expecting, allowing Him to renew our souls.

FAITH STEP: *Where are you trying to run ahead of God? Where do you feel weary and faint? What if your weariness is God's way of telling you to slow down and wait on Him?*

—Keri Wyatt Kent

AUGUST 19

"The Son is the radiance of God's glory and the exact representation of his being, sustaining all things by his powerful word. After he had provided purification for sins, he sat down at the right hand of the Majesty in heaven." Hebrews 1:3 (NIV)

The darkness in the cave settled over our family, blacker than any darkness I'd experienced before—sound-muffling, heavy blackness with no shades of gray. My eyes strained, but couldn't find even a pinpoint to focus on. My son squeezed my hand, and nearby my daughter gave a nervous giggle from my husband's arms.

The park ranger's voice was almost swallowed by the weight of the emptiness. "Now I'll use my flashlight to point out unique features of this cavern."

The mild light of a few double-A batteries exploded like the sun. Suddenly quartz formations glistened like diamonds embedded into the walls of the cave. Stalactites glowed with vibrant, limestone white. Even better, my children's eyes sparkled with wonder. The radiance of the flashlight revealed incredible beauty, impossible to see in the darkness.

There are many days that the world feels like a dark, forbidding cave. Evil has twisted and distorted the beautiful world God created and damaged our relationship with Him and each other. God's glory is all around us, but we need the radiance of Jesus to illuminate it for us. In fact, without Jesus, my image of God would be full of fear of the unknown and invisible—the same sort of fear I felt far beneath the ground in the dark cave. Because Jesus came in the flesh, He lit up the truth about God's love for us and illuminated what had seemed frightening and unknowable. He continues to guide us in finding the beauty hidden in our every day.

FAITH STEP: *Ask Jesus to reveal God's glory to you in a fresh way today— perhaps bringing unexpected light to a place that feels dark.*

—*Sharon Hinck*

AUGUST 20

"God...has in these last days spoken to us by His Son...
being the brightness of His glory and the express
image of His person." Hebrews 1:1–3 (NKJV)

The other day I was walking with my three-year-old, Adelaide, when she looked up in the sky and said, "Mommy! I see God!"

I looked, and all I could see was the sky—a beautiful shade of blue, like a silk curtain stretched across the heavens—but the sky nonetheless. I admitted to my daughter that all I could see was sky. "But the heavens do declare the glory of the Lord," I assured her.

"You can't see Him, can you, Mommy?"

"Nope."

We walked a little farther, she displaying obvious pity for my lack of vision.

"What does God look like, Adelaide?"

She didn't miss a beat. "Jesus."

I'm not sure what was going on with my three-year-old that day. What I am sure of, however, is that what Adelaide said is biblically correct. Jesus is the "express image" of God. Everything we are able to know of Him shows us something of God's character.

When Jesus walks on water, we see God's power. When He heals the sick, we see God's compassion. When we see Jesus with children, we see God's tenderness. And when we see Jesus on the cross, we understand something of God's fierce longing for a relationship with us. We see His love.

FAITH STEP: *What is your favorite story of Jesus? What does it reveal to you about the expressed heart of God?*

—Gwen Ford Faulkenberry

AUGUST 21

"If you, God, kept records on wrongdoings, who would stand a chance? As it turns out, forgiveness is your habit, and that's why you're worshiped." Psalm 130:3–4 (MSG)

*I*n the more than forty years that I've been walking with Jesus, I've grown, I've learned, I've had faith and trusted. And also, I haven't. I've sinned, I've ignored the truth, I've doubted and I've been afraid. I've gone through seasons of rebellion—some that people could see, and some that I kept well-hidden. I've made some pretty big mistakes, and if my track record is anything to go on, I'm not done making them.

Even when we become all-new people and are washed shiny clean by Jesus, we're going to continue to sin. The surest path to less sin is to stop trying to do it on our own, and surrender. We learn this paradoxical lesson quite slowly. When we focus on clinging to Jesus, like a branch to a vine, we do better than when we try to stand on our own. As Paul commiserates in Romans 7, sometimes we do that which we don't want to do; we battle daily with sin.

The Bible is clear: sin is part of our condition. But confession and repentance bring us into the light of grace. And even though we won't be perfect until we're in heaven, He can change us in the here and now into grace-filled people.

Jesus is the one who rescues us from ourselves, who continues to forgive us. As this psalm reminds us, Jesus is a habitual forgiver! What a promise. Written centuries before Jesus' birth, this verse points prophetically to the everlasting mercy of God and the life, death and resurrection of Jesus.

FAITH STEP: *Spend some time confessing specific sin in your life—patterns of thought, actions or attitudes. Receive His abundant forgiveness, and then spend some time worshipping Jesus for His habit of forgiveness, for His ever-renewing mercies.*

—*Keri Wyatt Kent*

AUGUST 22

"Though he slay me, yet will I hope in him." Job 13:15 (TNIV)

$\mathcal{W}$e got our dog from the local animal shelter, and she had been an outdoor dog her entire life. We wanted to train her to live inside our home, so we began crate training.

Every night and every time we left the house, we would try to entice her to go into her kennel, a crate large enough for her to stand up and turn around in, but small enough that she wouldn't go to the bathroom in it since dogs don't do that close to where they sleep.

The first time, she went into the kennel blithely, but after we shut the door on her and she realized she couldn't get out, she was very unhappy. The next time we tried to get her into her kennel, she resisted and it became a war of wills. No treats would induce her to enter that kennel. At the advice of our dog trainer, we forced her into her kennel that time and every other time for several months.

She thought we were torturing her. And, of course, we couldn't explain why it was good for her. But she still "forgave" us each time we let her out. She trusted in our love for her to let her out of that kennel and not leave her there, and she was loyal in her love for us.

Although Job wasn't a dog, he was just as loyal to God despite not understanding God's reasons for his suffering. He had to trust in God's love for him, the same way our dog trusts in our love for her. Jesus asks us to do the same thing—to trust in His love for us and to remain in that love.

FAITH STEP: *Are you going through a difficult time right now? It's hard to be like Job and continually hope in the Lord, but take some time to pray and ask Jesus for help. He wants us to have that kind of loyalty to Him.*

—Camy Tang

AUGUST 23

"Don't copy the behavior and customs of this world, but let God transform you into a new person by changing the way you think. Then you will learn to know God's will for you, which is good and pleasing and perfect." Romans 12:2 (NLT)

Think back to your high-school chemistry class, particularly when the teacher would mix chemicals to create a reaction, possibly a puff of smoke or other special effects. You learned the word catalyst—something that causes that which it comes in contact with to change. In our lives, Jesus is a catalyst for transformation. When we come into contact with Him, He changes us. Jesus forgives us, but beyond that, He changes our thinking. Once that happens, Jesus challenges us to be salt and light in a dark world. Both salt and light are catalysts—they cause change. I want to "live salty and shiny," as my friend Caryn Rivadeneira writes in *Grumble Hallelujah*, but there's a tension—to be in the world but not of it, to be relevant without being conformist.

What if the behavior and customs of this world are based on how unbelievers think? And not copying their behavior begins by not going along with their patterns of thinking? What if the way to not copy the customs of this world (greed, social climbing, etc.) is to focus on Jesus? To open ourselves to the promise of the second part of this verse—the part where God transforms us, changes our thinking—and that change will transform our behavior. Yes, our lives should be different, but not because we avoid certain sins or behaviors. They should be different because we engage in certain radical behavior: caring for the poor, practicing extravagant generosity, loving our neighbor, loving our enemy—things Jesus told us to do.

FAITH STEP: *Today, pray that Jesus would "transform you into a new person by changing the way you think." What old ways of thinking and behaving will you have to let go of in order for that to happen?*

—*Keri Wyatt Kent*

AUGUST 24

"But I see another law at work in me, waging war against the law of my mind and making me a prisoner of the law of sin at work within me. What a wretched man I am! Who will rescue me from this body that is subject to death? Thanks be to God, who delivers me through Jesus Christ our Lord!" Romans 7:23–25 (NIV)

*B*ang! The screen door slammed behind me. I stomped out to the garden, pulling on my work gloves. I was angry. Angry at the pickup truck that had cut in front of me in traffic. Angry at the cashier who had overcharged me. Angry at my son for talking back. Angry at my husband for not understanding. Angry at the world.

Yanking up handfuls of weeds, my gloves were soon dark with moist dirt. I worked my way along the neat rows and my breathing slowed. My thoughts calmed.

I noticed how rapidly some weeds had shot out runners, tangling themselves among my green beans and cucumbers, choking out life. I pictured my angry feelings. Each bitter thought spread gnarled fingers into my heart—choking off love. And like the nettles and quackgrass, they kept coming back. There was only one Gardener who could help me in this battle.

"Jesus, tear out those dangerous weeds in my soul. Don't let sin take root in me."

His love and forgiveness washed over me, and then I felt His nudge to pray specifically for each person I felt had wronged me. I began to pray with each clump of weed I pulled. "Lord, protect the stranger in the pickup who was in such a hurry. Father, bless the overworked cashier. Help my son with his frustration. Touch my husband with Your joy today."

Soon my garden was free of weeds, able to thrive and produce again; and my heart was fertile ground, ready for the fruit He wanted to cultivate in me.

FAITH STEP: *How is the garden of your heart? Have you noticed any weeds? Ask Jesus to deal with the deep roots.*

—Sharon Hinck

AUGUST 25

"Thanks be to God, who always leads us as captives in Christ's triumphal procession and uses us to spread the aroma of the knowledge of him everywhere. For we are to God the pleasing aroma of Christ among those who are being saved and those who are perishing." 2 Corinthians 2:14–15 (NIV)

*M*mm…I love the scent of something tasty baking in the oven. Anyone for ooey-gooey lasagna? Banana bread? Chocolate-chip cookies? Can you smell them already?

The aromas of savory seasonings and sugary sweetness have a way of wafting through doors and windows, seeping into furnishings and clothing, captivating everyone in their path with the promise of satiating hunger.

The sense of smell is powerful. Just imagine sticking your head in a dumpster and taking a whiff—suddenly your pleasant daydreams of lasagna and banana bread and cookies scatter in the odoriferous breeze.

God's followers carry a powerful aroma that either draws others to want the good stuff of knowing Jesus or sends people running. Jesus Himself drew those in need of His gentle healing and compassionate spirit. Those were the ones who also tended to be open to hearing unpopular truth from Him, whereas those who weren't aware of their own need often rejected His presence.

Someone whose heart refuses to be drawn to Jesus' aroma of salvation will reject Him no matter how godly our conduct may be. However, we never know when our paths will cross with that of someone who may need the refreshing scents of Jesus' love and grace.

Wear the aroma of His Spirit throughout this day, and be part of satisfying someone's spiritual hunger for eternity.

FAITH STEP: *Find a small, empty bottle and label it "Aroma of Christ." Place it where you get ready for the day as a reminder of whose aroma you're giving off to all you come in contact with.*

—Erin Keeley Marshall

AUGUST 26

"Not that I have already obtained all this, or have already arrived at my goal, but I press on to take hold of that for which Christ Jesus took hold of me." Philippians 3:12 (NIV)

One of my friends endured successful heart surgery, and was happy to put the difficult experience behind her. However, the surgeon wanted to follow up with her in a year. She would have preferred to close the file on the whole experience. Waiting for the next appointment was unsettling.

My husband juggles many projects at work. He loves the feeling of getting one completed and out the door, but each time he does, it seems three more appear on his desk. I battle my e-mail inbox, struggling to keep up on answering mail, but each day more appear reminding me that work is never fully finished.

My friends and I who are parents have poured love into our children's lives. Yet sitting at a high-school graduation ceremony, the realization smacks us between the eyes that our role as parents isn't a closed file. We will never stop caring, praying and longing to be a good influence in our children's lives.

All of life is a challenge to live with open files—those parts of life that are still in process, whether medical uncertainties, open-ended work projects or parenting. We also live in the midst of open files in our personal development: the longings unfulfilled, the habits that lurk in the background waiting for a moment of weakness, the uncertainties not yet resolved.

I used to think that becoming a Christian closed all files—signed, sealed, delivered. Clear answers to all questions. Every trial explained by a clear purpose.

But I've learned to know and love God even more in the open files—the uncertainties—the unfinished race. While we're here on earth, we haven't yet reached our goal. The work God has called us to is still in progress. The Holy Spirit's sanctifying work isn't finished in our hearts. Because Jesus took hold of us, we can press on.

FAITH STEP: *What are the open files in your life? Thank God for all the works in progress that He is completing.*

—Sharon Hinck

AUGUST 27

*"You don't nurse your anger and don't stay angry long,
for mercy is your specialty. That's what you love most.
And compassion is on its way to us." Micah 7:18 (MSG)*

"*I*'m gwumpy," two-year-old Calianne announced. She crossed her pudgy arms, blew out her nostrils, furrowed her brow and stuck out her bottom lip to prove it.

I stifled a smirk. "Why are you grumpy, sweetheart?"

"Because I'm gwumpy."

Turns out her brother had ticked her off by not sharing a toy, and she wasn't over it yet.

I called Paxton into the room, got his take on what happened and then recalled a friend's wisdom about asking and offering forgiveness. She had been teaching her own preschool-aged son that when someone apologizes, it's important to speak the words "I forgive you." I thought her insight was brilliant.

As my friend had pointed out to me, there are two parts to making forgiveness complete. When someone apologizes, acknowledging that we forgive that person helps us release leftover resentment. It's as if verbalizing "I forgive you" helps free the other person from ongoing guilt and frees our own spirit from being soured by bitterness.

Jesus told us to forgive over and over again, too many times to count (Matthew 18:21–23), and He modeled verbalizing forgiveness in His conversation with the woman accused of adultery. (See John 8:2–11.)

Pax and Cali offered and accepted forgiveness. Then they hugged and sped off to their next adventure.

And I went back to my task with a heart lightened by witnessing a picture of Jesus' forgiving, merciful Spirit.

FAITH STEP: *Who has crossed your mind as you've read today's devotion? If your heart feels burdened by a grudge, take the freeing step of verbalizing forgiveness.*

—*Erin Keeley Marshall*

AUGUST 28

"God is our refuge and strength, a very present help in trouble." Psalm 46:1

*M*y aunt Gerry was treated for melanoma on her heel five years ago. Since then, she had been cancer-free, until a spot showed up last month on her liver. Because of blood-clotting issues, she cannot have surgery. So the doctor recommended a less-invasive procedure to treat the tumor on her liver.

The way it was described, it seemed the procedure was fairly simple. My aunt, as well as the rest of us, expected it wouldn't be especially painful. We were wrong. In reality it was a horrifying experience. After a month's time, she is finally starting to feel better, and get her sense of humor back.

I visited her the other day and she was telling me about being half-awake during the procedure. She told me to imagine a Roto-Rooter going through my groin on the way to my liver. We laughed about it now, because we can. She related to me, rather theatrically, that at one point during the procedure she remembers yelling, "Jesus! Help me! Oh, Jesus! Help me be able to stand this!" It was so funny we both laughed till we cried.

On my way home, however, I thought more about it. Even though it is funny to imagine her yelling for Jesus during the procedure, the truth is that it is also completely normal and right—exactly what she should have done. What all of us should do in a similar situation, or any situation, for that matter.

FAITH STEP: *Is there a need in your life today? It could be a matter of life and death, or it could be something small. Nothing is too big for Jesus, and nothing that concerns us is insignificant to Him. Call out His name! He stands ready to help.*

—*Gwen Ford Faulkenberry*

AUGUST 29

"The people who walked in darkness have seen a great light. For those who lived in a land of deep shadows—light! sunbursts of light!" Isaiah 9:2 (MSG)

I accepted Jesus into my heart as a little child—I was maybe five or six years old. I remember the day clearly: going into my room after a particularly compelling Sunday-school message, praying on my knees and then opening the door of my room to find the hallway of our little suburban ranch house flooded with light. I remember walking to the living room, where the brightest sunlight I'd ever seen was streaming through the picture windows, filling the room—and my freshly redeemed soul—with light.

I don't know that casual observers would think that I had "walked in darkness" in my preschool years, before I made a decision for Christ. And yet the Bible says all have sinned. All. Even little kids. I knew what sin was, even as a child. I knew the times I'd lied or been naughty. My mother will attest I was a little sinner, even then. As we all are.

But these words about Jesus, penned centuries before His birth, remind us that although we all live in the shadows, and walk in the dark, we can come into the light. And then, the Bible says, we are to take that light to others. As Jesus' followers, we're meant to shine, so that others can find their way out of the dark.

The question is, Do I shine? Or do I mostly complain? Do I bring light, or merely find fault? Does my ability to trust Jesus draw others toward Him, or does my fear and negativity push them away? I want to be a light, but sometimes, my whining is the bushel basket I put over my own light.

FAITH STEP: *Would people who know you describe you as someone who brings Jesus' light? Ask Jesus to show you where you can shine more brightly.*

—*Keri Wyatt Kent*

AUGUST 30

*"And, lo, I am with you always, even unto
the end of the world."* Matthew 28:20 (KJV)

When the plane landed in Hong Kong late at night, I stumbled out into a new world. The humid air tasted like a combination of jasmine and bus fumes. Taxis darted like minnows. Radios blared tinny songs in Cantonese. I'd been invited to teach dancers on an outreach team for Youth with a Mission, and was excited to meet the people I'd be working with, but because of flight delays, the mission base was tucked in for the night when I arrived. The staff had a place for me in the women's dorm, but didn't want to disturb everyone, so I was shown to a tiny guest building.

Jet-lagged and disoriented, I curled up on the cot that filled most of the room as the darkness pressed in around me. I'd never been away from my husband and two young children for this long, and I'd never been this far away from my comfortable Midwestern home. The enormity of the distance hit me. I felt completely alone.

"Lord, are you here? I've landed. I made it safely. Thank you. But I need to know you're here."

A silly prayer. Theologically, I understood that God is omnipresent. He's everywhere. But I'd never had to test that truth in such a distant place before. Immediately the warm sense of God's presence reassured me. His still small voice whispered to my soul. Joy flooded me as I hugged His promise to my heart—a promise proven in a new way. He was with me.

Since that time, I've experienced other places that felt as frightening as the end of the world: a cold, lonely MRI machine; the bedside of a friend who lost her baby; the graveside of loved ones. But in every single place, He has kept His promise. There isn't a place too far or an experience too frightening for Him. He is always with us.

FAITH STEP: *What are some of the unusual places where you've experienced God's presence? If you're in a lonely, frightening place right now, ask Jesus to show you He is there with you.*

—*Sharon Hinck*

AUGUST 31

"The tongue is a small member, yet it boasts of great exploits....
How great a forest is set ablaze by a small fire! And the tongue
is a fire.... No one can tame the tongue—a restless evil, full of deadly
poison. With it we bless the Lord and Father, and with it we curse
those who are made in the likeness of God. From the same
mouth come blessings and cursing...this ought
not to be so." James 3:5–10 (NRSV)

The tongue is so small yet with such capacity to be cruel. It's easy to let my tongue run wild. It is tempting to let something spill out—disgust with a difficult friend or family member, dislike for someone who disagrees with me, gossip—those juicy tidbits of information that may or may not have a basis in truth. Yet a word, once spoken, can never be harnessed, recaptured or controlled.

Envision the pure, innocent mind of a child. Picture that child being exposed to something improper or shocking. That young mind cannot erase those images once embedded in its psyche. They will stay with them forever. Neither can I erase hurtful words I speak. They embed themselves in people's minds and grow like seeds in dark, rich, loamy soil. Their produce is negativity, doubt, lowered self-worth, insecurity, hurt. No one can control or undo what harm these spiteful or injurious words might do. They are like feral things that cannot be ensnared.

The spoken word can be as sharp and dangerous as a blade, wounding and potentially deadly. In order to honor Him I must keep my mouth and my mind in sync—always focused on what honors the Lord.

FAITH STEP: *Avoid hurtful, careless or thoughtless words today.*

— Judy Baer

September

SEPTEMBER 1

*"Don't give holy things to dogs, and don't throw your pearls
in front of pigs. They will stomp on the pearls, then turn
around and attack you." Matthew 7:6* (CEB)

One of the most irreplaceable, valuable things we possess is our time. We cannot go out and buy more time, we cannot go into the kitchen and whip up a couple of extra hours.

And yet time is one of the things we squander the most easily. We waste time, we spend time doing things that sap our energy. If someone asked you to give them money, you might decline, but when they ask you for your time, how do you respond?

There's nothing wrong with giving someone your time, but I have often been sucked into commitments I should have avoided by thinking—well, it's only a few hours of my time. I forget time is a pearl of great price.

This odd saying of Jesus forces us to consider: what are the holy things I possess? What are my pearls—the things I value most, the things that are rare and precious to me?

My stuff is not holy. My possessions are not my pearls. But the hours I have each day—these are precious. As my children get older, and move toward independence, I realize I do not get these days to do over. When other people try to demand those pearls from me, sometimes the most holy thing I can do is refuse.

One of the more countercultural ways I spend time with my family is to take a weekly Sabbath. The Bible tells us the Sabbath is to be kept holy. Those precious hours, when I set aside my work and busyness to focus on my relationships with God and my family—they are pearls. In order to protect them, I sometimes have to say no to the requests of others. I think Jesus would approve.

FAITH STEP: *What do you need to say no to in order to protect the holy things in your life? Think particularly of your schedule—have you thrown your pearls before pigs?*

—*Keri Wyatt Kent*

SEPTEMBER 2

"I have seen you in the sanctuary and beheld your
power and your glory. Because your love is better than life,
my lips will glorify you." Psalm 63:2–3 (TNIV)

We continue to fall in love with Jesus anew each day. His Holy Spirit is inside us, reminding us of His love, and that love isn't just better than our lives—His love makes our lives worth living. His love makes our lives richer, brighter, deeper, bolder.

Yet despite what His love does for us, we often neglect to glorify Him. Glorifying Jesus is not just thanking Him for the good things He gives us. The first definition of glorify is "to cause to be or treat as being more splendid, excellent, etc., than would normally be considered."

So glorifying Jesus can be saying things to others that lift Him up, that give Him splendor and make Him even more excellent. He's already splendid and excellent, but our words make Him more splendid and excellent in other people's eyes. We can help others see how awesome He is.

Glorify also means "to honor with praise, admiration, or worship; extol." So we should never stop thanking Him and praising Him for what He does for us. We should also praise Him for who He is, His character and majestic qualities. We should praise Him simply because He's awesome.

FAITH STEP: *Glorify Jesus today, whether in your words to others or in your words to Him. Look for opportunities to glorify God, simply because His love makes our lives magnificent.*

—Camy Tang

SEPTEMBER 3

"Brothers and sisters, think of what you were when you were called. Not many of you were wise by human standards; not many were influential; not many were of noble birth. But God chose the foolish things of the world to shame the wise; God chose the weak things of the world to shame the strong." 1 Corinthians 1:26–27 (NIV)

A mission trip to the Czech Republic started as a simple idea. I had friends who were Czech and I'd been there a few times. I'd fallen in love with Prague, and it saddened me to know that most of the Czech people didn't believe in God. Not long after I started looking for opportunities to serve, one presented itself. I was asked to lead a team of eighteen people there on a mission trip. I was sure the mission board was mistaken. I'd never been on a mission trip before. I didn't know how to teach English as a second language—or to train others to do so. It was during this time I ran across a quote by Hudson Taylor, a missionary to China: "God uses men who are weak and feeble enough to lean on him." Because I didn't know what I was doing, I depended on God even more.

I shouldn't have been surprised that in all the areas I was weak, God's strength shined through. He provided the people, the training materials and the funds. He was with our team every step of the way as we interacted with people from a different culture.

The greatest joy came on the last night when the mission director gathered our team together. "I've never been so impressed with a team of people. You are loving and energetic. You didn't let fear stop you, but you reached out to the Czech people with Christ's love."

I smiled as he said those words. I knew our success wasn't from our training or wisdom. All we achieved was a result of our dependence on God.

FAITH STEP: *Consider where you would go on a mission trip if God opened the door. Why would you go there? Do you think God put it on our heart for a reason? Pray and ask Him to show you when the time is right.*

—*Tricia Goyer*

SEPTEMBER 4

"But a man named Ananias, with the consent of his wife Sapphira, sold a piece of property; with his wife's knowledge, he kept back some of the proceeds, and brought only a part and laid it at the apostles' feet. 'Ananias,' Peter asked, 'why has Satan filled your heart to lie to the Holy Spirit and to keep back part of the proceeds of the land?…You did not lie to us but to God!' Now when Ananias heard these words, he fell down and died…. After an interval of about three hours his wife came in, not knowing what had happened. Peter said to her, 'Tell me whether you and your husband sold the land for such and such a price.' And she said, 'Yes, that was the price.' Then Peter said to her, 'How is it that you have agreed together to put the Spirit of the Lord to the test?"… Immediately she fell down at his feet and died." Acts 5:1–5, 7–10 (NRSV)

Satan is still trying to make us stumble.

Ananias and Sapphira's sin wasn't how much they gave, but that they lied to God and to His people about it. They said they'd given more than they really had when, actually, they'd held some back for themselves. They tried to deceive God. What's more, they'd ruined their testimony about their faith.

Are we trying to deceive someone to make them think better of us?

Sin is both knowing what we should do and not doing it and failing to do what we know we should be doing. These are the acts of omission and commission.

Sapphira, wife of Ananias, knew her husband hadn't given the disciples all he should have and yet she tolerated it. She lied about holding things back from them. She chose her husband's side over the truth and over God. The sin was not having saved some money for themselves but for lying and saying that they had given it all to God when they really hadn't. They put Him to the test.

The result for them was tragedy. Nothing must come before the Lord! Nothing.

FAITH STEP: *What are you tolerating or overlooking? Is there something you should speak up about and are remaining silent? Why? Ask God what He wants you do and take action.*

— Judy Baer

SEPTEMBER 5

"But the Advocate, the Holy Spirit, whom the Father will send in my name, will teach you all things and will remind you of everything I have said to you. Peace I leave with you; my peace I give you. I do not give to you as the world gives. Do not let your hearts be troubled and do not be afraid." John 14:26–27 (NIV)

My kids and I get up early—they have to be out the door by 6:45 am to catch the bus. They make their own lunches and get their own breakfast, so I really don't need to be up, but I still rise early in order to have a few minutes with them. Besides, it takes me a while to wake up, and if I sit and drink coffee while they get ready, the grogginess clears in time for me to start working once they leave the house.

During one particularly difficult season of life, I would stand, waiting for the coffee to brew, and I would sigh, without realizing it. My son, who is very tuned in to subtlety, came and stood next to me one morning and gave an exaggerated sigh. I looked at him. "What?" I asked. "That's you," he said, sighing loudly again.

I hadn't even been aware. It got to be a running joke. When I would sigh, one or both kids would loudly sigh as well. "That's just how I wake up!" I would say. But there was more, below the surface, trying to escape in those sighs. I was weary, emotionally. I'd let life's challenges trouble my heart. I'd ignored Jesus' gift of the Holy Spirit, and the supernatural peace He gives to His children.

Sometimes, sighing is our troubled heart's way of crying out to Jesus. I began to pay attention to my sighs, and rather than sink into sadness, I would use them as a reminder to pray, to receive the peace that Jesus promises.

FAITH STEP: *What are the things that make you sigh? Are they perhaps something to pay attention to, a reminder to pray and to ask Jesus for the peace He promises to His children?*

—*Keri Wyatt Kent*

SEPTEMBER 6

*"He humbled you, causing you to hunger and then feeding you
with manna, which neither you nor your ancestors had known,
to teach you that people do not live on bread alone but on every word
that comes from the mouth of the Lord." Deuteronomy 8:3 (TNIV)*

I love bread. I can honestly say I'm passionate about it. I love crusty Italian bread with holes the size of the Grand Canyon. I love French bread with its soft, almost creamy center and crisp crust. I love the sturdy but soft Greek bread holding the marinated meat of a gyro. I love thin naan with its darkened bubbles across the surface.

I think God deliberately used bread in this passage as opposed to other things we eat—like vegetables or meat—because the Word of God is like bread. Nourishing, comforting, filling. Just as bread can be varied, Scripture can hit me in different ways depending on where I am in my life.

God can test us with trials in our lives to show us that we need Him more, or so that we find we need Him in a different way. We often see trials as ways the devil is torturing us, but Jesus tested His own disciples to determine that they were faithful. It wasn't just so He could know their faith, but also so that the disciples could grow and mature in their faith.

When in trials, digging into the Bible is often the only way to stay sane. And while in those different stages of your life, the Word of God is like bread—it can be different each time you read it, but it's always filling. It's hard to thank God for our trials, but they can show us how to depend on Jesus more, just like we depend on bread to survive.

FAITH STEP: *Are you struggling with something right now? Take the time to read more of God's Word, and find sustenance, comfort and fulfillment there. Eat the bread of heaven and find a new way to cling to Jesus.*

SEPTEMBER 7

"If you preach, just preach God's Message, nothing else; if you help, just help, don't take over; if you teach, stick to your teaching; if you give encouraging guidance, be careful that you don't get bossy." Romans 12:7–8 (MSG)

To put it nicely, some people say I'm a born leader. To be more honest, there are times when I can get bossy. I remember one time when I was on vacation with a friend.

"Go to the room and get our coats and I'll make reservations for dinner," I told her.

I can still remember the shocked look on my friend's face. "I'm not one of your kids," she told me. "You don't need to boss me around."

That was a gentle reminder that I need to talk through plans with people and not just announce what I think others need to do.

The same thing can happen when I start serving others, sharing God with them. I can see the changes they need to make in their lives and my nature is to tell them what I think they need to do. Over time I've learned that Jesus knows even better than me—shocking, I know!

Through the years I've learned I don't need to tell others what to do. Instead I need to point them to Jesus. Jesus will be there for them when I'm not. Jesus can see what's in another person's heart when I can only judge their outward actions. More than that, Jesus is never bossy. Jesus can guide in gentle ways, bringing others to the right path without pushing them there. I'm so thankful for that.

FAITH STEP: *Is there someone you'd like to "boss around" (in a positive way, of course)? Instead of sharing your opinion, pray and ask Jesus to speak to that person's heart in ways you can't.*

—*Tricia Goyer*

SEPTEMBER 8

"Do you not know that in a race the runners all compete, but only one
receives the prize? Run in such a way that you may win it. Athletes exercise
self-control in all things; they do it to receive a perishable wreath, but we an
imperishable one. So I do not run aimlessly, nor do I box as though beating air;
but I punish my body and enslave it, so that after proclaiming to others I
myself should not be disqualified." 1 Corinthians 9:24–27 (NRSV)

"So whether you eat or drink, or whatever you do, do everything
for the glory of God." 1 Corinthians 10:31 (NRSV)

$\mathcal{I}$'m so competitive. I enjoy winning and feel like a failure when I don't.
I'm unhappy to play second fiddle. If I start something, I like to finish
it—in style. Some say I have a type-A personality.

It's strange then, why I sometimes slack off where the Lord is concerned.
Winning takes intention and discipline. A race is a good metaphor for the
journey I'm on. My crucial disciplines are prayer, worship and study of
God's Word. I cannot grow without it. I can't go at them half-heartedly
and expect to make progress. This isn't a stroll we are on, but a full-out
run! If it means giving up something, do it. If it means sacrificing self,
it's worth it. This is the life-race we're meant to be on! Everything we do
should be for God's glory, not our own. If an action won't honor God, I
must refuse to do it. Persist in Bible study and prayer. It is the exercise of
the soul.

Satan is ready to trip us every chance he can. We need to be ready!

FAITH STEP: *Pray, "Lord, help me to put all my energy and obedience toward*
pleasing You. Don't let me grow lazy. Like an athlete readying for a race, help me
to plunge myself into the discipline of the Word and the delight of prayer. With
Your help, it is a race I can win."

—Judy Baer

SEPTEMBER 9

"And when Jesus had cried out again in a loud voice, he gave up his spirit. At that moment the curtain of the temple was torn in two from top to bottom." Matthew 27:50–51 (TNIV)

$\mathcal{I}$ didn't fully understand the role of the curtain in the temple until I read the Old Testament and the description of the tabernacle. To separate the Most Holy Place, which housed the ark of the Covenant, from the Holy Place, where only the priests could enter, there was a curtain to shield the priests—or perhaps shield the Presence of God. God's holiness could not be exposed to human sinfulness.

It was hard for me to conceive of God's holiness until I read about how priests were struck dead when they didn't respect the holiness of the ark. God's holiness is like a furnace, burning white-hot and pure, but incredibly deadly. We are too fragile to survive if we get too near it.

So when the curtain ripped in two at Jesus' death, that was incredibly significant. The curtain wasn't like a kitchen curtain or drawing-room drapes. The curtain was huge and extremely heavy and thick. The power to rip it in two was already immense, but the power that enables us to be in the presence of God's holiness is even greater. It brings more significance to the blood that covers us and covers our sins.

FAITH STEP: *Do you view Jesus as holy, or do you just view Him as a friend or a father? We cannot forget Jesus' burning, white-hot holiness. We need to live our lives and respect that holiness, because we were bought with a price that enables us to stand in the furnace.*

—Camy Tang

SEPTEMBER 10

"As Jesus started on his way, a man ran up to him and fell on his knees before him. 'Good teacher,' he asked, 'what must I do to inherit eternal life?' 'Why do you call me good?' Jesus answered. 'No one is good—except God alone. You know the commandments: "You shall not murder, you shall not commit adultery, you shall not steal, you shall not give false testimony, you shall not defraud, honor your father and mother."' 'Teacher,' he declared, 'all these I have kept since I was a boy.' Jesus looked at him and loved him. 'One thing you lack,' he said. 'Go, sell everything you have and give to the poor, and you will have treasure in heaven. Then come, follow me.' At this the man's face fell. He went away sad, because he had great wealth." Mark 10:17–22 (NIV)

*W*hy is it that we consider Jesus' private conversation with Nicodemus ("you must be born again") true for all people, but Jesus' public conversation with this young man to be only for him? Certainly, this passage isn't saying that everyone who wants to follow Jesus should sell all their worldly possessions and give the money to the poor, right? Then again, could it be that we are missing something in this story?

Jesus tells this man two things: to let go of his wealth and to follow Him. So often we're so focused on the financial implications of this verse—did He really mean we should sell all our stuff?—that we miss the obvious invitation. Jesus says, to this man and to us, "Follow me. Don't stop at merely believing certain things in your head, or keeping certain rules. But follow—orient your life around our relationship. Do as I do. Walk with me."

If we follow, we realize that our stuff doesn't matter. We see that when we're reborn, everything changes.

FAITH STEP: *What are you holding tightly to, that Jesus may be asking you to release, so that you can truly follow Him? What is one small step you could take today to follow Jesus?*

—Keri Wyatt Kent

SEPTEMBER 11

*"For the wages of sin is death, but the gift of God is eternal
life in Christ Jesus our Lord." Romans 6:23 (NIV)*

*M*y teenage daughter is a hard worker and a born saver. She works a part-time job and babysits, and socks away her wages in the bank. She loves watching her little nest egg grow. She's using her earnings to help pay for a trip this summer to Spain with her high-school foreign-exchange club.

My dad, also a saver, told her when she'd saved a certain amount, he'd give her a "bonus check" as an incentive to continue saving. She was even more motivated to not fritter the money away at the mall; she kept saving until she reached the goal, and was excited when her grandfather sent her the promised bonus.

Wages don't magically appear in your bank account—you have to earn them. And while my dad's generous bonus was a gift, my daughter had to earn it by saving up to meet a goal. It was a conditional gift.

Eternal life, on the other hand, is a free gift, utterly and completely. It is pure grace. Earning it is impossible.

What we earn by our sin is death. Not just someday—living a life focused on self-indulgence may feel like freedom, but it's actually a kind of death, right now. Staying stuck in sin is not really living.

But we have a choice—to stay miserable, or accept the free gift of God's grace and find life. We cannot earn it, and we don't have to clean up our act to be good enough to receive it. We have to let go of our sin, admit we're a mess and in need of rescue.

FAITH STEP: *Have you accepted Jesus' free gift of eternal life? Even if you've prayed to accept Him, are you living in the freedom of that gift, or are you still living as though you're trying to earn His love? Today, open your hands and heart, and remember that His grace is abundant, sufficient and new every morning.*

—Keri Wyatt Kent

SEPTEMBER 12

*"Now faith is assurance of things hoped for, the
conviction of things not seen." Hebrews 11:1 (ESV)*

The Bible is full of examples of acts of obedience. Obedience is not my strongest quality. When I look to Scripture, I see Noah, who pleased God by respecting His warning and building the ark. He must have been a laughingstock, but he did it anyway. I don't like being made fun of. I avoid it whenever I can. But, like He did for Noah, the Lord might have something He wants me to do that's out of my comfort zone.

What is the ark I'm supposed to build today? In what is God asking me to be obedient that might be uncomfortable, awkward or embarrassing? Is it to reach out and befriend someone whom my neighbors or friends make fun of? To lead a Bible study that I feel incompetent to lead? To speak up about something that is happening in my community or church that doesn't honor Him?

Abraham was called by God to set out for the place in which he was to receive his inheritance without knowing where he was going!

Can I follow God and remain comfortable when I don't know what's next? I have a light in Jesus that pierces the darkness right in front of me, but it only shines so far. With Christ I must take only one step at a time and wait for Him to illuminate the next. It's like jumping off the high dive and then checking on the way down to make sure there's water in the pool. With Christ, however, I am assured that there's always water in the pool.

FAITH STEP: *If your next act of obedience and faith feels unclear, ask for illumination and wait for God's answer.*

— Judy Baer

SEPTEMBER 13

"When I kept silent, my bones wasted away through my groaning all day long. For day and night your hand was heavy on me; my strength was sapped as in the heat of summer. Then I acknowledged my sin to you and did not cover up my iniquity. I said, 'I will confess my transgressions to the Lord.' And you forgave the guilt of my sin." Psalm 32:3–5 (TNIV)

I don't know why it takes me so long to admit when I'm wrong. Is it a pride thing? Is it a desire to be right all the time? Is it my wanting to feel superior over other people? Is it embarrassment that I was so insistent, but now I'm backtracking what I said? Is it an idea that I have to be perfect to be liked and accepted?

If I don't confess my wrongs, it eats inside me, like a cancer chewing through my bones. It feels like my sin has become acid in my stomach. And I feel ugly, dirty, soiled.

This is not how God wants me to be. Jesus wants to forgive my sin. It's the reason He died for me. But I need to confess it or else my relationship with Him is strained, like a rubber band stretched too tight. I need to release the tension.

The wonderful thing is that confession makes me feel one hundred times better. It's not just the weight of guilt being lifted, but also the fact that Jesus loves me so completely that confession restores our relationship. There are no grudges or lingering hurt. He never asks us to be perfect little Christians—but He does ask us to come clean when we're wrong.

FAITH STEP: *Is there something you're not confessing? Some wrong you've done or said? Confess it to Jesus. Seek His love, His will for you.*

—*Camy Tang*

SEPTEMBER 14

"But where sin increased, grace increased all the more." Romans 5:20 (NIV)

*A*rgghhh! I cringed as the car ahead of me putzed along. I could run faster than this!

Convinced of that fact, I glanced at the speedometer and cringed again. Oops. My bad.

The car was going the speed limit and, lo and behold, probably spared me a speeding ticket from the police officer whose car I just noticed hiding off the side of the highway.

Those old speed limits. They're oh-so-easy to break.

But today I felt convicted by how often I try to justify ignoring them with excuses of I'm running late; everybody does it; five miles over is acceptable—so what's another two?

I teach my kids that laws protect us, but when I feel stifled by them, I'm not sure I'm truly on board with the necessity of some laws—at least for me. As I typed that, rest assured I realized the audacity of that admission. But in all honesty there's a strong thread of entitled feelings within me that claim I have the right to break certain laws and expect God's protection regardless.

Laws point out our sins. That's been their purpose since God created the Law—capital L—for His people thousands of years ago.

Jesus allowed that car to be ahead of me today. Through it, He showed me the greater grace He loves to shed on us despite our sin. I deserved a ticket. He could have made sure I got one. Knowing He didn't do so doesn't make me less guilty, as if it were okay because I got away with it. Knowing He showed me grace reminds me of my need for that grace.

Jesus loves offering grace to people when He knows we'll be moved to live for Him because of it. He's the Master at transforming lifestyles of sin into lifestyles of grace.

FAITH STEP: *What rules do you struggle to obey? How have you experienced Jesus' grace in your life?*

—Erin Keeley Marshall

SEPTEMBER 15

"Who then will condemn us? No one—for Christ Jesus died for us and was raised to life for us, and he is sitting in the place of honor at God's right hand, pleading for us. Can anything ever separate us from Christ's love? Does it mean he no longer loves us if we have trouble or calamity, or are persecuted, or hungry, or destitute, or in danger, or threatened with death?… No, despite all these things, overwhelming victory is ours through Christ, who loved us." Romans 8:34–35, 37 (NLT)

When she first got her license, my daughter got pulled over for not stopping completely at a stop sign. She wasn't speeding and there were no other cars in the quiet residential area intersection, but she couldn't deny that she hadn't made a complete stop. She was absolutely beside herself with regret.

A good family friend is an attorney. He offered to go with her to court. A kid who's had her license less than a month would have trouble convincing a judge to grant court supervision. I accepted his generous offer. I didn't want my daughter to get off the hook completely, though. She had to pay a fine (out of her own money), but if she avoided tickets for a year, the transgression wouldn't go on her record.

In Romans 8, Paul uses courtroom language: are we condemned? There's evidence to convict us. We are guilty of sin. But we have a loving advocate, Jesus, who pleads our case.

When I can't figure out how to pray, when I'm at a loss for words, it is comforting to know that Jesus is at the right hand of the Father, pleading for me. Interceding for me. Why? Because He loves me. And the Bible promises that nothing can separate me from that love.

FAITH STEP: *Do the challenges of your life make you doubt that Jesus loves you? Spend some time thanking Jesus for being your advocate, for pleading your case. Thank Him that you can have victory, not on your own merits but because of His love for you.*

—*Keri Wyatt Kent*

SEPTEMBER 16

"Because of the miraculous signs Jesus did in Jerusalem at the Passover celebration, many began to trust in him. But Jesus didn't trust them, because he knew human nature. No one needed to tell him what mankind is really like." John 2:23–25 (NLT)

I tromped backstage at the theater where I'd been working for months. As I made my way to the dressing room to prepare for the evening's performance, a few conversations broke off. Other actors didn't meet my eyes when I offered a cheerful, "Hello."

I shrugged and got into costume, trying to ignore the whispers and sideways glances. After the curtain call, when everyone else had left for the night, one of my friends walked out with me. "You really don't know?"

"What's going on? People are acting so weird."

She sighed and told me that one of the trusted staff members had been saying things about me. Untrue, hurtful, insulting things. Now rumors were burning up the backstage.

Shock drained the blood from my face. The gossip was ridiculous, and I knew friends would eventually see the truth. What hurt so badly was that a trusted colleague would do this to me—smirking and spreading lies that had no purpose but to wound.

That night I cried over my Bible asking God to help me figure out how to deal with this betrayal. He led me to this verse in John—an odd little verse I'd never noticed before.

I shook my head as I read. Doesn't love expect the best? Isn't trust the default attitude to offer? Gently, God showed me that love was not the same as naïveté. Jesus didn't collapse in shock and disillusionment when He saw the thoughtless and sometimes cruel choices people made, because He knew human nature. He carefully chose where to put His trust. He also knew the difference between those who only befriended Him for what they could get out of Him, versus true followers. Somehow, acknowledging what Jesus saw—what mankind is like—helped me on the road to forgiveness and deeper wisdom in where I placed my trust.

FAITH STEP: *Think about ways to focus more trust on Jesus and a little less dependence on other people.*

—*Sharon Hinck*

SEPTEMBER 17

"Therefore, there is now no condemnation for those who are in Christ Jesus, because through Christ Jesus the law of the Spirit who gives life has set you free from the law of sin and death." Romans 8:1–2 (TNIV)

We know we were set free from eternal damnation when we accepted Jesus Christ. We also feel freedom as we live our lives, serving Him and feeling His pleasure in us, knowing He is guiding us and taking care of us.

Freedom is a powerful thing. Anyone who has been a prisoner of some sort, even if being tied up for a game of cowboys and Indians, understands the unique feeling of relief when freed.

When Jesus set us free from the law of sin and death, He meant complete freedom. Not just from our sins, but also from our past:

Past actions that we're ashamed of, with guilt that sometimes strangles us.

Past relationships where we were hurt, where the pain still cuts and makes us bleed even today.

Past lifestyles that present dark, dangerous temptations to our new lives.

Jesus set us free, so take steps to truly break free. Release your past in your mind so that Jesus can release your heart and your soul. Breaking free doesn't mean you live your life perfectly from now on, that you'll never do anything you're ashamed of, or that you'll never feel hurt again. But breaking free means your past is not a set of manacles chaining you and holding you down, or holding you back. Jesus wants you to be free.

FAITH STEP: *What in your past is chaining you down? Breaking free isn't usually a quick and easy thing, so pray for Jesus to help you to be able to give your past up to Him. Remember that He's with you every step of the way. Pray for Him to help you with these early steps so that you can walk forward and not backward. Pray for the wisdom you need to break free.*

—*Camy Tang*

SEPTEMBER 18

"The Lord is my shepherd, I lack nothing. He makes me
lie down in green pastures, he leads me beside quiet
waters, he refreshes my soul." Psalm 23:1–3 (NIV)

*M*ama needs a time-out, I thought as I closed my children's doors at naptime.

Actually, the need for time-outs is not exclusive to children and their parents. We all need those.

Even Jesus needed to get away for refreshment. Check out Luke 5:16 to find out what He did to recoup His energy and refill His spirit; He often got alone to pray. He learned from His heavenly Father the importance of taking Sabbath rest, which God spoke so much about in the Old Testament. Back then it wasn't optional. God's people would put aside their work for R&R. No ifs, ands or buts about it—God spelled it out clearly in the Ten Commandments.

I love how the NIV and NASB word Psalm 23:1–2: "The Lord is my Shepherd.... He makes me lie down." One way or another, Jesus will help us take the rest we need, whether we do it of our own volition or we crash and burn from mental or physical fatigue. In John 10, Jesus refers to Himself as our Shepherd. As His sheep, our first instinct needs to be to follow Him for our own good.

A few years ago my husband and I committed to put aside work one day a week to prioritize rest and rejuvenation. Our chosen day is Sunday. In the years since then, I've been amazed how my efficiency improves for the week! Instead of cringing over missing a day to "get things done," I actually get more done throughout the week, and I feel more clear-headed and energized.

When I live by Jesus' wisdom and prioritize Sabbath rest, my "cup" truly does overflow, and I thrive in His goodness and love that follow me all my days.

FAITH STEP: *At a loss to fit in Sabbath rest? Pull out your planner and jot it down. Now it's on the to-do list, not to be shifted.*

—*Erin Keeley Marshall*

SEPTEMBER 19

"No testing has overtaken you that is not common to everyone. God is faithful, and he will not let you be tested beyond your strength, but with testing he will also provide the way out so that you may be able to endure it." 1 Corinthians 10:13 (NRSV)

Am I so different from everyone else? Are my temptations more difficult to resist or more alluring, more dangerous than the temptations of others I know?

But it's so hard, Lord! I have wants and needs. I don't like to deny myself anything. It just doesn't seem fair.

"Blessed is anyone who endures temptation. Such a one has stood the test and will receive the crown of life that the Lord has promised to those who love him. No one, when tempted, should say, 'I am being tempted by God'; for God cannot be tempted by evil and He tempts no one" (James 1:12–13, NRSV).

Blessed, You say? Can't I be blessed any other way? Something easier, perhaps?

"But when one is tempted by one's own desire, being lured and enticed by it; then, when that desire has conceived, it gives birth to sin, and that sin, when it is fully grown, gives birth to death. Do not be deceived, my beloved" (James 1:14–16, NRSV).

Am I being deceived right now? Is my impulse to gamble more than wanting to have a little fun? Are the angry things I say when I know I am in private more than harmless venting? Is the inclination to make up stories or tell fibs more dangerous than I think?

"Live by the Spirit, I say, and do not gratify the desires of the flesh. For what the flesh desires is opposed to the Spirit, and what the Spirit desires is opposed to the flesh; for these are opposed to each other, to prevent you from doing what you want" (Galatians 5:16–17, NRSV).

I am free in You, Lord: free of my urges and desires, free of temptation, free to live with an eye to eternity. Praise You!

"For sin will have no dominion over you, since you are not under the law but under grace" (Romans 6:14, NRSV).

FAITH STEP: *Think of a temptation you face on a regular basis. Use Scripture to help you form your prayers for strength.*

— *Judy Baer*

SEPTEMBER 20

"On a Sabbath Jesus was teaching in one of the synagogues, and a woman was there who had been crippled by a spirit for eighteen years. She was bent over and could not straighten up at all. When Jesus saw her, he called her forward and said to her, 'Woman, you are set free from your infirmity.' Then he put his hands on her, and immediately she straightened up and praised God." Luke 13:10–13 (NIV)

One of the things I love most about Jesus is His boldness. He loves and heals fearlessly. In fact, you could argue that Jesus actually loved the Pharisees enough to challenge their legalism. It's like He's saying, "Come on, guys. Don't you want to be set free from thinking you have to keep the rules to earn God's favor?"

I imagine this woman, painfully twisted and bent, like an old tree, from arthritis or osteoporosis. And yet she is in the synagogue. She doesn't let her handicaps keep her from worship. Still, she's burdened, weighed down.

Sometimes I feel like this woman—weighed down by life's challenges, or other people's expectations. I long for freedom, to stand up straight and just joyfully praise God. But no matter how hard I try, just like this woman, I can't heal myself. I can't manufacture joy and release. It only comes from the healing touch of Jesus.

When the woman stands, the first thing she sees are the eyes of Jesus. And the first thing she does is praise Him. What an example! Jesus later calls this woman "daughter." Such affirmation brought her emotional and spiritual healing as well, I think.

FAITH STEP: *Think of a specific situation in your life where you feel crippled. (Maybe in a relationship, in your job or even in your church.) Today, let Jesus step into that situation. Allow Him to heal you, so that you can praise Him.*

—Keri Wyatt Kent

SEPTEMBER 21

"You, then, why do you judge your brother or sister? Or why do you treat your brother or sister with contempt? For we will all stand before God's judgment seat." Romans 14:10 (TNIV)

*R*ecently, I was on the receiving end of a snap judgment. A woman sent a hurtful e-mail accusing me of something I didn't do. It made me feel like she'd beat me with a baseball bat, especially because I was innocent and she had no right to say such things to me. It took three pots of tea and the advice of a good friend for me to respond graciously to her.

We all know it's wrong to make snap judgments about people or to condemn them without getting the full story. We know it's not what Jesus would want us to do. We know that when we do it, it could be that we're being ignorant of the story behind the person's actions. The other person may have a really good motivation for being a certain way or doing certain things.

Granted, sometimes we make a snap judgment and we're right, but how often does that happen? And the times we're wrong usually cause more damage than it's worth, so we know we shouldn't make snap judgments. We should give people the benefit of the doubt, and we should be patient and considerate to others, giving them a chance to explain themselves.

We know all this in our heads, but we still make snap judgments anyway. It's almost automatic.

I'm hoping this experience will make me rethink the next time I might make a snap judgment against someone else. I want to remember how hurt I felt so that I'll hesitate before doing something that might make someone else feel the way I did.

FAITH STEP: *Have you been hurt by someone else making a snap judgment about you? Remember that hurtful feeling so that you won't be so quick to hurt someone else. Have you made a snap judgment against someone? Go to them and apologize, or just talk to them to understand their side of the story. React the way Jesus would want you to react.*

—*Camy Tang*

SEPTEMBER 22

"It is written: 'As surely as I live,' says the Lord, 'every knee will bow before me; every tongue will confess to God.'" Romans 14:11 (TNIV)

We read Scriptures and know that when Jesus comes again, everyone will be judged. Jesus will show Himself to be the one true God, and all the scoffers will willingly bow before Him, confessing He is the Lord.

But the Jesus coming again and the Jesus with us now are one and the same. The Jesus who sat and ate dinner with tax collectors is the same Jesus who was transfigured on the mountain, whose appearance made the disciples tremble in fear. The Jesus who blessed the prostitute anointing Him with expensive perfume is the same Jesus who died for her sins on the cross and then rose from the dead.

People scoffing Jesus now don't realize how powerful He is, and sometimes their attitude affects us, even though we don't want it to. We lose sight of the Jesus in Revelation with the sword coming out of His mouth and instead focus on the "softer" Jesus who wanted to bless the little children. We underestimate Jesus' power and might in the face of calm, logical atheists touting evolution and charismatic speakers who say there are many ways to God.

FAITH STEP: *Take a moment to look at your own vision of who Jesus is. Have you lost sight of His power and might? Ask for Jesus to send you reminders of His power today so that you can live your life more aware of who He really is.*

—Camy Tang

SEPTEMBER 23

*"Jesus replied, 'No one who puts a hand to the plow and looks
back is fit for service in the kingdom of God.'" Luke 9:62 (NIV)*

Smoke steamed from the hood, the van puttered and gasped, and my
husband pulled to the side of the road. Four hot, cranky kids wailed from
the back seats. Our family had been through a rough patch—several years
of financial struggle, relationship issues, and the normal exhaustion of
raising small children—and we were on our way to our first vacation in
years. We'd prayed so hard that God would refresh us, strengthen us and
help our family grow closer. Instead, our second day on the road the van
died, stranding us in a small town in Canada. The part needed to fix the
car couldn't arrive for a week, and the cost of repairs was the last straw in
our financial stress. In a moment of utter frustration, I told God I didn't
think I wanted to follow Him anymore. I'd given my life to serving Him,
and it seemed life just went from one relentless struggle to the next.

I repented soon after, but was shocked at how I'd looked back from
the plow. Jesus often spoke of counting the cost of following Him and the
long-term commitment required. Only a decade earlier in a college class,
I'd told a professor I'd die for my faith rather than deny it. It didn't take the
threat of a firing squad to make me question the wisdom of following Jesus—just a broken-down car, more debts and a disrupted vacation. Shame
hit me as I confronted my lack of commitment. I'd been so confident I
would follow Jesus anywhere, but the ordinary hardships of life made me
doubt His love.

We were able to rent a van and continue our drive to the mountains. The
grandeur of alpine forests and snowy peaks, the sheer size and beauty of
God's creation, spoke deeply to my heart and reminded me that no matter
how big my problems seem, He is bigger. I made a quiet commitment to
put my hand to the plow and keep my focus on Jesus in the coming days.

FAITH STEP: *Are there situations that have made you pull back from whole-
hearted trust in following Jesus? Invite Him to renew your faith today, and make
a new commitment to keep your eyes on Him.*

—*Sharon Hinck*

SEPTEMBER 24

"The Lord is my shepherd, I lack nothing. He makes me lie down in green pastures, he leads me beside quiet waters, he refreshes my soul. He guides me along the right paths for his name's sake." Psalm 23:1–3 (TNIV)

*R*ecently, I had a very scary moment when I was lost in a city. My friend had guided us to where I needed to drop her off. The directions were very straightforward, which I was relieved about because I had forgotten to bring our GPS unit to guide me home.

After I dropped her off, I faithfully backtracked to the freeway, but then discovered that while there was an off-ramp from the freeway, which I had used earlier, there wasn't an on-ramp to get back onto that freeway. I drove right under the freeway and was in completely foreign territory.

I panicked. I didn't know what street I could follow that would parallel the freeway so that I could somehow find a new on-ramp. It was nighttime and there weren't many places open where I could park and ask someone, plus the neighborhood didn't look very safe.

I called my husband to ask him to check a map website on his computer and guide me home. He had to figure out where I was to begin with, then how to guide me to the nearest freeway on-ramp.

Usually, when I read this psalm, I think about fuzzy white sheep following a shepherd through rolling green hills. But after my experience, I realized that Jesus as my shepherd is like my husband guiding me home through those dark city streets with the scary-looking drug dealers on the corners. Jesus is there to lead me safely through both the dangerous neighborhoods and pretty meadows of life.

FAITH STEP: *Remember that Jesus is your shepherd and is there to guide you. Today, actively look to Jesus for guidance through the problems you face rather than giving in to stress or fear. Take time out to say a quick prayer and ask for help. And in the quiet, happy moments today, remember to stop and thank Him for leading you there.*

—Camy Tang

SEPTEMBER 25

"No one has ever seen God; but if we love one another, God lives in us and his love is made complete in us. This is how we know that we live in him and he in us: He has given us of his Spirit." 1 John 4:12–13 (NIV)

When my daughter was three, she had a crisis of faith. "I want to believe in Jesus, but I can't see Him!" she wailed, with characteristic drama.

I assured her that Jesus existed, and loved her, even though she could not see Him. "He put you in our family, and so when I love you and hug you, that's Jesus loving you," I tried to explain. "Jesus loves you through other people, especially your parents!" She looked skeptical.

We've been having that conversation (or some form of it) for years. But the cool thing is, now my daughter is seventeen, and she leads a group of three-year-olds in the Sunday school at our church. She's served faithfully there for several years. She lets Jesus love those kids through her.

I've always found this idea somewhat astounding. As I once heard Henry Cloud say, "God uses people. People are God's Plan A. There is no Plan B." In other words, God communicates His truth to people not with neon lights across the sky, but through the actions and words of other people. It's how He cares for the poor, how He teaches truth, how He loves three-year-olds, seventeen-year-olds…and forty-year-olds.

This verse says that God's love is made complete when we love each other. Part of how you love God is by loving others. And we can do that not on our own, but because we have His Spirit in us.

FAITH STEP: *Whom do you need to love today, so that they can experience God's love?*

—Keri Wyatt Kent

SEPTEMBER 26

"May the God who gives endurance and encouragement give you the same attitude of mind toward each other that Christ Jesus had, so that with one mind and one voice you may glorify the God and Father of our Lord Jesus Christ." Romans 15:5–6 (NIV)

The middle-school choir members blinked up at me. Dacia poked Roberta. Timothy yawned loudly. Jerome shuffled in late. I tapped the baton on my music stand and everyone sat up taller. "From the beginning."

The pianist plunged into the introduction and we dove into the anthem.

One of the more hyperactive boys charged forward in the music, trying to drag the rest of the choir behind him. Then the sopranos belted out the melody, but drowned out the male voices to a dim mutter. I waved my arms around ineffectually. Tempos clashed, notes collided and each verse was a new opportunity for uneven stops and starts.

The music teacher was on maternity leave, and I was just helping out for a few weeks. I suddenly had a new appreciation for her work.

A choir can't function without unity. Chords won't blend if each singer is ignoring the other vocalists, the accompaniment, and the musical director. On the other hand, when all the singers focus on a common goal, share the composer's vision for the piece, and follow the director's dynamics and tempo, a choir can become one organic voice that creates a beautiful moment of transcendent art.

Romans 15 tells us that God wants us to unite with others to glorify God with one heart and mouth. Glorifying God encompasses more than singing. It's how we serve others as the Body of Christ, how we reach out to share truth with the world, as well as how we worship. The spirit of unity is as challenging for us as it was for my middle-school choir. Thankfully, God provides a clue when He tells us it will happen, "as you follow Christ Jesus." I'm so grateful that in our efforts to unite as followers of Christ, we have a director with the confidence and skill to lead us into beautiful harmony.

FAITH STEP: *Let's fix our eyes on Jesus and follow His tempo today.*

—Sharon Hinck

SEPTEMBER 27

"Christ is just like the human body—a body is a unit and has many parts; and all the parts of the body are one body, even though there are many." 1 Corinthians 12:12 (CEB)

Over the last decade, I've had the privilege of speaking to women all over the country. When I lead a retreat, I tell them I'm not just there as a speaker, but also as a listener.

One of the recurring themes among the women, at least the ones who are honest, is loneliness. They feel alone, even if they are married, have kids and have friends. They don't feel they are fully known, and yet, they are afraid of letting their guard down.

Some are lonely because they are self-focused—they want someone to love them and be their friend, but they never consider looking for someone who needs a friend, someone that they can give love and friendship to. They're focused on getting, rather than giving. These types are going to continue to be lonely until they start being other-focused.

When we spend time alone with Jesus, why do we do it? Time with Jesus refuels us and fills us, so that we can love others. We receive love from Jesus so that we can share it. We also receive love from Jesus so that we are not demanding that others meet the need that only He can fulfill.

Yes, we can experience Jesus' love individually, but we also experience it, in a richer way, in community. Because we have the Spirit, we can be conduits of God's love to others. And we can receive God's love through others. Together, we can accomplish more together than any of us could on our own.

FAITH STEP: *Today, spend some time with Jesus and let Him fill you up, so that you can love others. Rather than focusing on your own loneliness, look for someone who is lonely that you could reach out to.*

—*Keri Wyatt Kent*

SEPTEMBER 28

"The Lord is my light and my salvation; whom shall I fear? The Lord is the stronghold of my life; of whom should I be afraid?" Psalm 27:1 (NRSV)

*W*hen I am afraid I can't hear the Lord. My anxiety blocks out every good thing. It takes over my body. I tremble; I cannot sleep. My mind runs wild imagining the worst. There is no light or respite in fear. It's a fog that overtakes me and I can't see past the present moment. It is blinders that hide from me the many blessings I have been given. Gratitude dissolves. Hope disappears. It's like quicksand. The more I struggle, the deeper I am entrenched. I'm like a terrified child who is sure this bad situation will not—cannot—end.

I must look to Jesus, to find His outstretched hand, His comforting gaze, the movement of His Spirit. Alone, I'm drowning and I cannot swim.

Through the clamor these are the words I long to hear. Trust Me. Don't be afraid. Rest in My arms today.

FAITH STEP: *Look for Scriptures that talk about alleviating fear and worry. Comfort yourself with them today.*

— *Judy Baer*

SEPTEMBER 29

"I am the vine; you are the branches. If you remain in me and I in you, you will bear much fruit; apart from me you can do nothing." John 15:5 (NIV)

I'm a person who often judges my own worth on performance and accomplishment. I'm a bit type A, hyperproductive. Use whatever label you like, it doesn't bother me—I get things done, and that is what matters to me.

So much of this performance mentality carries over into my spiritual life—in fact, may have been fostered by my religious upbringing. I grew up in a church where people would, with a straight face, ask you how many people you'd led to the Lord. And look concerned if your number was too low. And then walk into church service where we would sing, without a trace of irony, "Just As I Am."

I tried really hard to bear fruit, by witnessing or doing good deeds. I worked very hard at "remaining" or "abiding" in Jesus—by reading and memorizing Scripture, praying, going to church—all kinds of doing.

Reading, memorizing, praying, witnessing—all are good things, if they flow out of our connection to Jesus. But sometimes, we do such things in an attempt (subconscious, perhaps) to impress Jesus or try to earn approval.

But that is not what abiding is about. Jesus said, "apart from me you can do nothing." Rather than making plans and asking Jesus to assist, I need to learn to let Him make the plans. I have to trust that fruit will be the inevitable result of a life spent clinging to Jesus.

FAITH STEP: *So often, we have a little time with Jesus in the morning and then disconnect our little branch to go off into our day. Today, keep the image of the vine and branch in your mind. Have no other goal than abiding, turning your thoughts and heart toward Him, for a few seconds at a time, as you go through your day.*

—*Keri Wyatt Kent*

SEPTEMBER 30

*"The Lord is close to the brokenhearted and saves those
who are crushed in spirit." Psalm 34:18 (TNIV)*

There was a time in my life when I was clinically depressed. My parents took me to a psychologist who helped me a lot, but what really healed me was giving my life to Jesus that summer.

It was really hard because the depression made me feel like a squashed bug on the sidewalk. I didn't want to do anything for myself, much less someone else. I can understand what the Psalmist means to be "crushed in spirit." My soul felt trampled.

Even when I gave my life to Jesus, it was a sort of desperate, last-ditch effort. "Please, Jesus, help me not to kill myself." I didn't want to exist anymore. I felt so broken and tired and achy and transparent. I was ready to be blown out like a candle in the wind.

It didn't feel like Jesus was near me. I felt a little stupid praying to Him when I couldn't tell if He was even there. And right after I gave my life to Jesus, I had expected some choir of angels to come down or for me to feel lighter or happier. But I didn't feel anything.

But in the weeks that followed, I started suddenly being aware of a comforting presence with me. The feeling crept up on me slowly until one day, I realized I didn't feel alone anymore.

We all go through times when our spirit is flayed and beaten. It's even harder because we don't feel like Jesus is there. Those are times we need to just cling to the knowledge that Jesus is close to the brokenhearted. Don't give up.

FAITH STEP: *Write down Psalm 34:18 on an index card and keep it with you in your purse or pocket so that you can remind yourself daily. It will help you trust in the Word of God where He promises to be with you when you are brokenhearted, even if you can't feel Him. God never breaks His promises.*

—Camy Tang

October

OCTOBER 1

"Let the one who boasts, boast of the Lord." 1 Corinthians 1:31 (NRSV)

$\mathcal{I}$ found myself being proud today. I did a good job at work. Someone praised me and I felt myself puff up with pride. I was pleased with myself and the way things turned out. I know I'm good at certain things and this certainly proved it.

But I'm singing my own praises, am I not? Priding myself on a job well done? That's a slippery slope, I know. Pretty soon I'll forget that the Lord had a hand in this and begin to think it's all about me.

I read the headlines in self-help books about changing, taking charge, being the person I dreamed I could be. Many self-help gurus say that I'm in charge of my life, that I rise or fall as a result of my own actions. That no one has control over me but me.

But it's not true, is it? None of this happened because of me. Without Christ, there's nothing good that I can do. It's all ashes. Only with Him can I really succeed. There is no one to brag about but Jesus. I must never mess with the Father's glory or intrude or lay claim to the holy works of God.

FAITH STEP: *Give credit and praise to God for everything good you do today.*

OCTOBER 2

"As a prisoner for the Lord, then, I urge you to live a life worthy of the calling you have received." Ephesians 4:1 (NIV)

One of the greatest gifts my parents gave me was permission to listen to the voice of my own gladness. My father told me that I could do anything with my life; his only hope was that I would enjoy my work as much as he enjoyed his.

My father was not called to be a missionary or a pastor, a teacher or some other vocation that people label as noble. He ran a small company that sold sandblasting and spray-painting equipment. But he ran it well, and ethically. He demanded hard work from his employees, but never asked them to do more than he was willing to do as well.

In *Wishful Thinking: A Seeker's ABC*, Frederick Buechner writes: "The place God calls you to is the place where your deep gladness and the world's deep hunger meet." Christians have two callings. The first we must heed is the call to follow Jesus. (See Romans 1:6–7.) We share that with all our brothers and sisters in Christ; it is a general calling. But each of us also has a specific calling, whether it is to run a company or write books or to be a mom, or an orthodontist, or whatever. Romans 1:1 says that Paul was "called to be an apostle." That was his specific calling.

The voice of my own gladness (and the world's need) called me to be a writer. And I think I enjoy my work as much as, maybe more than, my dad enjoyed his.

What is God calling you to do? If you don't know, the question to start with is what brings you joy? And then, how will you respond to that call?

FAITH STEP: *If you followed your "deep gladness" where would it lead you? Have you given some time in prayer to asking God about your specific calling?*

—*Keri Wyatt Kent*

OCTOBER 3

"You watched me as I was being formed in utter seclusion, as I was woven together in the dark of the womb. You saw me before I was born. Every day of my life was recorded in your book. Every moment was laid out before a single day had passed. How precious are your thoughts about me, O God. They cannot be numbered!" Psalm 139:15–17 (NLT)

It's easy to realize that God created me and made my life. It's easy to know that God has all my days laid out for me, but every moment? This moment?

This moment when I'm still twenty pounds overweight.

This moment when there are dishes in my sink.

This moment of weariness and a tense neck.

This moment of deadlines and disasters on the evening news.

Jesus is Lord of Creation, and He's the Lord of dailyness.

Jesus knit me together, knowing that I'd never look like a supermodel.

Jesus strengthens me, knowing that it's the dishes, the laundry and the vacuuming that makes me weary.

Jesus holds me, when I'm uptight and out of sorts.

Jesus comforts me when the worries of this world weigh me down.

Every moment was laid out for me, and the plan was for Jesus to be in those moments. If God put such care in creating me, why wouldn't He put equal detail into the planning of each day with Jesus smack in the middle of it?

FAITH STEP: *Consider the moments that made up the last twenty-four hours. How often did you invite Jesus in? Now consider the twenty-four hours that still stretch ahead of you. How can you do better with welcoming Him into those moments?*

—Tricia Goyer

OCTOBER 4

"Hope does not disappoint, because the love of God has been poured out within our hearts." Romans 5:5 (NASB)

I hosted a book club in my home a while back. One time a lady joined our group who hadn't been there before. Her name was Kim, and she was in a wheelchair.

We had a special time of prayer for her, but before that I asked her to tell us her story. The details she related pierced my heart because I could so closely identify with her life—her life before, that is. She was in her late thirties, with four children, a teaching job she loved and a very active life. Basically overnight, because of lupus, she became paralyzed from about her ribcage down.

The horror of Kim's story as she related it was almost too much to bear. I believe it would have been too much for her to bear had it not been overshadowed by her hope that God works all things together for the good—even things like this. Kim went on to tell us about a new ministry the Lord had opened up for her at school: She listens to students' problems and offers them hope in their lives. She said even those in the most desperate situations will look at her in her wheelchair and listen when she shares with them the hope she has in Jesus.

As sisters in Christ, we have agreed with Kim to pray for a miracle—that her body be restored. But meanwhile, it's a beautiful thing to witness the miracle Jesus has wrought—and keeps nurturing in her spirit. What a difference hope in Him makes!

FAITH STEP: *Are you looking for a miracle today? Perhaps the miracle God has for you is to give you more of Jesus in your inner life, even as He restores the outward things that concern you, in His time and His way.*

—*Gwen Ford Faulkenberry*

OCTOBER 5

"The person without the Spirit does not accept the things that come from the Spirit of God but considers them foolishness, and cannot understand them because they are discerned only through the Spirit." 1 Corinthians 2:14 (TNIV)

*I*s there a nonbeliever you've been trying to talk to about Jesus? Are they argumentative with you? Or are they evasive, not answering your questions or cleverly twisting the topic around? Or are they passive-aggressive, pretending to pay attention to you just to make you go away?

We don't want to become buzzing flies, irritating nonbelievers with our words about Jesus, but when we care about someone, we want them to experience the abundant life Jesus offers. We want them to understand.

The problem is that they may not be able to understand. The Bible says that certain things are impossible for nonbelievers to grasp because a person needs the Holy Spirit to give divine wisdom so we can understand things about God. It makes sense: God is so infinite and powerful, our puny minds wouldn't be able to comprehend Him and His will if we didn't get a bit of supernatural help.

So then how can a nonbeliever understand about Christ?

First of all, trust that the Spirit can speak to someone no matter how you might have screwed things up. Second, don't give up, because the Spirit can speak to them through you. Third, take a look at the exact words and phrases you use when you speak to your nonbelieving friend or loved one. They may be common words you use with your church family, but would they really make sense to an outsider? Is it possible that the words you use would make a nonbeliever feel alienated? The meanings of words change so quickly in our culture, so make sure that there's no negative connotation with the words you choose. Is there a different way you can phrase things?

FAITH STEP: *Spend time in prayer for a nonbeliever in your life whom Jesus has laid on your heart. Ask for wisdom in how to speak to that person, and pray for the Spirit to help him or her understand about Jesus. Don't give up. Jesus can reach your nonbelieving friends in ways you don't see.*

—Camy Tang

OCTOBER 6

*"Always be humble and gentle. Be patient with each other,
making allowance for each other's faults because of your love.
Make every effort to keep yourselves united in the Spirit, binding
yourselves together with peace." Ephesians 4:2–3 (NLT)*

My husband and I recently celebrated our twentieth wedding anniversary. I'd love to tell you that it's been two decades of bliss. Um, not exactly.

Don't get me wrong—we love each other. I would love to tell you that both of us have always been humble and gentle, patient and peaceful—and as a result, unified and never in conflict. If you are married yourself, you know that's not true. If you're not married and think it might be, sorry to burst your bubble. Part of the reason marriage takes so much effort and commitment to make it work is that both parties involved are human beings. We're not perfect.

We both love Jesus and each other. We have amazing children. We laugh together and can talk about pretty much anything. And yet marriage is hard. I love structure and crossing things off my list; he likes keeping his options open. The families we grew up in could not be more different. I'm a Cubs fan; he's a White Sox fan. We are pretty much opposites on the Myers-Briggs profile.

As a result, we've had conflict. Getting along has required hard work, some painful conversations and a willingness to forgive each other repeatedly.

Unity doesn't just happen—in a marriage or any relationship. In our friendships or families, we have to choose to be patient. Unity flows from our efforts to be humble, gentle, patient. We cannot manufacture such benevolence on our own. So how does it happen?

The phrase "in the Spirit" gives a hint. Jesus prayed for His followers to have unity, via the Spirit. Unity is elusive and fragile, unless we have Jesus.

FAITH STEP: *Read this passage in several different versions of the Bible. Pick your favorite and memorize it. Write down ways to live it out in your marriage or other important relationships.*

—*Keri Wyatt Kent*

OCTOBER 7

"If anyone wishes to come after Me, he must deny himself,
and take up his cross and follow Me." Matthew 16:24 (NASB)

*W*e all face situations in which we may feel left out, unappreciated, unloved. Those can be extremely painful. I try to avoid such situations as much as possible, but found myself in one the other day. While processing the hurt, and praying over what to do with it, the above verse came to mind.

It seems when we come across these challenges one way of dealing with them is to let the hurt eat us up inside, and morph into anger and bitterness. This takes a huge amount of energy. It demands our focus, and we lose our joy. But Jesus' way is better. He says, "Deny yourself, pick up your cross and follow Me." In other words, "Die to it. Let it go. And let Me lead you into resurrection life" (MSG).

Following Jesus in death to self is a daily choice, and sometimes moment by moment. In the moment His words came to my mind, I felt the knot in my stomach loosening. I don't have to do this, I thought. I don't have to be angry. I don't have to let it matter so much. I can choose another way. His way.

The way of the Kingdom is the way of the cross. We die with Jesus to be raised with Him. He is the proper focus—not our issue or even our pain. Like the old hymn says, "the things of earth grow strangely dim in the light of His glory and grace."

FAITH STEP: *Are you hurting because someone has slighted you in some way? Take it as an opportunity to die to yourself, pick up your cross and follow Jesus. His way will lead you out of death into beautiful, joy-filled life.*

—*Gwen Ford Faulkenberry*

OCTOBER 8

"Enter through the narrow gate. For wide is the gate and broad is the road that leads to destruction, and many enter through it. But small is the gate and narrow the road that leads to life, and only a few find it." Matthew 7:13–14 (NIV)

A few years ago my husband and I hiked a remote area of the Ottawa National Forest. We've done a lot of hiking, including sections of the Superior Hiking Trail, so we felt fairly confident. But the old-growth forests provided a new experience. Instead of clear paths cutting through thick underbrush, we found stretches of huge trees in all directions, with smooth forest floor coated with a bed of fallen leaves. No dirt path visible. Nothing to indicate which way to go, except for small trail markers nailed to trees.

At first, we could scan into the distance and spot the next marker and know which way to head. But sometimes trail markers were missing. We found several broken off, or resting in the dirt near the base of a tree.

When the trail seemed to disappear, I forged ahead. Eventually I pulled to a stop. "I have no idea where I'm going."

My husband muttered, "That never stops you." We backtracked to the last marker and tried a new direction until we found the elusive next symbol.

Our hike that day reminded me of the adventure of following Christ. He might give me a glimpse of the final destination, but most of my life journey, I'm aiming just for the next small trail marker up ahead. My steps lead through rocky terrain, beautiful vistas and swampy bogs. Often God's guidance is as clear as the white diamond markers on tree trunks, giving me courage for tough climbs and wet slogs. Other times, I struggle to see the path. I flounder in a likely direction for a while and then need to backtrack a bit, stand still and listen until Jesus gets me back on track. His narrow path is the only one that will lead me safely through the wild forests of my life and home to my eternal destiny.

FAITH STEP: *Ask Jesus to show you clear trail markers for the next step in your journey on His path.*

—*Sharon Hinck*

OCTOBER 9

*"I am the true vine, and my Father is the vinedresser. Every branch in me
that does not bear fruit he takes away, and every branch that does bear
fruit he prunes, that it may bear more fruit. Already you are clean because
of the word that I have spoken to you." John 15:1–3 (ESV)*

The current economic recession has not been easy for many families. I
know people who have lost their homes, or been forced to sell and down-
size. Our income has been cut by more than half in recent years.

God has used this time of economic challenge to prune me—to strip
away the nonessentials. I don't like pruning, but I long for the resulting
fruitfulness: to be more like Jesus, and to make a difference for Him in
this world.

Our culture is far removed from vines and branches—our food comes
wrapped in cellophane or cardboard. Unless we take a tour of Napa, we
may never even see a vineyard. It's easy to forget that pruning is an essential gardening task, which actually results in fruitfulness.

In the original Greek text, the word translated "takes away" (sometimes
translated "cuts off") is airo. An ancient practice of vinedressers was to
prop up unproductive vines with trellises, improving air circulation and
hence productivity. Airo, some scholars feel, refers to that nurturing practice, rather than a more violent lopping that the English implies.

As my material wealth has been pruned, contentment, patience and
long-suffering have shyly unfurled, like hesitant buds in spring. I'm more
compassionate toward the poor, more tender. I'm also more likely to pray
for God's daily provision, and see what comes as gifts from His hand, not
my own. My job is not to try to keep the Father from pruning, but to cling
always to Jesus, and trust.

FAITH STEP: *Where do you need to be pruned? Where do you need to be lifted
up, cleaned up, so that you can be fruitful? What practices do you have in place
in your life to keep you clinging like a branch to a vine?*

—Keri Wyatt Kent

OCTOBER 10

"But blessed are those who trust in the Lord, whose confidence is in him. They will be like a tree planted by the water that sends out its roots by the stream. It does not fear when heat comes; its leaves are always green. It has no worries in a year of drought and never fails to bear fruit." Jeremiah 17:7–8 (TNIV)

New ventures can be scary. Going on a trip somewhere new, or starting a new ministry at church, or starting on a new work project—it's hard to take that first step. What if you get sick away from home? What if no one's interested in the new ministry? What if you do a terrible job on the new project? There are always too many fears and too many unknowns, and we like to be in control of our environments.

But sometimes new ventures are exactly what we need. Jesus does not want us to become complacent in our faith—He wants us to be working for Him. His Word is alive and active, and if we obey His Word, then we will be too.

Trees may look delicate and pretty, but they have deep, deep roots, often deeper and larger than the part of the tree above ground. Those roots are fed by water we can't see either, and they have a remarkable ability to survive.

In this passage, Jesus compares us to trees. If we are trees, we also have a deep root system in Jesus Christ. We are watered by the immense reservoir of strength and power through the Holy Spirit. And the fruit we bear has eternal consequences.

FAITH STEP: *Pray and ask Jesus to show you how you can "branch out" and serve Him in new ventures. Don't be afraid, because you're anchored in Christ and His power.*

—*Camy Tang*

OCTOBER 11

"Some of you will rebuild the deserted ruins of your cities. Then you will be known as a rebuilder of walls and a restorer of homes." Isaiah 58:12 (NLT)

I have a confession. In recent years I have become an HGTV addict. Maybe addict is exaggerating a bit, but I have done my share of home renovations and have gleaned many home-improvement ideas from watching do-it-yourself shows. In all honesty, the process is a contentious one, as any "healing" journey can be. But the results? Oh, I love the results!

Improving our earthly living spaces brings some satisfaction, but it can't compare to the perfect, forever home Jesus is fashioning for us with Him someday. (See John 14:2–3.) Acts 3:20–21 (CEV) says, "That time will come when the Lord will give you fresh strength. He will send you Jesus, his chosen Messiah. But Jesus must stay in heaven until God makes all things new, just as his holy prophets promised long ago."

Sometimes when I look around at the sorrows of life, I feel anxious for that time to come soon. The prophet Isaiah wrote a lot about the messiness of living on earth. He informed the Israelites that they could play a part in God's restoration. If they'd turn back to the Lord, they could be rebuilders instead of continuing on as demolishers.

Jesus was a carpenter while He lived here, and I'm guessing His craftsmanship was superb. But more important than building and repairing furniture and homes was the rebuilding He did of souls. While we're waiting for Him to return, we can serve as apprentices in His miraculous renovation of worn-out hearts and crumbling lives.

You can always find people in need of Jesus' precision craftsmanship. Will you show His love by being part of His restoration work?

FAITH STEP: *Find or buy a good-sized nail to place in a visible spot. Let it remind you of the nails the world used in an attempt to demolish Jesus' ministry; then let it prompt you to take an active role in Jesus' rebuilding of lives.*

—Erin Keeley Marshall

OCTOBER 12

"But God remembered Noah and all the wild animals and the livestock that were with him in the ark, and he sent a wind over the earth, and the waters receded." Genesis 8:1 (TNIV)

*N*oah was stuck in that ark for a hundred and fifty days. That is a really long time to live in a floating barn.

He probably felt pretty neglected by God after a while. After all, the entire earth was covered with water, and he and his family were the only human beings left, drifting in a ship on a vast ocean. He might have felt God had forgotten all about him.

Are you feeling like God might have forgotten you too? Maybe you're going through some really rough things emotionally. Maybe you're contending with difficult people. Maybe you're under a lot of pressure from work or other people in your life. There's no end in sight, and you feel like God has left you hung out to dry.

But Jesus doesn't forget us. He has very specific timing that we may not understand. He has a very good reason for doing things when He does them.

After hearing Lazarus was sick, Jesus deliberately waited two days before heading toward Bethany. By the time He got there, Lazarus had been buried for four days. Both Mary and Martha said to Him, "If you had been here, my brother would not have died." They didn't understand His timing. They must have been able to calculate, from the timing of their message, that He hadn't come right away. Imagine their amazement when He raised Lazarus from the dead.

Jesus has not forgotten you. Trust in His timing—it might be something you need to learn or work through, it might be to give someone else enough time, or it might be to show the enormity of His power.

FAITH STEP: *You can trust that His timing will always be for your good. Cling to your trust in Jesus. You are not forgotten.*

—Camy Tang

OCTOBER 13

"It is God who arms me with strength and keeps my way secure. He makes my feet like the feet of a deer; he causes me to stand on the heights." 2 Samuel 22:33–34 (NIV)

*M*y SUV rounded the curve and climbed farther uphill. A moment later I saw the deer and instinctively braked.

We stared at each other briefly before he leaped effortlessly up the steep hillside. After making sure no vehicle was behind me, I gazed at the graceful animal as he joined two others waiting at the top.

I marveled at how perfectly God had fit the deer to move easily in their environment. Although deer begin life on trembling legs, Jesus strengthens and fine-tunes their muscles to handle rocky, hilly terrain with majestic grace.

Jesus works similarly in us by giving us the power we need to make it in the challenges of our environment. According to 2 Corinthians 1:21 (NLT), "It is God who enables us, along with you, to stand firm for Christ." In the challenges of living well for Jesus, His power in us gives us what we need to stand…and to stand firm. That concept is echoed in 1 John 2:13–14 (MSG): "Your fellowship with God enables you to gain a victory over the Evil One."

Jesus' vision for you is a victorious one. Just as deer wear the dignity and grace of their Creator, so do you. With Him, you can say, "Christ gives me the strength to face anything" (Philippians 4:13, CEV).

Whatever the heights of your challenges, Jesus desires to tone your spiritual muscles to handle them. Stand firmly on the truth that His strength empowers you.

FAITH STEP: *What are you facing that needs a fresh vision of Jesus helping you to stand firmly in His power? Ask Him to give you what you need for your current environment.*

—Erin Keeley Marshall

OCTOBER 14

"Follow God's example, therefore, as dearly loved children and walk in the way of love, just as Christ loved us and gave himself up for us as a fragrant offering and sacrifice to God." Ephesians 5:1–2 (NIV)

My husband and I are both tea drinkers. I fuel my writing work with pot after pot of Irish Breakfast or English Teatime with some Darjeeling or Good Earth to keep things interesting. Ted chases down supper with a big mug of iced tea. Plain old Lipton is his preference, and we brew up a pitcher every day or two to keep in the fridge.

In the morning, when I'm blinking owlishly, trying to figure out what day it is, Ted brews a pot of morning tea and brings a mug of steamy heaven to me. And when I notice the pitcher in the fridge is close to empty, I brew another batch of iced tea for him.

Now logic would say that it would be just as easy for Ted to brew the iced tea for himself, and for me to make the hot tea for myself. Both tasks take about the same amount of time.

But by doing it for each other, the tea means more. It becomes a gift of love.

Thinking about that phenomenon made me wonder about other places in my life where I could apply that concept. Living in Christian community means sometimes doing something for others even when they could do it for themselves. Community also means accepting gifts of love even when I could have managed on my own. It's interdependence. It's a choice to look out for the needs of another.

FAITH STEP: *Can you think of someone in your life who could use some Orange Pekoe with a little lemon and sugar? Maybe they don't look like they need it, but offer it anyway. Our small acts of love can make a huge difference to the people around us.*

—*Sharon Hinck*

OCTOBER 15

"Are you tired? Worn out? Burned out on religion? Come to me. Get away with me and you'll recover your life. I'll show you how to take a real rest. Walk with me and work with me—watch how I do it. Learn the unforced rhythms of grace. I won't lay anything heavy or ill-fitting on you. Keep company with me and you'll learn to live freely and lightly." Matthew 11:28–30 (MSG)

One of the most dangerous words in the English language is the word yes. Many of us grew up learning to try to make people happy—in the name of unselfishness, we took care of everyone except ourselves. We said yes indiscriminately.

The word yes seems so nice. And sometimes it is the appropriate response. We think it is more generous, nicer, even more Christian to say yes. However, every time we say yes to one thing, we have said no to an infinite number of other possibilities. So we have to choose carefully what we say yes and no to.

A few years ago, I had said "yes" too many times. I had speaking engagements three out of four weekends for several months in a row. When I described my travel schedule to people, I actually would tear up in frustration. I needed a rest.

Frederick Buechner writes, "When you find tears in your eyes, especially unexpected tears, it is well to pay the closest attention." So I did. And I realized I was tired and burned out. I needed to learn the unforced rhythms of grace, to say yes sometimes, but also to say no sometimes, even to good things, in order to say yes to Jesus, to keeping company with Him. I began to see that living freely and lightly requires me to say no, so that I can say yes to Jesus.

FAITH STEP: *Reread today's verses. Which word or phrase resonates with you? Spend some time journaling about how you feel. What is one thing you can say no to, so that you can say yes to Jesus?*

—Keri Wyatt Kent

OCTOBER 16

*"For he will command his angels concerning you to
guard you in all your ways." Psalm 91:11 (TNIV)*

A few months ago, my friend was involved in a very bad car crash. A drunk driver T-boned her minivan, narrowly missing injuring her children in the backseats. My friend ended up with a broken foot and a bone fragment in her knee.

After surgery and rehab, she was ready to drive again. I asked her if she was afraid to drive, and she said she was a little nervous, but "if it's my time to go, it's my time to go." She wasn't going to worry about getting into another car crash because she knew it wasn't in her control.

In his work *Ethandune, And Other Poems*, James Williams writes, "Man is immortal till his work is done." We can trust that our lives are in God's hands, in God's plans. He won't take us until He determines it's time. He doesn't go by what we think we still need to do or regrets on what we haven't yet done.

Jesus said, "Who of you by worrying can add a single hour to your life?" He is ultimately in control of your life. But that thought shouldn't make us apprehensive. Instead, we trust that Jesus knows what He's doing. If we continue to obey Him and live each day to the fullest, we'll know that He'll be pleased with the way we numbered our days.

FAITH STEP: *Do you worry about your life, your husband's life, your children's lives? It's natural to want to protect them, but we also need to remember that Jesus is the ultimate protector. Surrender your worry to Jesus, daily if you have to, and instead focus your energy on living each day as if it's your last.*

—Camy Tang

OCTOBER 17

*"The Lord is my strength and shield. I trust him with
all my heart. He helps me, and my heart is filled with joy.
I burst out in songs of thanksgiving." Psalm 28:7 (NLT)*

Tonight my eighteen-year-old daughter brought a friend to dinner. Halfway through the meal my daughter looked to her dad: "You should share about the time you felt God leading us to move two thousand miles away." Everyone around the table smiled. First, because it's a cool story. Second, because we know that story leads to a dozen more about how God has done great things in our family's life.

In Joshua 4:6–7, we read, "In the future your children will ask you, 'What do these stones mean?' Then you can tell them, 'They remind us that the Jordan River stopped flowing when the Ark of the Lord's Covenant went across.' These stones will stand as a memorial among the people of Israel forever" (NLT).

We don't have many memorial stones today, but we still need to be active in sharing stories of God's faithfulness to our children or those whom God has brought into our lives. It's through our personal stories that people understand how God has been our strength and our shield. Through our faith stories they understand the basis of our faith and trust. When those we care about see joy on our faces and hearts overflowing with thanksgiving, their faith in God will grow too. To share these stories is to share how God worked, and will encourage us to believe He will continue to work in every part of our lives.

FAITH STEP: *Share one of your favorite God stories with a new friend today.*

—Tricia Goyer

OCTOBER 18

*" 'Does Job fear God for nothing?' Satan replied. 'Have you not put
a hedge around him and his household and everything he has? You have
blessed the work of his hands, so that his flocks and herds are spread
throughout the land. But now stretch out your hand and strike everything
he has, and he will surely curse you to your face.' " Job 1:9–11* (TNIV)

I admit I'm a fair-weather sports fan. I'll idly watch a game on television if my husband is watching, but I didn't start to actually care about our local team until they started having a winning season, unlike true sports fans who've been avidly following this team through thick and thin, sunshine and rain.

Whether you care about sports or not, we need to take a lesson from those sports fans. Jesus does not want fair-weather fans. He wants us to stick with Him even when things get tough, even when things don't make sense, even when we feel like we're all alone.

How it must have hurt Him when His disciples ran away on the Mount of Olives. True, they were facing a crowd of armed men, but the feeling of being abandoned is something none of us ever likes to feel.

The most famous lesson in fair-weather fans is in the story of Job. God allowed all kinds of terrible misfortune to happen to Job, but he never cursed God. His friends and his wife were examples of various kinds of fair-weather fans, but Job was a true sports fan, in it for the long haul. He remained true to God's nature and character. He didn't abandon God just because God allowed something unexpected.

Are you going through trials right now? Take a page from Job's book. He was emotionally honest with God, but he could still say, "The Lord gave and the Lord has taken away; may the name of the Lord be praised."

FAITH STEP: *Don't be like Jesus' disciples. Instead, trust in God's character and wait for Him to bring you through this.*

—Camy Tang

OCTOBER 19

"'For who has understood the mind of the Lord so as to instruct him?' But we have the mind of Christ." 1 Corinthians 2:16 (ESV)

*M*y fingers stumble over the piano keys as I squint at the hymnal. The notes are a blur and I can't make sense of them. Why am I hitting all the wrong notes? I rub my eyes. Of course. I forgot my glasses. I fetch them from the other room and am soon back to playing with renewed confidence and ease.

Anyone with vision problems knows the feeling when things don't look right. No matter how beautiful a painting is, if you can't bring it into focus, it's a confusing mass of colors. A book of poetry could have lyrical, transcendent lines, but those words can't stir your spirit if they are only gray squiggles. But with glasses or contacts, we can again see things the way they are meant to be seen.

I wish it were as simple to correct my spiritual focus. Much of my life, I seem to squint myopically at the world around me, unable to see the beauty in my cranky neighbor, the holy grace in another pile of laundry and the precious opportunity in a work setback. When I look into a mirror, my vision problems are especially bad as I only see flaws and inadequacies obscuring the image of a beloved child of God.

I need to look through new eyes. Thankfully, God gives us that ability. We have the mind of Christ. We can view the world, others and ourselves through a new perspective—one that brings God's grace into clear focus.

FAITH STEP: *Is there something in your life that doesn't look good to you? Ask God for the mind, the perspective, the vision of Christ and take another look. Can you see His beauty hidden in that situation?*

—Sharon Hinck

OCTOBER 20

"But as for me, it is good to be near God. I have made the Sovereign Lord my refuge; I will tell of all your deeds." Psalm 73:28 (TNIV)

This world often feels like opposite sides of a tug of war. A deadline at work pulling me in one direction, church volunteering in another, volleyball games pulling me this way, housework dragging at my feet.

I plan to do my morning devotions, but the demands of the day sometimes intrude, so I say a quick prayer and head out the door.

But this is like visiting your parents, giving them a hug and then saying, "Sorry, gotta dash. See you next year!" You wouldn't do that. You visit them to spend time with them, to be close to them.

The things in this world can be distractions that pull us away from Him. Don't let it happen. Zealously guard your time with the Lord each morning. If you have to, institute a rule that the kids and the husband have to be both bleeding and burning before you'll be drawn away from your precious time with Jesus.

You want to be near to Jesus. It's when we're close to Him that He whispers to us. It's when we're quiet with Him that He gives our hearts true rest and peace. It's when we make Him an undistracted part of our day that He becomes our emotional shield and spiritual refuge.

FAITH STEP: *Make it a priority to draw near to Jesus and stay there for a while.*

—Camy Tang

OCTOBER 21

Love is patient.... 1 Corinthians 13:4 (RSV)

*U*gh…how we hate to wait! Ever gotten bent out of shape over a delayed flight? A backed-up doctor's office? A long checkout line? A microwave that takes too long?

I once heard one way to know if you're impatient is if you punch thirty-three seconds on the microwave timer because it takes less time than punching the three and then the zero—they're at least two inches apart!—but then you cringe because you end up waiting longer!

I had to chuckle the other day during an e-mail conversation with my mom. She has her hands full with a day job, an evening business, marriage, grandparenting, church activities and on and on. Like many of us, she found herself wishing for more time on the clock. Initially I agreed with her, until it hit me. Who are we kidding? We'd just pack in more to-dos, only to moan about still not having enough time!

And then in the midst of all this moaning, I read that love is patient. Wow, that verse convicts me like none other. Plain and simple. In several Bible versions, the beginning of 1 Corinthians 13:4 reads the same. Real love is patient, with no clarification of "unless your day gets too crazy."

One thing that can be particularly difficult to wait on is an answer to prayer. But during those waiting times we can experience Jesus' patient love for us. He often shows extreme patience in sending His answer because He loves us too much to let us settle for an incomplete one. When we give Him time to perfect His provisions, we don't rob ourselves of His best, and we don't diminish His joy at providing just what we need.

Love Him enough to wait for His loving response.

FAITH STEP: *Meditate on Jesus' promise that "Peace I leave with you; my peace I give you. I do not give to you as the world gives" (John 14:27, NIV). Ask Him to help you wait peacefully and patiently instead of restlessly.*

—Erin Keeley Marshall

OCTOBER 22

"He said to them, 'Go into all the world and preach the gospel to all creation.'" Mark 16:15 (TNIV)

It's easy to get into a good routine as Christians. Spend time with Jesus every morning. Pray for the people on our prayer list. Go to church on Sunday, and maybe go to a midweek Bible study. Volunteer at church, whether as a Sunday-school teacher or a greeter or an usher or maybe a deacon. We have a nice schedule that allows us to serve God without being burned out. We know we're pleasing God with our actions.

Or are we? Jesus gave a very clear command: Go. Not "stay and preach" but "go and preach."

Go where? Overseas? Across the country? It's easy to assume that's what He meant. And for some of us—maybe for you—that's exactly what He wants for you, to step way outside your comfort zone and your ZIP code in order to serve Him. In order to serve others. And perhaps to be transformed yourself.

But there are other places to "go" too. Do people at your workplace know you're a Christian? "Go" to work and start speaking Jesus' words to your co-workers.

How about the parents at your child's school? Do you interact with them and get to know them? "Go" and invite them to church or Vacation Bible School.

Do you know your neighbors well? If not, then "go" and get to know them. Show your faith in your actions and your kindness. Let them see Jesus in you.

FAITH STEP: *There are lots of places if you start brainstorming—your child's sports teams, or music groups, or language classes. Your sewing circle, knitting friends, scrapbooking gatherings. Take the time to think of where you can "go" to preach the gospel. And then go!*

—*Camy Tang*

OCTOBER 23

"Elisha said, 'Go around and ask all your neighbors for empty jars. Don't ask for just a few.'" 2 Kings 4:3 (NIV)

How big is your God?

That's a silly question. He's as big as ever. He's the God who created the world, parted seas, raised the dead, paid for our salvation with his Son's life.

Maybe a better question is, How big is your faith in your God?

Yesterday I spent time praying over various needs—mine, my family's, my loved ones', the world's. As I laid concerns at Jesus' feet, I yearned for a reminder that He would be as big—if not bigger—than what I hoped for.

And then this morning I read the story from 2 Kings 4:1–7 of the poor woman and her oil jars. It spoke directly to my prayers.

Elisha knew absolutely that he served the limitless God. I love how he instructed the woman to collect jars and then added, "Don't ask for just a few." He knew that God would provide beyond what the woman knew to ask for. The oil flowed until the woman and her sons ran out of jars—which leads me to assume it would have kept flowing if they had collected ten times as many jars!

Many generations later Jesus met another desperate woman with great big faith. (See Luke 8:43–48.) She had been sick for twelve years, but she knew that all she needed for complete restoration was to draw close enough to touch his robe. She didn't need a specific prayer formula, educated words, impressive skills, the right look. Nope. A little bit of Jesus was enough for her need. Imagine how much more fulfillment a whole lot of Jesus brings.

Tap into His limitless resources, draw close and let Him keep nourishing your faith.

FAITH STEP: *Ask Jesus to make your faith as big as He is, not merely as big as your logic.*

—Erin Keeley Marshall

OCTOBER 24

"And we all, who with unveiled faces contemplate the Lord's glory, are being transformed into his image with ever-increasing glory, which comes from the Lord, who is the Spirit." 2 Corinthians 3:18 (TNIV)

*W*hen you take off a veil, you're vulnerable. A veil is to obscure or completely hide your face, and revealing your face puts you in a place where you're exposed and defenseless.

Jesus wants that vulnerability from us because if we're not vulnerable, we can't be fully connected with Him. He talks about us abiding in Him, and that kind of oneness doesn't happen if we're not completely open to Him.

When we first give our lives to Christ, we're very open with Him—after all, we've surrendered our will and hearts to Him. But as time passes and you walk along a different path, learning new things, other areas in your life pop up and maybe you don't completely surrender those areas to Jesus. They might seem innocent enough—why bother to ask Jesus what school to send your daughter to? Or whether to buy that house or not? Or if you should quit your job or take a job at a particular company?

But Jesus wants us to be unguarded with Him. He never asked Peter, James or John to put a veil over their faces when Jesus was transfigured. Jesus was exposed and so were they. So why would He want you to not offer up all areas of your life to Him?

FAITH STEP: *Take time to pray about any areas in your life that you haven't opened up to Jesus. Where are you defensive? Where have you protected yourself? What have you walled off apart from Jesus? Offer them to Him. Take off your veil.*

—Camy Tang

OCTOBER 25

"For I resolved to know nothing while I was with you except
Jesus Christ and him crucified." 1 Corinthians 2:2 (NIV)

Each time I read this verse, I gulp. Can I really aspire to this sort of single-minded focus? Can I learn to value Christ so much that everything else becomes like nothing by comparison?

When we were newlyweds, my husband and I went on a backpacking trip in the Grand Teton Mountains with a youth group. As we prepared, we learned about priorities. When you have to carry everything on your own back for miles of hiking in high elevations, you get wiser at deciding what matters most. I've heard that some experienced backpackers will even cut off the handle of their toothbrush to reduce the weight of their pack by another fraction of an ounce.

Before we left, I looked around our apartment. I liked our microwave, our books, our piano. I enjoyed a dresser full of clothes and a curling iron on the bathroom counter. But for our adventure in the mountains, all I really needed were the basics of survival. Ten days lugging a tent, sleeping bag and food taught me a lot about how much is nonessential.

Sometimes in our walk of following Christ, we get bogged down by the nonessentials. There are plenty of interests, activities or ambitions that feel important. They aren't necessarily bad things. But they sometimes threaten to crowd out the central purpose of life. When we're serious about following Christ through the difficult climbs of discipleship, we want to pare down to what matters most: knowing Him and His crucifixion.

FAITH STEP: *Think about the backpack of your spiritual life. Are there any nonessential things weighing you down?*

—*Sharon Hinck*

OCTOBER 26

"Jesus answered, 'I am the way and the truth and the life.'" John 14:6 (TNIV)

I couldn't have been more surprised when I received an e-mail from an old boyfriend. He was someone I cared for greatly during my teen years and his confessions of love shocked me.

I started to wonder, "What if…?" Suddenly my good marriage didn't look as great as I thought it was; it seemed dull, safe, unromantic. I became discontent with my husband and the life I was living.

I was drawn to my ex-boyfriend's comments, and over the next week I e-mailed him a few times. When he continued his wooing words, I talked to my husband and my friends and followed their advice to break off communication. I e-mailed him weeks later, letting him know I was committed to my husband. I also prayed for one thing most of all: truth. I prayed that my eyes would be open and that I wouldn't be drawn away by lies.

The more I prayed, the more I realized Jesus is truth. The more I spent time with Jesus, the Truth, the more the lies revealed themselves. The truth was my husband loved me and had committed his life to me. The truth was that anyone who was trying to break up my marriage and family was not after my best interest and was not from God.

Jesus revealed deeper truths too, that my relationship with my old boyfriend was something I needed to confess. Even though Jesus had forgiven me at my moment of salvation, I needed to look at that time through eyes of Truth—through Jesus' eyes. Jesus had been there all along wanting to love me even as I turned to another.

Jesus is the way and the truth and the life. Anything that doesn't agree with Him and His way is a lie.

FAITH STEP: *Think back to old relationships and consider the truth of the situation through Jesus' eyes. Pray and thank Jesus for revealing His way and giving you His life.*

—Tricia Goyer

OCTOBER 27

"A new command I give you: Love one another. As I have loved you, so you must love one another. By this everyone will know that you are my disciples, if you love one another." John 13:34–35 (NIV)

When I was nine, my family moved. That same year, I grew four inches and got glasses. I was the geeky new kid at school whose pants were always too short and always had her nose in a book. My best friend was the school librarian.

It was a lonely time, an awkward phase that lasted until I went to high school. I got contact lenses, found pants that fit and realized that all that reading had made me smart, which provided a peer group of other geeks. I also found friends in the Campus Life group at my school.

Since then, I've grown more adept socially, though I'm still introverted. But I've learned that part of what it means to follow Jesus is to love others. It's not optional. Jesus says, "you must love one another."

Sometimes people hurt or disappoint us. Friendship is wonderful, but sometimes challenging. But Jesus says, love anyway. And then, sends people to us.

In *The Four Loves,* C. S. Lewis wrote, "For a Christian, there are, strictly speaking, no chances. A secret Master of the Ceremonies has been at work. Christ, who said to the disciples 'Ye have not chosen me, but I have chosen you,' can truly say to every group of Christian friends 'You have not chosen one another but I have chosen you for one another.'"

Over the years, Jesus has led me to friends He's chosen for me, though I might not have chosen them for myself. These friendships bring both joy and pain. But they have formed me spiritually. They have provided a place for me to obey Jesus' command to love Him by loving others.

FAITH STEP: *If you feel lonely, consider that others may also need a friend. Take a step to build a new friendship or deepen an existing one.*

—Keri Wyatt Kent

OCTOBER 28

"Though he slay me, yet will I trust him." Job 13:15

Lindsay is a very special young lady to me. I have known her since she was just a little girl coming to my house for music lessons. As she has grown up I have had the privilege of being a part of her life and nurturing her relationship with Jesus.

Several years ago, Lindsay was diagnosed with a rare disease called idiopathic chondrolysis. She spent several months in a wheelchair, but through God's answer to much prayer the disease went into remission and she was able to walk again. Though she deals with pain in her joints, her high-school years have been relatively normal and full of activity.

Just this past week she had a scare, however. It seemed the disease was flaring up again, and Lindsay spent a few days in bed. Her mom made an appointment at Children's Hospital with the doctor who supervises her care.

I was committed to praying for Lindsay that day and checked her Facebook page for updates. As she headed to the hospital, she wrote this status on her wall:

Off to Children's Hospital—so ready to find out what is going on! God has granted me one miracle and I pray He has another one in store. I trust we will get good news! But, whatever news the doctor has for me I am determined to receive as a blessing, believing Jesus knows best and He is in control of my life.

Later that night I found out that the news was good, and I rejoiced with Lindsay and her family. However, it is that original post that stays with me even now, challenging and inspiring me to greater heights with my Savior. I want a heart like that—a heart that stands ready to receive whatever He gives, trusting His goodness and sovereignty, resting in the promise of His blessing.

FAITH STEP: *Jesus, I trust you with _____ , and receive Your blessing. I believe You know best and You are in control of everything.*

—*Gwen Ford Faulkenberry*

OCTOBER 29

"Jesus replied: 'Love the Lord your God with all your heart and with all your soul and with all your mind.' This is the first and greatest commandment. And the second is like it: 'Love your neighbor as yourself.'" Matthew 22:37–39 (NIV)

"*I* luff you sooo much, Mama." My tiny daughter wore her most dreamy expression as she crooned those words. That was just before she wrapped her arms around my neck and melted me on the spot. It's said that good things come in small packages, and that's very true when it comes to our children.

It's also true about the little word *love*. A small package, those four letters hold true power.

Popular views of love give us feel-good images of traipsing through fields of wildflowers with the object of our affections. Love does feel great. But those simplistic views can easily underestimate love's true power, so how about taking a few minutes to consider what real love really is?

True love has muscle, toned from neverending use. With practice and unselfish discipline, it digs down to the trenches where it's needed most, where nothing else will do to meet a need. Love can heal the deepest hurts and model life-changing lessons. It has guts and doesn't shy away from unpopular truth. It forgives at its own expense, for the good of someone else. In fact, love is all about someone else.

Jesus said the greatest two commandments are to love God and others. We've read and heard that a few dozen times. Notice, though, how we're to love: with everything. With our whole beings—heart, soul and mind.

Love has what it takes, whatever it is. Jesus models that kind of love, the type we absolutely can count on.

May our loved ones be able to count on our love that way, through Jesus' power in us.

FAITH STEP: *Brainstorm three creative ways you can show someone you love them this week.*

—*Erin Keeley Marshall*

OCTOBER 30

"Finally, beloved, whatever is true, whatever is honorable, whatever is just, whatever is pure, whatever is pleasing, whatever is commendable, if there is any excellence and if there is anything worthy of praise, think about these things." Philippians 4:8 (ESV)

*I*t's been said that insanity is doing the same thing over and over and each time expecting the results will be different. Surely this is true of my thoughts as well. What I think, I will find. If I prepare myself to meet with negativity, discouragement or hostility, I am sure to see it. But if I plan for acceptance, positivity and friendliness, then that is what I will discover. If my mind is negative, my life will be too. If I don't change how I think about things, with positivity and hope in the Lord rather than doubt and despair, no matter how much I desire it, nothing new can happen.

My mind is strong and stubborn but the Holy Spirit is stronger. He can help me manage my mind, corral my thoughts, attitudes and decisions and focus them all toward Christ. The insanity of doubt and gloom can be replaced with wisdom, reason and joy.

FAITH STEP: *Don't do the same thing over and over and expect the results to be different. If you find yourself doubting, whining, complaining or expecting the worst, turn it around. Instead of "I hate rain," think "my garden is being watered." Jesus has brought joy into our lives. Live like it!*

— *Judy Baer*

OCTOBER 31

"Surely the lowborn are but a breath, the highborn are but a lie. If weighed on a balance, they are nothing; together they are only a breath. Do not trust in extortion or put vain hope in stolen goods; though your riches increase, do not set your heart on them." Psalm 62:9–10 (TNIV)

I recently read the story about a husband and wife who had a rocky marriage. They took the extreme measure of moving to a foreign country to try to salvage their relationship. They had to simplify to enormous measures—no car, no television, no high-paying jobs. Without all the distractions of their "stuff," they found their hearts and souls healing. They grew closer to God and closer to each other.

Jesus warns about riches in numerous places in the Gospels, and sometimes it's easy to gloss over the words, to let the meanings slip in one ear and out the other. After all, most of us aren't rich. We're "comfortable" or "content." Yet we have closets of clothes, spare rooms with boxes, garages full of stuff.

I'm not saying to sell everything you have and give the money to the poor, nor do you have to go live in a foreign country. But if you simplified your life—if you got rid of more stuff than you're comfortable giving away—would you be able to hear Jesus better without the physical, emotional and spiritual clutter? After all, this world is passing away, and our bodies with it. Can we simplify, getting rid of our things and trusting Jesus for our memories, for the lessons learned, for the needs we have?

FAITH STEP: *Take a moment to really pray and see if you're holding on to things or to riches that are distracting you from Him. Pray for help to get rid of it. Be willing no matter how drastic it might be, because Jesus will be more than enough for all your needs.*

—*Camy Tang*

November

NOVEMBER 1

"But the seed on good soil stands for those with a noble and good heart, who hear the word, retain it, and by persevering produce a crop." Luke 8:15 (NIV)

*I*n the past several years, the economic recession has cut my family's income, forced us to drastically reduce our expenses. And yet it's been a time that has strengthened my faith, in part because there's little else to cling to.

One of Jesus' richest parables is about the seeds that fall on various types of soil—hard-packed, rocky, thorny and good. On any given day, any of these could describe the condition of my heart—some days are better than others. I want to have good "heart soil" every day, every minute, but that's not something I think anyone can manufacture. It simply results from faith and perseverance. Luke's version of the parable says that good soil results from hearing and retaining the Word. This raises some questions: Do we hear? And how do we retain the Word? Does this mean memorizing Scripture? Or is it something more?

The way to hear God's Word is to read your Bible or hear it taught at church. Are these regular habits in your life? Do you make it a regular practice to hear God's Word?

The Greek word translated "retain" in this verse is katechō. Reading other verses with that same Greek word can shed light on its meaning. For example, Hebrews 10:23 says, "Let us hold unswervingly [katechō] to the hope we profess, for he who promised is faithful" (NIV). One way to retain the Word is to memorize it.

I can improve the soil of my soul by hearing God's Word, holding unswervingly to it, persevering in faith, even when times are difficult. Clinging to Jesus will produce a crop of spiritual fruit that my sheer effort could never produce.

FAITH STEP: *Spend some time thinking about the soil of your heart. Is it soft and open to God's Word? When you hear God's Word, do you retain it, hold unswervingly to it? Memorize today's verse.*

—Keri Wyatt Kent

NOVEMBER 2

"Even before he made the world, God loved us and chose us in Christ to be holy and without fault in his eyes." Ephesians 1:4 (NLT)

My mom married my stepdad when I was four, but I always felt like part of the package deal rather than a bonus feature. Our relationship was fine. My stepdad was good enough to me—he provided a home and made sure I always had everything I needed, yet deep down my heart longed to be chosen.

After I accepted Jesus into my life, I felt the same way. I knew Jesus loved me, but He loved everyone, right? Did God really love me and choose me for me?

Even before he made the world…that phrase makes my heart sing.

Even before he made the world…I was chosen in Christ. The sacrifice Jesus made was to make me holy and without fault. Yes, I had to accept God, but He was waiting for me, loving me as I journeyed to Him. Even though I am just one person in a sea of faces, God looks to me and says, "I want that one."

John 15:16 (NLT) speaks of this too: "You didn't choose me. I chose you. I appointed you to go and produce lasting fruit, so that the Father will give you whatever you ask for, using my name."

Jesus didn't just choose us to be His; He also chose us to impact others. It would have been enough to be accepted and forgiven, but Jesus also chose me to join Him in all the amazing things He wants to do on earth.

Today I have a good relationship with my stepdad—better than I had growing up. Part of that is because I'm more thankful for what my stepdad gave me rather than hurt over what I didn't have. But another part is that because Jesus chose me, I'm able to impact others—my stepdad included—for Him.

FAITH STEP: *Read Ephesians 1:4 out loud, personalizing the text. "Even before he made the world, God loved ME and chose ME in Christ to be holy and without fault in his eyes." Write those words on a note card and pull it out during times you need to feel Jesus' love in a special way.*

—*Tricia Goyer*

NOVEMBER 3

*"Can any one of you by worrying add a single
hour to your life?" Matthew 6:27 (NIV)*

often coaxed my grandma to tell me the stories of her life. She lived in Latvia during World War II and endured a Communist occupation and then a Nazi one, an escape across the Baltic, and five years in a displaced-persons camp. She had every reason to live in fear, but instead she taught me a lot about the futility of worry.

As a young parent I faced battlegrounds too, even though my circumstances were much easier. I didn't have bombs exploding nearby or tanks rolling across the farm. I didn't have to worry about how far I could stretch cabbage soup to feed hungry mouths.

But in our overachieving, more-more-more culture, I felt swept into expectations I didn't know how to meet. Rushing children from play practices to music lessons to sports. Tutoring, allergy shots, orthodontics. Life felt out of control. Parenting seemed to be a specialized skill that was more about keeping up than providing love and discipline. My anxiety level increased as I tortured myself with a grandiose picture of what it meant to be a woman, a mom, a person—a picture I didn't match.

Visiting my grandma always helped. She had lived through events beyond her control, and knew that anxiety turned our eyes away from God. She saw every hour of her ninety-nine years as a gift from God's hand.

When I read Jesus' words about worry, I think of my grandma. Sometimes life feels out of my control because it is. I couldn't control every aspect of my children's childhood. I can't change some of the difficult and painful challenges in my life today either. I can't fix every person or problem. But when I feel overwhelmed, I can put the situation in Jesus' hands, knowing He does have my days and my hours safe in His care.

FAITH STEP: *What are your top three worries today? Can you place them in Jesus' care today?*

—*Sharon Hinck*

NOVEMBER 4

"[Jesus] said to the man, 'I tell you, get up, take your mat and go home.'" Mark 2:10–11 (NIV)

"*F*ree at last! Free at last! Thank God Almighty I'm free at last!"

I'm finished with my workout for another day! And like many folks, I have a love-hate relationship with exercise. I love the idea of it. I love how I feel after I finish. Sometimes I even love the process and knowing the purge of stress and calories will feel good the rest of the day.

The hardest part of most challenges is getting started—the first step of action. It marks a crucial turning point. The challenge of the first step is a timeless one, and it applies to faith as well.

God does a great deal to carry us through life. However, He does require that we take an initial step in faith, even when the challenge ahead seems insurmountable.

Consider His instruction to His people on the brink of receiving the Promised Land (Joshua 3). He was ready to part the Jordan River so they could cross. However, they needed to step out in faith before He cleared the obstacle—at flood stage, no less: "As soon as the priests…set foot in the Jordan, its waters flowing downstream will be cut off and stand up in a heap." Those waters looked dangerous, but the people needed to make the first difficult move in faith that He would deliver them.

Consider also the paralytic Jesus healed in Mark 2:10–11. In order to experience healing, the man had to act in faith by obeying Jesus' instruction to get up and walk. How easy it would have been for him to give the excuse, "But I can't, Jesus." The man had many more reasons to doubt Jesus than to believe him. But all he needed was one good reason to stand up in faith. Jesus Himself was that one good reason.

Jesus is your one good reason too. Accept the challenge, and then step out and find out Jesus is enough.

FAITH STEP: *What faith step sounds too difficult but continues to nag your thoughts? The first step is yours to take.*

—*Erin Keeley Marshall*

NOVEMBER 5

"This was in accordance with the eternal purpose that he has carried out in Christ Jesus our Lord, in whom we have access to God in boldness and confidence through faith in him." Ephesians 3:11–12 (NRSV)

I have so much doubt sometimes—about God, about myself, about my salvation. It happens in weak moments, when I'm tired, when I've heard too much negativity and pessimism, when I've surrounded myself too long with those who don't know the Lord. Then there is bleakness in my thoughts, hopelessness, despondency and fear. Then I pray for help not to open my mind to Satan's lies or to rumor or scandal, to trivial nonsense, to the inane and insignificant. My life can't be strong and uplifting when my mind has sunk into the pit. It is then that I must look upward and pay attention to the Lord. His desire is to redeem my sinful self.

The more time I spend in the Word, the more He reveals to me and the more I understand. Life is too complicated to live without instruction! And the directives are in His Word.

FAITH STEP: *Just like you plan for a fire emergency, make a plan for the times doubt strikes. Spend time fortifying yourself in Scripture today.*

— Judy Baer

NOVEMBER 6

"Ask, and it shall be given you; seek, and ye shall find;
knock, and it shall be opened unto you." Luke 11:9

The head of our university is a busy woman. She has about a thousand things going on all of the time, situations and people demanding her attention from every direction. It's a hard job and she balances it well.

The other day we had a meeting scheduled. I had been working on a proposal for her, trying to get a study-abroad program started at our school. It was pretty involved, as I'd consulted with others with similar programs, surveyed our student body and drawn up plans for how to approach our first student-travel opportunity. I was pretty jazzed to share it all with her and hopefully get the ball rolling. Then her secretary called and told me the meeting was postponed. The boss was too busy; we'd have to reschedule.

It happens to everyone, doesn't it? Life gets in the way; we get busy and have to change plans with people, tell people to wait or wait ourselves on something we feel is important. It's the human condition.

Thankfully, it's not Jesus' condition. He is never late, never too busy, never unable to devote His full attention to us. We never have to reschedule. He sees us as individuals and we are all vitally important to Him. There are no hoops we have to jump through, no balancing of other interests, no hierarchy to His love.

FAITH STEP: *Go to Jesus with whatever you need—now. He's more than available; He's waiting to hear from you.*

—Gwen Ford Faulkenberry

NOVEMBER 7

"Blessed is the one whose transgressions are forgiven, whose sins are covered. Blessed is the one whose sin the Lord does not count against them and in whose spirit is no deceit." Psalm 32:1–2 (NIV)

The transactions of grace are, in many ways, inexplicable. We sin; Jesus pays the price and does not count it against us. He forgives, with extravagance verging on spoiling.

I have been married for more than two decades. I'm astounded at how many times I have had to forgive, and how many times I would have to ask for forgiveness, in order to maintain a healthy marriage.

I'm also the mother of two teenagers, who are the greatest joys of my life. I made plenty of mistakes raising them and I'm sure I'll make more. But when I make those mistakes, I admit it to them. I apologize, ask for their forgiveness, and they sweetly grant it (okay, sometimes not right away). If I could give one bit of parenting advice, it would be to apologize to your kids when you mess up. They'll be more likely to do the same. Let this Psalm be true of your family.

Our own willingness to forgive is more than merely magnanimous. It provides us a window into the heart of Jesus, who forgives.

When we are willing to love another person, we catch a glimpse of how we are loved. We peer into the heart of Jesus, the One Who covers all sin.

FAITH STEP: *Is there someone you need to forgive today? If it seems impossible, think of what Jesus has forgiven you of. Forgiveness does not require the other person to apologize. It only requires that you release the hurt that you keep allowing yourself to feel.*

—Keri Wyatt Kent

NOVEMBER 8

*"Lord, the Lord Almighty, may those who hope in you not be
disgraced because of me; God of Israel, may those who seek you
not be put to shame because of me." Psalm 69:6 (TNIV)*

We are ambassadors for God. He knows we're sinful and we're not perfect, but we're still here to represent Him to others.

If you're upset with your spouse, you try to be considerate of the kids and not hash things out in front of them. If you're frustrated at work, think professionally and present your concerns to your boss logically and calmly rather than in a rash tirade. If you're annoyed with a family member, don't insult him in front of your entire clan.

It's the same with how we represent Jesus. We try to be thoughtful of those who don't know Him. We don't want to be the ones to give them a bad impression of Jesus. No matter how tired or upset we are, we need to be mindful of nonbelievers, in the same way we'd be considerate of our kids, our boss, our family.

Think of your relationships with nonbelievers in your life. Are you being a good witness of Jesus' love, patience, kindness, sensitivity? Or are you giving them a wrong impression of what a follower of Jesus ought to be? Nonbelievers tend to lump all "Christians" together, so how are you breaking a stereotype or showing that not all believers are hypocrites?

FAITH STEP: *Pray for Jesus to help you to be more considerate of the people He's trying to reach. Ask Him to give you His love for them, and pray for the patience (gulp!) and self-control you need to serve Jesus when you're with those people.*

—Camy Tang

NOVEMBER 9

"Beloved, do not imitate evil, but imitate good. He who does good is of God; he who does evil has not seen (discerned or experienced) God [has enjoyed no vision of Him and does not know Him at all]." 3 John 1:11 (AMP)

The disciple John saw Jesus and was perhaps His closest friend, and that relationship changed John for life. While we know Jesus by reading about Him, John walked by His side, felt Jesus' touch, leaned against Him for support.

Before I accepted Jesus as Lord, I went through a rough spot in my life. I made bad choices and hurt many people. I also hurt myself. For years, even though I'd accepted that Jesus forgave me, I had a hard time forgiving myself for the pain I'd caused.

One morning during prayer, God put an image in my mind of my "dark" years. I saw myself in a black room, walking in complete darkness and groping around to find my way. God reminded me that's how things were before I allowed the light of Jesus into my life. I stumbled because I couldn't see, and in the process I got hurt. I also hurt others. When I opened the door and welcomed Jesus into my heart, His light was there to show me the way. I knew which way to go. I stumbled far less.

That image helps me to have compassion on those who don't know the love and light of Jesus and who've not accepted Him into their lives. There are so many who don't even realize they're stumbling. There are so many who haven't experienced Jesus as John did, or even as I have. They need someone to introduce them to the Light.

FAITH STEP: *Take a moment to consider someone you know who is walking in darkness. How would having Jesus' light change them? What can you do to bring light to that person?*

—*Tricia Goyer*

NOVEMBER 10

"For the past twenty-three years…the Lord has been giving me his messages. I have faithfully passed them on to you, but you have not listened." Jeremiah 25:3 (NLT)

$\mathcal{I}$’ve had a couple of Jeremiah days this week. You know, those days when everything you do seems destined for failure?

Take today, for instance. It started out great. I dropped my kids off at school and made it to the grocery-store checkout lane in record time. Then as I watched the items drop into the bags, I opened my purse…and remembered that my wallet was at home in yesterday's Bible-study tote. No wallet, no groceries, which meant a trip back home and a serious loss of time.

I can't stand wasting time. Resting, I like. But wasting time I can't afford is a tough pill to swallow. Not only that, but it irks me to feel yet again that my brain isn't what it used to be.

However, I believe the Holy Spirit had begun whispering to me even before I discovered my goof. Although I felt disappointed, deep in my spirit I was calm. Calm!

As I re-drove the round-trip to the store, wallet in hand, I asked Jesus to show me some purpose in my mistake, some way He could redeem the loss of time. You know what? He immediately reminded me of this half-written devotion about days full of failures. At that point it was a mish-mash of thoughts, but this flub and the victory of a calm spirit provided the wrap-up I needed to bring this writing to completion. I had been praying for a sweetening of my spirit in the midst of busyness—and true to Himself, Jesus showed that His power is perfect (and purposeful) in my weakness. (See 2 Corinthians 12:9.)

Hallelujah for Jeremiah days that reveal Jesus at work despite our limitations! (See Romans 8:28.)

FAITH STEP: *Write out Romans 8:28 and 2 Corinthians 12:9. Post them where you'll see them next time a Jeremiah day strikes.*

—*Erin Keeley Marshall*

NOVEMBER 11

"Be kind and compassionate to one another, forgiving each other, just as in Christ God forgave you." Ephesians 4:32 (NIV)

"For if you forgive others when they sin against you, your heavenly Father will also forgive you. But if you do not forgive others their sins, your Father will not forgive your sins." Matthew 6:14–15 (TNIV)

I was sitting at lunch with a longtime close friend, complaining (again!) about something my husband had done or neglected to do. She listened compassionately, but then firmly asked: "Keri, have you ever forgiven Scot for just being who he is?"

This friend knows a thing or two about extravagant forgiveness. As her alcoholic father was dying, unrepentant about the many ways in which he had damaged his family, she went to care for him. She had to forgive him for being who he was.

Forgiveness is a daily practice for Christ followers. The word forgiving in Ephesians 4 implies an ongoing activity. Jesus tells us to forgive when others sin against us, not if. It's going to happen again and again.

So often, I want to hold on to grudges, build a case out of a thousand small injuries. But Jesus strictly warns that God won't forgive us if we don't forgive others. Further, lack of forgiveness keeps us in pain: "When you refuse to forgive, you are giving the person who walloped you once the privilege of hurting you all over again—in your memory," Lew Smedes, a former professor at Fuller Theological Seminary, says. "The first person who benefits from the forgiving is the person who does the forgiving. Forgiving is, first of all, a way of helping yourself to get free of the unfair pain somebody caused you."

FAITH STEP: *Who do you need to forgive today? Who is hurting you over and over, in your memory? Let yourself be free of that pain by forgiving that person, even if they are unrepentant or unaware of the pain they caused.*

—Keri Wyatt Kent

NOVEMBER 12

*"As the bridegroom rejoices over the bride, so
your God will rejoice over you." Isaiah 62:5 (NASB)*

One of the best days of my life was my own wedding day, when I got to dress up like a fairytale princess and marry the handsome prince. It was seven o'clock in the evening. The atmosphere of the church was charged with excitement. Inside the doors of the sanctuary there were 450 guests waiting. Outside, in the foyer, my dad and I watched for our cue. We were both tearfully happy. He cradled my arm in his big hand like a piece of fine china. As the bridal march sounded forth, we walked down the aisle, past smiling faces of well-wishers. My heart felt like it might beat out of my chest. Then I saw him: my prince, Stone Faulkenberry, the one my heart loves.

He stood at the end of the aisle in a black tux with tails, tall and strong and beautiful. His face was resplendent with joy. His shining blue eyes were transfixed on me and me alone. My racing heart stilled. In that moment I felt completely loved, completely honored, completely home. Moving forward to take his hand, nothing else mattered except that I was his and he was mine.

Sometimes it's hard for me to imagine the God of the universe taking this kind of delight in human beings, but He does. In Matthew 25, Jesus calls Himself our bridegroom. It's the perfect analogy for perfect love. Picture this: the Prince stands on the threshold of heaven in all of His amazing glory. He looks down through time and finds me, even in my less-than-a-princess state—and He finds you. A radiant smile breaks out across His face. His fiery eyes glow with pride. From that moment forward, nothing else matters, because we are His, and He is ours.

FAITH STEP: *Close your eyes for a minute and receive the joy that flows over you from your Prince of Peace. Take His hand and hear Him whisper in your ear: "You are loved. You are honored. In Me, you are home."*

—Gwen Ford Faulkenberry

NOVEMBER 13

"Woe to you, scribes and Pharisees, hypocrites! For you clean the outside of the cup and the plate, but inside they are full of greed and self-indulgence. You blind Pharisee! First clean the inside of the cup so that the outside also may become clean.... For you are like whitewashed tombs, which on the outside look beautiful, but insides they are full of the bones of the dead and of all kinds of filth. So you also on the outside look righteous to others, but inside you are full of hypocrisy and lawlessness." Matthew 23:25–28 (ESV)

*S*ometimes I feel like a dirty cup, like my favorite white one I use for tea. It looks pretty on the shelf, shiny and bright, but if I peer inside it is blackened and unsightly with dark stains where others cannot see.

I work hard to make people think well of me, but how hard do I work to please the Lord? There are two kinds of holiness—external holiness and internal holiness. The Pharisees were concerned with external holiness—the impression they gave to others, how righteous and pious they could appear to be yet they didn't take care of the condition of their insides, their internal holiness.

I do that sometimes. I make sure everyone thinks I'm kind and giving, honest and true yet what's going on in my mind, I'd never want to reveal to the world—pettiness, envy, crabbiness, ingratitude. I don't want to be a hypocrite—I'm done with being stained and nasty. Jesus' grace cleans me up, forgives me, washes me that I might be unsoiled again.

Only by Jesus' grace and forgiveness can we change the condition of our cups. Praise Jesus for the gift of salvation.

FAITH STEP: *What is dirtying your "cup" right now? What is tarnishing your internal holiness? Is there something in your life that you need to take care of? Search yourself, answer the question and ask God for help to put to rest what is holding you back.*

– Judy Baer

NOVEMBER 14

"The Lord is my light and my salvation—whom shall I fear? The Lord is the stronghold of my life—of whom shall I be afraid?" Psalm 27:1 (TNIV)

Jesus and His disciples were in a boat when a terrible storm came up. The disciples woke Jesus up with their panicked cries that they were going to die. Jesus quite calmly said, "You of little faith, why are you so afraid?" Then He casually rebuked the storm and they were all safe. He knew He was more powerful than a puny storm—after all, He spoke the world into being. A storm was nothing compared to His power.

He asked the disciples why they were afraid to make the point that when they're with Him, they have no reason to be afraid. Jesus is more than capable of keeping things from falling apart.

Sometimes, we're not fearing a situation—like a storm—but we're fearing ourselves. We don't trust ourselves to do things right. But whether we're fearing a situation or ourselves, we're not believing Jesus is able to solve any problems that arise. We're thinking our screw-ups are more powerful than Jesus, and that's just ridiculous. He's able to give us the help and strength we need. He's infinitely bigger than any of our failures.

FAITH STEP: *Do you fear anything inside yourself? Are you insecure about anything in particular? Give it up to Jesus and walk forward, despite the fear. Trust Jesus to take care of you. You have no reason to fear.*

—Camy Tang

NOVEMBER 15

"Our Father who is in heaven, hallowed be Your name. Your kingdom come, Your will be done, on earth as it is in heaven. Give us this day our daily bread. And forgive us our debts, as we also have forgiven our debtors. And do not lead us into temptation, but deliver us from evil. For Yours is the kingdom and the power and the glory forever. Amen." Matthew 6:9–13 (NASB)

As a child, I thought the Lord's Prayer contained the words "my will be done." Even after I'd been told otherwise, I still didn't want to believe it. How could anyone know what I needed and wanted better than me? God was smart and all, but could I trust Him? I knew He was around somewhere, watching over me, but how could He know what was best for me—what translated in my childish vernacular was what I wanted?

It took me several years to let down my guard, to really put my weight down where God was concerned. It was just how I treated flying. Granted, I'd get on the plane but I'd hover my feet above the floor so as not to put too much extra pressure weight on the plane. Logical? No. Fanciful thinking? Yes.

Then I decided to test Him, just a bit at a time. I turned something over to Him and waited for results. God didn't disappoint. Things still turned out fine. In fact, some things turned out better than fine! So I gave Him a little more responsibility for my life. And more. And more. Eventually I realized that there were things He could handle even better than me. What's more, even when things weren't going my way, I didn't feel alone. We're in this together, God and I. I don't have to tough things out alone.

Yes, Lord, Thy will be done. It is far better than mine.

FAITH STEP: *As you pray the Lord's Prayer today, think about what each word means. It is how Jesus taught us to pray.*

— Judy Baer

NOVEMBER 16

"But I call to God, and the Lord will save me. Evening and morning and at noon I utter my complaint and moan, and he hears my voice. He redeems my soul in safety from the battle that I wage, for many are arrayed against me." Psalm 55:16–18 (ESV)

I was brought up to be polite, to mind my manners. Especially when praying—quiet reverence was all I'd ever seen modeled. So this Psalm rubs me the wrong way. It seems to espouse complaining and moaning to God, all day long. As if that were okay.

Then again, I didn't have to fight many battles in my sheltered, suburban life. I can't remember a time when many were arrayed against me. Sure, there was some teasing and even a bit of bullying endured in junior high, but really, it was minor.

But for many women, daily life is a battle. A few years ago, I got to interview a young woman from Sierra Leone, a small country in West Africa. When she was a teenager, Ruth was tricked into leaving her hometown and then sold her into sexual slavery. She was eventually rescued from the brothel where she'd been held captive.

Ruth has endured war, rape, slavery. But eventually, she found Jesus. Today, she works with the Faith Alliance Against Slavery and Trafficking (FAAST) in Sierra Leone, educating others about human trafficking. Many refuse to believe that trafficking happens, or they blame the victims. Ruth bravely says, "It does happen, it happened to me."

Ruth's story put this Psalm in a whole new light for me. Should we not be complaining to God on behalf of our sisters who continue to be held captive? If we don't, who will?

FAITH STEP: *Visit www.faastinternational.org to learn more about the ongoing problem of sexual slavery both in the United States and around the world. Pray boldly for the women and children who are trafficking victims, and learn what you can do to help.*

—Keri Wyatt Kent

NOVEMBER 17

"Listen! For all these years I have been working like a slave for you, and I have never disobeyed your command; yet you have never given me even a young goat so that I might celebrate with my friends. But when this son of yours came back, who has devoured your property with prostitutes, you killed the fatted calf for him!" Luke 15:29–30 (NRSV)

Do you hear the envy and resentment in the voice of the brother of the prodigal son? He, after all, was obedient to his father and always did what he was told but he'd never been given a party or even a goat! Now his wastrel brother comes home and everyone celebrates. Does that seem fair? It certainly didn't to this hardworking sibling.

But who was hurt by this pique of jealousy? Not the prodigal son who was at last home with the father he loved. Not the father, who was overjoyed at the return of the son he thought was lost to him. Probably not any of the celebrants either, who were enjoying themselves at the party. The only one truly hurt by the envy was the jealous son.

Have you carried things around in your heart—anger, resentment, bitterness or antagonism—over a perceived hurt or slight? Do you feel like a martyr because you believe you are the only one who does things the way they should be done? Do you feel alienated and separate from friends and family because of your way of thinking? If so, the lack of forgiveness in your heart is only hurting you!

FAITH STEP: *Today choose to be forgiving no matter what happens, just as Jesus was. Decide not to let feelings that eat at you take over. Make your mind up not to take offense. Choose forgiveness.*

— *Judy Baer*

NOVEMBER 18

"Hallelujah! Praise God from heaven, praise him from the mountaintops; Praise him, all you his angels, praise him, all you his warriors, Praise him, sun and moon, praise him, you morning stars; Praise him, high heaven, praise him, heavenly rain clouds; Praise, oh let them praise the name of God—he spoke the word, and there they were!" Psalm 148:1 (MSG)

A child's prayers have to be some of the sweetest words ever spoken.

In recent months my two-year-old daughter Calianne has begun to add her prayers at mealtimes and bedtime. Just as her dad and I have enjoyed listening to her older brother talk to God, we love the privilege of witnessing her communicate with her friend Jesus.

Two reasons I love her prayers are 1) they come straight from her heart—whatever is topmost in her thoughts, and 2) they're all about giving thanks. She's typically eager to pray, and she usually says something like this:

"Tanks you, Jesus, for pink fire trucks and for Daddy and Mama and Paxton-boy. And tanks you, Jesus, for doggies and yogurt and mine cozy bed. Amen—Go get it!"

I adore the "Go get it!" she adds to the end. We have no idea where she heard it; she said it came from her head. Knowing her, it probably did. Anyway, because her prayers are loaded with thanksgiving instead of requests, the "Go get it!" isn't a demand that Jesus do her beckoning. It's more like she's cheering Him on and praising Him: "You go, Jesus! You're the best!"

My children inspire me to be simple before Jesus, to praise Him with my first thoughts, to cheer Him on for being Him—for being my victorious Savior, attentive Friend, holy Lord and mighty King.

The unhindered, childlike approach to faith that Jesus spoke of in Luke 18:16–17 shows itself in how we communicate with Him. Let's bless Him with prayers of trust-filled praise. Go get it!

FAITH STEP: *What typically characterizes your prayers? Praise? Requests? Complaints? Thanksgiving? Desperation? Trust? Offer it all to Him, paying special attention to praise and give thanks.*

—*Erin Keeley Marshall*

NOVEMBER 19

*"Instead, speaking the truth in love, we will in all things grow up
into him who is the head, that is, Christ."* Ephesians 4:15 (TNIV)

One thing I count on in my friendships is that my friends and I tell each
other the truth even if it's hard to say it or hear it. But preparing myself to
talk to a friend is almost as stressful as actually doing it. I worry about how
they'll take it, I worry that I won't communicate effectively, and I worry
that I'll forget something or inadvertently say something hurtful. I worry
that they'll be insulted and walk out on me, and I worry that things will be
tense between us. I worry that I'll be abandoned.

I recently had to tell my friend some bad news, but I was so worried
about it that I prayed a lot beforehand. When I finally told her, she took it
really well, and I'm sure my prayers contributed to that. She appreciated
that I told her the truth. All my worry was for nothing.

Sometimes you just need to tell the truth even if it will make you unpopular, even if your friends will abandon you. Isn't that what Jesus did?
He spoke bluntly to the Pharisees, the ones most likely to understand Jesus' words. But Jesus didn't couch His words in flattery or ease into the
conversation with them. He had to tell them that they were being hypocrites. And His fight with them led to the crowd of men who came to ar-
rest Him on the Mount of Olives, where His friends all abandoned Him.

Is there something you haven't yet told someone in your family or one
of your friends? What's holding you back?

FAITH STEP: *Give it up to Jesus in prayer—after all, He knows what you're
going through—and trust in Him to help you through whatever difficult things
you need to say.*

—Camy Tang

NOVEMBER 20

"The Lord does not look at the things people look at. People look at the outward appearance, but the Lord looks at the heart." 1 Samuel 16:7 (NIV)

Azar Nafisi was a professor at the University of Tehran, and as the regime in power grew stricter and stricter, virtually every book she thought was important to teach was banned. Instead of kowtowing to this attempt at government control over education, Nafisi decided to hold class in her home. A banned book club, if you will, made up of mostly young women.

A particularly powerful image I remember from Nafisi's memoir, *Reading Lolita in Tehran*, is when a group of female students come through Nafisi's door. Disguised in chadors that cover everything but their eyes, they begin to shed their outer garments as soon as they are safe inside her foyer. It is then that each one comes to life, according to the writer. Their individual characters emerge like butterflies from cocoons.

I believe all women can probably relate to that imagery of the outer coverings. It doesn't have to be a chador. It can be the clothing one's Christian denomination approves. Or the creed. How about skin color? Bank account? Disability? Dress size? It can even be a smile that says "everything's okay" or a frown that says "don't come too close."

With us, just like the women in Professor Nafisi's book, it is when we peel off those layers, letting other people see what's underneath, that we truly can be free. Hidden behind our veils of pride, shame, pretension, fear—we isolate ourselves from others. It's a form of bondage, and Jesus came to set the captive free!

Sometimes we find layers we didn't even know existed, in ourselves and others. But freedom to be who we are in Christ—and giving other people that freedom—is worth it. As Paul writes, "It is for freedom that you were set free."

FAITH STEP: *Throw off any layers of self you're carrying around—and let His beauty shine through!*

–Gwen Ford Faulkenberry

NOVEMBER 21

"Jesus is 'the stone you builders rejected, which has become the cornerstone.' Salvation is found in no one else, for there is no other name under heaven given to mankind by which we must be saved." Acts 4:11–12 (NIV)

At Thanksgiving, we gathered friends and neighbors around an abundant table. The holiday provided a lot of bonding time with my kids, especially with my teenage son, because I put him in charge of decorating the table. He and I had a great time shopping for fabric, cheap glasses to use as vases, river rocks from the craft store. We gathered curly willow branches and fresh sage sprigs from the backyard, mini-pumpkins from the farm stand. My son went to work painting branches and pumpkins, arranging them precisely. His artistic talents dovetail with our family mission of hospitality.

We used river rocks as place cards, with each person's name written on their rock. After dinner, we instructed each person to take their rock, and write on its smooth surface what they felt thankful for this Thanksgiving. Then, we went around the table and shared our thoughts.

We piled up the rocks, to create a sort of altar. I shared the story from 1 Samuel, where Samuel builds an altar and names it Ebenezer, which means "stone of help," to commemorate how God had answered prayer and helped Israel in a key battle. (See 1 Samuel 7.)

Jesus is our rock. Jesus is our Ebenezer, our stone of help. He is the cornerstone, the very foundation of our faith, which we can lean on and trust. When we take a few moments to remember specific ways that He has helped us thus far, we build a little altar in our hearts. When faith wavers, we can look at the altar and be assured that He will help us again.

FAITH STEP: *Take a smooth stone and a permanent marker, and write a reminder of Jesus' help on it. Put it somewhere you can see it each day.*

—*Keri Wyatt Kent*

NOVEMBER 22

"Rejoice always. Pray continually. Give thanks in every situation because this is God's will for you in Christ Jesus." 1 Thessalonians 5:16–18 (CEB)

*O*utside, the snow is not so much falling as swirling, driven in cloudlike, dancing sheets. The storm, predicted for days, gathers strength, after a slow but steady morning with an inch or two of accumulation and ordinary (for Chicago) winds. A foot or more of snow, combined with fierce winds, is supposed to fall in the next day or so.

School is already canceled for tomorrow, and my kids will be home soon, rejoicing that they have a snow day tomorrow. I'm thankful that I've got beef stew simmering in the Crock-Pot: dinner is not only taken care of, but also perfuming the house with a beef-and-garlic fragrance that's wonderfully welcoming on this stormy afternoon.

The Greek word translated "thanks" in this verse is eucharisteo, meaning to be grateful, to express gratitude. If the word looks familiar, it's because we use it to describe the sacramental meal we also call communion, the Eucharist. In the Eucharist, we remember Jesus. We proclaim, in the words of the liturgy, His resurrection. In remembering His act of supreme love, how could we feel anything but grateful? And when we give thanks, when we are grateful, when we eucharisteo: do we not proclaim Christ's presence in the world, do we not feast on the goodness of His presence with us? What if giving thanks is not merely a way to feel better, but a way to shine the light of Jesus in a dark world, to proclaim His resurrection?

As the snowstorm gathers strength, I'm grateful for the roof over our heads, for heat and light (which will hopefully stay on during the storm!), for food on the table, for my family gathered in safe, so many small blessings. In the midst of the storms of your life, what will you rejoice over, pray about and give thanks for?

FAITH STEP: *Take a few moments to list ten things you are grateful for today.*

—*Keri Wyatt Kent*

NOVEMBER 23

"Many that are first shall be last; and the last first." Mark 10:31

*M*y favorite Flannery O'Connor story is called "Revelation." It's about a woman named Mrs. Turpin who thinks she is righteous, and thanks God that she is not like the "white trash" she sees around her or the former slaves who work on her farm. The first scene is in a doctor's office, and readers are privy to the inner dialogue of Mrs. Turpin as she passes judgment on everyone else in the waiting room. A girl named Mary Grace, whom Mrs. Turpin pities because of her ugliness, is reading a book, but she seems to be able to discern Mrs. Turpin's self-righteous thoughts. In a surprising outburst, Mary Grace throws the book at Mrs. Turpin, giving her a black eye and screaming at her. What she yells is always a source of hilarity in my classes: "Go back to hell where you came from, you old warthog!"

In the next major scene, Mrs. Turpin is standing by the hog pen on her farm, contemplating what just happened. She goes through stages of anger, self-pity and finally, honest searching. Her revelation occurs when she sees heaven open, and a great procession of people. In front are the former slaves, white trash and other miscreants. They are singing, dancing and shouting hallelujah. At the back of the line is Mrs. Turpin herself, along with all of the other people she thinks of as worthy to enter the kingdom of God.

Readers want to despise Mrs. Turpin. But most of us can't, because she's too familiar. If my thoughts in a given moment were exposed to the world, it wouldn't always be pretty. Sometimes, like Mrs. Turpin, I can't see beyond the end of my own nose. Thank the Lord that He is faithful—by His grace—to shake me up, and remind me that all my righteousness is really just filthy rags. Without Jesus, I'm nothing but an old warthog!

FAITH STEP: *Are you in need of a "warthog" moment? Ask Jesus to reveal any areas of pride that may be hidden in your life. Submit them to Him, and walk in the freedom of His righteousness, which covers you no matter what.*

—*Gwen Ford Faulkenberry*

NOVEMBER 24

"Then Jesus told him this story: 'A man loaned money to two people—500 pieces of silver to one and 50 pieces to the other. But neither of them could repay him, so he kindly forgave them both, canceling their debts. Who do you suppose loved him more after that?' Simon answered, 'I suppose the one for whom he canceled the larger debt.' 'That's right,' Jesus said." Luke 7:41–43 (NLT)

On a fairly regular basis, the high-school youth group at our church has guest speakers who share a dramatic testimony: they'd been a drug addict, or a gang member, or engaged in some other spectacularly sinful lifestyle. Then they found Jesus, and He turned their life around.

I heard similar stories in my own youth group growing up and felt my own testimony was a little, well, trivial. I grew up in a Christian home, went to church every week, accepted Jesus as my Savior, and now, went to youth group every week in addition to church on Sundays. Boring. What had I been saved from, exactly?

This conversation in Luke occurs when Jesus dines at the house of Simon the Leper, a Pharisee. A sinful woman bursts in and anoints Jesus with costly perfume. The whole situation is scandalous, especially Jesus' reaction—He blesses and forgives her.

Why does Jesus ask this question about debt? Is He saying that Simon only has about a fifty-silver-piece debt toward God, while this repentant prostitute has a five-hundred-silver-piece one? I think Jesus was saying that Simon thought he had a smaller "sin debt"—but that all of us have absolutely no hope of ever repaying the debt of sin that we owe to God, and must throw ourselves on His mercy.

FAITH STEP: *Spend some time in self-examination. Even if we've been "pretty good" our whole lives and don't have an exciting testimony, we still have sinned—we've been jealous, angry, self-righteous or proud. Ask God to show you what you need to confess and repent of, to receive His forgiveness.*

—Keri Wyatt Kent

NOVEMBER 25

"In the seventh year of Jehu, Joash became king, and he reigned in Jerusalem forty years. His mother's name was Zibiah; she was from Beersheba. Joash did what was right in the eyes of the Lord all the years Jehoiada the priest instructed him." 2 Kings 12:1–2 (TNIV)

Christian mentors are wonderful. They guide us and help us on our way, whether spiritually or emotionally or both. They give of their time and wisdom, and they do it out of a desire to help, not because they're compensated.

But at some point you need to practice the wisdom you gained and to test the strength of your faith. You need to make your faith your own and not lean on another Christian's faith. You need to take responsibility for your own beliefs.

King Joash did fine while his mentor Jehoiada was alive, but once Jehoiada died, he started sinning against God. He did a complete 180, which was very sad because he had done such a good job while his mentor guided him. But perhaps his faith was not his own—it was borrowed from Jehoiada, and God wanted Joash to own his faith.

We shouldn't depend on another Christian so much that if they were gone, we would lose our faith. We need to make sure we own our faith for ourselves, depending on the Holy Spirit rather than another person. Jesus doesn't want lukewarm followers—He wants people 100 percent committed to Himself.

FAITH STEP: *Is your faith your own or do you rely heavily on another Christian to keep you accountable? How can you take control of your own faith? Write down some steps you can take this week.*

—Camy Tang

NOVEMBER 26

"As the men were leaving Jesus, Peter said to him, 'Master, it is good for us to be here. Let us put up three shelters—one for you, one for Moses and one for Elijah.' (He did not know what he was saying.) While he was speaking, a cloud appeared and covered them, and they were afraid as they entered the cloud. A voice came from the cloud, saying, 'This is my Son, whom I have chosen; listen to him.'" Luke 9:33–35 (NIV)

*K*ids are so honest. I remember times when my children have confessed they don't like their grandmother's cooking (ouch). Or times when they thought an older gentleman didn't smell very good. Times when they said those things horrified me, but I also understood. It takes time for children to understand how to filter their thoughts before they speak. They learn social graces the more they interact with others. We give children grace because, basically, they don't know any better…yet.

I smile to myself as I read about the comment added after Peter's declaration: "He did not know what he was saying." Peter was overwhelmed with this out-of-this-world experience and he reacted the only way he knew how: by speaking what he saw. Jesus, Moses and Elijah were present and they would need a way to stay out of the elements—and he would help.

The truth is, I'm more like my children—more like Peter—than I want to admit. I see something that catches my attention, and I try to analyze it in my small frame of reference. Thankfully God doesn't let me get carried away with my thoughts for too long. "Listen to my Son," God says. "Don't try to figure out everything for yourself."

Jesus is God's Son, sent to transform our thinking and our lives. In our walk with Him there will be moments that will surprise and delight us, but instead of reacting, we need to wait, listen and allow Him to tell us what His plan is all about.

FAITH STEP: *Think back to your days as a new believer. How were you different then than you are now? Pray and thank God for the growth and maturity you've experienced.*

—*Tricia Goyer*

NOVEMBER 27

"Why, my soul, are you downcast? Why so disturbed within me? Put your hope in God, for I will yet praise him, my Savior and my God." Psalm 42:11 (NIV)

$\mathcal{I}$ am generally an optimistic person. But a few years ago, I went through a season of melancholy. My marriage of fifteen years still wasn't easy—and I was realizing it would always require hard work. My kids were in junior high—and handling it well, but still, it's a tough age. My career felt, if not derailed, at least on an unproductive tangent. Life felt difficult.

I would stand at the stove—cooking dinner and listening to Norah Jones after a long day of work—and cry. It made no sense to me. I would ask myself, why am I so sad? I would pray, but feel guilty thinking I ought to be more joyful.

I remember finally calling a counselor, and trying to explain my uncharacteristic melancholy, and again bursting into tears. "I just need a little help," I said.

The Psalmist, in heartbreaking honesty, asks what most people ask at some time in their life: Why am I so sad? Then again, why not? Sometimes we are overwhelmed and sad, not because of our marriage, our kids, our career—but simply because we are.

Sometimes we need to talk it out, to come up with a new strategy, one that will allow us to redirect our hope. If we put our hope in our spouse, kids or career to make us happy, we'll be downcast and disturbed. When we stop hoping in people and things to make us happy, it frees them up to be a source—but not our only source—of joy. When we choose to hope in God, when we decide to praise our Savior, our faith grows. Jesus fills the empty space, and lifts us up.

FAITH STEP: *What do you need to do today in order to put your hope in God, to praise Jesus your Savior? How might deciding to do that bring you greater joy?*

—*Keri Wyatt Kent*

NOVEMBER 28

"He is despised and rejected of men; a man of sorrows, and acquainted with grief: and we hid as it were our faces from him; he was despised, and we esteemed him not." Isaiah 53:3

Throughout Scripture, Jesus is described with various titles and analogies. He is the Messiah, the Lamb of God, the Lion of Judah, the Good Shepherd, the Bread of Life, the Word made flesh, Emmanuel. Of all the wonderful depictions of Jesus, this raw, prophetic description in Isaiah often offers me the greatest comfort.

He is "a man of sorrows, and acquainted with grief." I know that God created the world, and that He is powerful. I know that God sent His Son and is loving and merciful. But when I'm facing loss, pain and grief that shreds me to the core, what I most want to know is that God understands—that He is acquainted with the pain I'm feeling.

When a ministry I had poured my life into for ten years had to close, my family had compassion, but no one could fully comprehend what the loss of that work meant to me, and I felt very lonely in my grief. In my tearful prayer times, I cried out to God, "No one understands how badly this hurts."

From the other side, I've faced the challenge of trying to offer empathy to a friend experiencing a struggle I've never faced: a house burned down, a child gravely ill or a husband's betrayal. Good friends listen, care and give the precious gift of support to each other as best we can, yet none of us can fully know what another person is going through. Only Jesus is fully acquainted with every bit of our experience. He is the powerful answer to our longing to be understood.

FAITH STEP: *Have you ever been disappointed when people haven't met your need to be understood? Bring all the details of your past or current heartache to the One who knows you intimately, understands you fully and loves you completely.*

—*Sharon Hinck*

NOVEMBER 29

"His master said to him, 'Well done, good and faithful servant.
You have been faithful over a little; I will set you over much.
Enter into the joy of your master.'" Matthew 25:21 (ESV)

I was having lunch one day with a friend and she told me a story that reminded me of the above verse. She said that she had taken her eighty-five-year-old mother-in-law to the doctor that morning. Because the older woman is in such poor health, it took much longer getting out of the house, to the doctor, in and out of the office, and back home than one might think. By the time it was over, a simple trip had taken the better part of the day.

My friend said that when they arrived back home, her mother-in-law had tears in her eyes. She said, "Thank you for taking me. I am sorry it took so long. I know you have better things to do with your time than this."

My friend's response was through tears as well. She said the Lord gave her the words to say, "Mother, I have nothing more important to do with my time than to take care of you. It is a privilege to be with you during this time of life."

When Jesus related the parable of the good and faithful servant in Matthew, I believe one of His points was to emphasize the value of little things. So often we tend to think of what is spiritual or important in grandiose terms, but in this parable, as well as in the life of Jesus, we see that the little things were often what concerned Him.

I believe there was no greater thing my friend could have done with her time that day than to minister to her mother-in-law. She won't get her name in the paper for it; in fact, no one much will ever know. But Jesus does, and for our faithfulness in little things, He says, "Enter into the joy of the Master."

FAITH STEP: *What "little thing" has Jesus assigned to you today? Do it with joy in your heart, knowing He sees and is delighted by your faithfulness.*

—*Gwen Ford Faulkenberry*

NOVEMBER 30

*"Let anyone among you who is without sin be
the first to throw a stone." John 8:7 (NRSV)*

I want to be slow to judge and quick to forgive. It is so easy to blame,
to censure, to disapprove of someone's behavior. It is arrogant to believe I
am on a moral high road. It is an illusion, this transitory pang of superior-
ity. As Romans 3:23 says, "For all have sinned and fall short of the glory
of God."

The Samaritan woman at the well in John 4:1–26 had had five husbands
and was currently living with a man who was not her husband. There was
plenty for Jesus to condemn in her behavior. Yet what did He talk about?
Living water, eternal life and worshiping the Father. His goal was to have
her change her heart and her actions and follow Him.

I must focus my eyes on forgiveness and telling others about Jesus, not
on finding fault, placing blame and harboring a critical spirit. I want to live
in the light of His love and mercy and remember that I am not without sin.

FAITH STEP: *Be aware today of the times you are tempted to judge someone for
their looks, behavior or attitude. Turn away from judgment.*

— *Judy Baer*

December

DECEMBER 1

"You show that you are a letter from Christ, the result of our ministry, written not with ink but with the Spirit of the living God, not on tablets of stone but on tablets of human hearts." 2 Corinthians 3:3 (NIV)

Christmas letters are subject to some bad press—teased for their predictable content: a résumé of each child's achievements, a collage of photos of people only vaguely remembered, or glitter-sprinkled tales of "here's what happened this year." I've sent and received each of those over the years. Still, I love Christmas letters. They always speak to me about our human condition.

Whether the letters are full of delightful vacations and career accomplishments, or the somber news of illness and death, they are always scented with a hint of bewilderment.

Has another year really gone by already?

When did our children grow from cuddly babies into college students?

How do we pick up the pieces now that a dear one passed away?

Why does life change so much?

As the letter progresses, that bewilderment often leads to a shift of focus and a beautiful testimony of faith. Yes, the year was full of births and deaths, vacations and layoffs, delights and horrors. Yes, time is grinding past at a relentless pace. But above it all, God is unfolding His plan. For the universe. For our lives.

I see glimmers of that unfolding each time I press open the creases of another Christmas letter. Friends give testimony to it in large fonts.

Life doesn't stand still while we struggle to make sense of it all, so breathing deep of the wonder, confusion and challenges that we all face is a comfort—as is the reminder that Christ brings meaning to all the ups and downs that fill each year. We are living letters to each other, sharing the beautiful story God is writing with our lives.

FAITH STEP: *Write a letter today, and share a way Christ has written on your life through His Spirit.*

—*Sharon Hinck*

DECEMBER 2

"And a woman was there who had been subject to bleeding for twelve years. She had suffered a great deal under the care of many doctors and had spent all she had, yet instead of getting better she grew worse. When she heard about Jesus, she came up behind him in the crowd and touched his cloak, because she thought, 'If I just touch his clothes, I will be healed.' Immediately her bleeding stopped and she felt in her body that she was freed from her suffering." Mark 5:25–29 (NIV)

This woman tiptoes up behind Jesus, touching Him secretly. Why? Because her bold move would have violated Jewish purity laws. A woman in her condition (or every woman's monthly condition) was considered unclean. She risked her life to touch this rabbi. But she's desperate and faith-filled, so she sneaks up in the crowd.

Immediately, she's "freed from her suffering." Healed! Even better, Jesus says, eventually, "Daughter, your faith has healed you. Go in peace and be freed from your suffering" (Mark 5:34, NIV).

The phrase is repeated: "freed from suffering." The one who was an outcast, taken advantage of by unscrupulous doctors, is now restored. Jesus calls her daughter—He values her. But what brought about her healing? Jesus did not come looking for her. She, with bold faith, sought Him out.

Are you, like this woman, debilitated not only by physical pain but also by shame? Where are you longing for freedom?

So many times when I've suffered emotional or physical pain, I find myself withdrawing, sitting in a corner waiting for Jesus to come and find me and perhaps join my pity party. This woman shows me another path: to risk, to take action, to seek Jesus, and to have the faith that will set me free.

FAITH STEP: *What specific situation is causing you pain or shame? What steps do you need to take to seek Jesus' healing touch? Where do you long to be freed? Talk to Jesus, and ask for His guidance as you take steps to be freed from your suffering.*

—Keri Wyatt Kent

DECEMBER 3

"The Lord thundered from heaven; the voice of the Most High resounded. He shot his arrows and scattered the enemy, with great bolts of lightning he routed them. The valleys of the sea were exposed and the foundations of the earth laid bare at your rebuke, Lord, at the blast of breath from your nostrils." Psalm 18:13–15 (NIV)

"*N*ot again," I muttered as the gruesome scene flashed on the TV screen. Advertising that show during early evening hours, when small children are still awake? Seriously?

Thankful my own children's attention was briefly diverted, I grabbed the remote and jabbed the Power button. They certainly didn't need to be exposed to haunting images at their young age. I certainly didn't need that kind of input either, for that matter.

However, the scene I glimpsed of fictitious evil got me thinking about the battles I can't see between Jesus and real evil. When I need a reminder of Warrior Jesus behind-the-scenes, I turn to Psalm 18, a passage I've loved for a long time.

I'm encouraged by filling my mind with true images of my Defender's ultimate power over evil. When it comes to rescuing His own, God moves heaven and earth, tearing down any stronghold that threatens the soul-security of those who shelter in His Son Jesus' saving grace.

While I revel in knowing that He is absolutely safe for me because I am His, I shudder to think of how dangerous He is to those who stand against Him. There truly is no greater safety and no greater danger than Jesus, depending on which side a person chooses to be on.

Nothing stops Him. Even Satan knows he can't stop Jesus. He hates that truth and continues to attempt to gain control—but he knows he is defeated.

May we understand that fact as much as God's enemies do.

FAITH STEP: *Read Psalm 18.*

—Erin Keeley Marshall

DECEMBER 4

"Soon afterward Jesus went with his disciples to the village of Nain, and a large crowd followed him. A funeral procession was coming out as he approached the village gate. The young man who had died was a widow's only son, and a large crowd from the village was with her. When the Lord saw her, his heart overflowed with compassion. 'Don't cry!' he said. Then he walked over to the coffin and touched it, and the bearers stopped. 'Young man,' he said, 'I tell you, get up.' Then the dead boy sat up and began to talk! And Jesus gave him back to his mother." Luke 7:11–15 (NLT)

About a year ago, a friend of mine lost her son to leukemia. He was only sixteen, and the loss was harsh, tragic, inexplicable. I read passages like this one, where Jesus thwarts death, and think—my friend is a deeply committed Christian, and she and hundreds of other people prayed for her son—why didn't Jesus intervene?

At the same time her son was ill, two other teenage girls I knew also had cancer. Both those girls were successfully treated, and are doing well. Why did Jesus heal them, but not my friend's son? My friend prayed just as much.

There may have been, in the village of Nain, other children who died that day or that year. Jesus did not, as far as we know, raise them from the dead. But when He sees a woman who will be devastated not only emotionally but also financially, Jesus is overcome with emotion.

Even if we have not lost a child, all of us experience grief and loss in this life. Sometimes Jesus intervenes, but sometimes, healing won't happen until we're in heaven. But this is what Jesus is like: He cares about all people—men and women. His heart overflows with compassion.

FAITH STEP: *Do you know someone who is grieving? How could you act as Jesus would, and let your heart overflow with compassion toward them? What specifically can you do to comfort them?*

—*Keri Wyatt Kent*

DECEMBER 5

*"I am the vine; you are the branches. If you remain in me and I in you,
you will bear much fruit; apart from me you can do nothing.... You did not
choose me, but I chose you and appointed you so that you might go and bear
fruit—fruit that will last—and so that whatever you ask in my name the
Father will give you." John 15:5,16 (NIV)*

*B*eing a homemaker is challenging because nothing lasts. I can fold
piles of clothes and when I turn around, a new pile of dirty laundry has appeared. Minutes after washing and drying the last dish and wiping down
the kitchen counter, someone strolls into the kitchen looking for a snack.
Perhaps because I've been a homemaker for many years, the phrase "fruit
that will last" stirs a deep longing in me. When so much of my day centers
around fleeting accomplishments, I'm all the more aware of how precious
it is to invest my time and energy in efforts that have eternal value.

That's why Jesus' invitation means so much to me. First, He explained
that if we remain in Him—a branch connected to the vine that holds and
nourishes it—we will produce much fruit. In our culture of busy activity,
this may not sound like an earth-shattering promise. We already feel like
we produce much. However, Jesus goes further and promises that the fruit
He brings through our lives will last.

Remaining in Him, we can reflect His love to others, encourage hearts
to worship Him, share His grace with those who haven't met Him yet—all
blessings that will resonate into eternity. In fact, as He produces fruit in
our lives, even the repetitive and ordinary tasks become part of the eternal
purpose. Folding laundry is no longer a never-ending and futile task, but
a way to model a servant heart. Writing reports at work is no longer busy-
work, but a place to practice diligence and build relationships.

Since we are grafted on to the vine of Jesus, everywhere we go, we bring
Him to a hungry world needing His fruit.

FAITH STEP: *What activities that are a necessary part of your life feel like they
have no lasting value? Can you look for ways Jesus might use them for His kingdom?*

—*Sharon Hinck*

DECEMBER 6

Reverence for God adds hours to each day. Proverbs 10:27 (TLB)

*A*t this moment in time we're preparing to move into a new house, I am under book deadline, and I have four children—including a very busy one-year-old. If I were to have an excuse not to take time to be with Jesus, this week would be it. Staying up every night until midnight, packing during the day and chasing a baby, you'd think I'd cherish every extra moment of sleep.

Yet my eyes still pop open in the morning. Not because I'm wide awake, but rather because my heart is hungry. I need Jesus. I need to read His Word and spend time with Him. After years of loving Jesus, my heart reveres Him. I stand in awe of what a difference spending time with Him makes in my life.

In Jesus' arithmetic, "subtracting" time from our busy day multiplies the potential of every moment. Because of our time with Him we have a clearer vision, a more peaceful heart and a more joyful spirit. When I spend time with Jesus, I better discern what to spend my time on. My day seems to work better, and in the way Jesus works the hours of the day seem to multiply too.

This week is busy, yes, but when I spend time with my Lord I can make it through the day better than I anticipated I could.

FAITH STEP: *Find at least two other times during the day to get away with Jesus. Think about times like the ten minutes when your biscuits are baking at dinnertime or the fifteen-minute break you have at work. Afterward, consider how that time focused on Jesus impacted the rest of your day.*

—*Tricia Goyer*

DECEMBER 7

"Happy are people who show mercy, because
they will receive mercy." Matthew 5:7 (CEB)

The word mercy brings to mind "the least of these"—the poor, unfortunate and marginalized. I think of people who are essentially victims in my mind, people who've had a tough time—homeless people or starving children in Africa.

Certainly, people who are disadvantaged deserve to be shown God's mercy. Jesus tells us that what we give is what we will get, when it comes to being merciful. And while we all want mercy shown to us, it's harder to show it to others.

But what if we're to show mercy not only to the downtrodden, but also to our enemies? Jesus has been challenging me lately to show mercy to people who criticize me. Who wrongly and unfairly attack me, persecute me, bother me. What would it look like to show mercy to the person who gossips about us at work, the extended family member who criticizes our decisions or tries to boss us around, or the "perfect" mom at the PTA meeting whose passive-aggressive comments make us feel small?

Extending mercy, especially to those who don't deserve it, is something we cannot do on our own. We need Jesus to help us. But when we do it, with His help, it brings us an amazing feeling of empowerment and joy.

The Greek word translated "blessed" in most versions and "happy" in this one is makarizo, meaning supremely blessed, fortunate, happy and well-off. I want that, but the question is, am I willing to walk the tough path that will bring me that blessing? Am I willing to love my enemies, to show mercy without expecting reciprocity, to leave justice in God's hands?

FAITH STEP: *Think of someone who has wronged or hurt you. Write a letter (you don't have to send it) to that person, forgiving them and showing them mercy.*

—*Keri Wyatt Kent*

DECEMBER 8

"Hezekiah trusted in the Lord, the God of Israel. There was no one like him among all the kings of Judah, either before him or after him. He held fast to the Lord and did not stop following him; he kept the commands the Lord had given Moses." 2 Kings 18:5–6 (NIV)

*E*ver have one of those days when you feel extraordinarily unremarkable? Maybe you woke up, looked in the mirror and decided it'd take too much work to feel good about yourself, so you crawled back into bed. Or maybe later in the day you couldn't find your groove in a meeting, and you felt your colleagues looking at you quizzically, as if they too knew you weren't all there.

We've all been there. It's human nature to want to feel special, one-of-a-kind, irreplaceable. Unfortunately, it's also human nature to doubt all that.

I love what 2 Kings says about King Hezekiah. Among the Old Testament list of kings and their failures and accomplishments, a good one stands out. Hezekiah was one such standout. In fact, "there was no one like him among all the kings of Judah."

In wondering what qualities made him excel, it's amazing to note what's said of him before and after that statement: "Hezekiah trusted in the Lord" and "he held fast to the Lord and did not stop following him; he kept the commands the Lord had given Moses."

Hezekiah was one-of-a-kind because he walked closely with God. As in our modern society, living by the Lord's ways was rare in Hezekiah's time.

Jesus also stood out on earth, but not because of any outward features. (See Isaiah 53:2.) The pure, holy, loving character of His heavenly Father shined through Him and brightened the world wherever He went.

Godliness is a beautifier and the measure of success that counts. How freeing to know that Jesus makes standouts of us when we follow Him.

FAITH STEP: *How is simple, pure faith remarkable to you? Live a remarkable day by focusing on Jesus' priorities for you, namely living and loving like He does.*

—*Erin Keeley Marshall*

DECEMBER 9

"See what great love the Father has lavished on us, that we should be called children of God! And that is what we are!" 1 John 3:1 (NIV)

It is 6:48 am, the exact time my children have determined they must walk out the door in order to catch the bus each morning. I send them off with words, since teenagers rarely tolerate a hug good-bye that early in the day.

"Have a good day," I tell them. "Good luck on your math test. I'll be praying for you."

I watch them, two coltlike blond teenagers in black parkas, their long legs striding down the sidewalk, ready to break into a gallop if they see the bus at the corner. I watch them, still sort of amazed that they are no longer babies. They move relentlessly toward adulthood and independence.

There's a pull in my heart when I see my kids—whether they are leaving for school, playing sports or just hanging out at home. Even when my kids misbehave or are difficult, I love them. It sometimes overwhelms me.

We are God's children: loved, chosen. We are not an inconvenience to Him. His love is extravagant; He has lavished it upon us. We do not have to pry scraps of affection from God's clenched fist. He pours it out with abundance. Because of Jesus, He has adopted us as His own.

The way we love our kids on our best, most unselfish day—that's not even close to how much God loves us, all the time. Now, loving my kids does not mean indulging their every whim. In fact, sometimes love means setting limits, telling them "no."

God's love is much the same—it sustains and holds us. It sometimes sets limits. The struggles of this life do not negate God's love for me, any more than the struggles my children face negate my love for them.

FAITH STEP: *Today, spend some time being quiet with God, receiving the love He wants to lavish upon you. Remember that, as His beloved child, you don't have to earn His favor.*

—*Keri Wyatt Kent*

DECEMBER 10

"As Jesus and his disciples were on their way, he came to a village where a woman named Martha opened her home to him. She had a sister called Mary, who sat at the Lord's feet listening to what he said." Luke 10:38–39 (TNIV)

I always felt a bit sorry for Martha, maybe because I am a Martha. I'm the organized one, getting things done, making sure the household runs smoothly. I don't do well with spontaneity or last-minute changes. If I ask you to do something, I am trusting you'll do it, and if you don't, it messes everything up for me.

I read this story and want to say, "Well, Jesus obviously doesn't know what's going on in the kitchen. If I were Martha, I'd tell Him that it's fine if Mary doesn't help me, but I don't want to hear any whining from Him when it's nine o'clock at night and dinner still isn't ready."

But I realize that Jesus isn't saying we should also allow the dishes to pile up in the sink while we read our Bibles together. He's talking about priorities.

Mary's first priority was Jesus. She could have picked better timing, in my opinion—like maybe after she'd done her work in the kitchen—but in putting Jesus first in her life, it enabled her to make better choices in other areas and to form better relationships with people, even her annoyed sister.

If you put Jesus first in your life, even over your love for your husband, it makes your marriage stronger. If you put Jesus first over your children, it enables you to raise them with more wisdom and love. If you put Jesus over the other things in your life that are important to you—like Martha's obsession with the perfect dinner party—then the important things are put into perspective and become even better.

FAITH STEP: *Where are you not putting Jesus first in your life? Over what areas? Pray for wisdom in rearranging your priorities. Choose what's better, and it won't be taken away from you.*

—Camy Tang

DECEMBER 11

"Listen! A sower went out to sow. And as he sowed, some seed fell on the path, and the birds came and ate it up. Other seed fell on rocky ground, where it did not have much soil and it sprang up quickly, since it had no depth of soil. And when the sun rose, it was scorched; and since it had no root, it withered away. Other seed fell among the thorns, and the thorns grew up and choked it, and it yielded no grain. Other seed fell into good ground and brought forth grain." Mark 4:3–8 (NRSV)

I mean to be good, rich, productive ground, but lately my days have been so hectic and demanding. There's driving the kids to school, being room mother, my job, making meals, cleaning the house, shopping, going to the gym, having my hair done, spending time with friends and family. I volunteer at the food pantry every week and drive my mother-in-law to her doctor appointments. That leaves little time for Bible study and fellowship. Sometimes it's difficult to squeeze in more than a few quick prayers during the day. I'm so busy.

But those things are thorns, aren't they? Thorns that choke out whatever I'm trying to do in the name of the Lord. I put them first and they squeeze out any time I might spend with Him. I've got it backward. If I don't put Jesus first in my day, I'll produce nothing of value. I've packed my days with activity, much of it for worldly pursuits. An overcrowded life chokes out what my Savior is trying to say to me. I'm deafened by the din of my own existence.

FAITH STEP: *Today, give up one chore, one hour, one thing on your to-do list and sit with Jesus. Be still and know that He is God.*

DECEMBER 12

"Woe to you, teachers of the law and Pharisees, you hypocrites! You give a tenth of your spices—mint, dill and cumin. But you have neglected the more important matters of the law—justice, mercy and faithfulness. You should have practiced the latter, without neglecting the former." Matthew 23:23 (NIV)

I grew up in a home where tithing was normal. When I got my first real job at age sixteen, my dad sat me down and told me that the money was, of course, mine to use as I saw fit. But, he said, he wanted to tell me that over the years, he had always tithed, that he recommended it, and that God promised to bless the generous. This made sense to me, and I made a habit of giving ten percent of all I earned.

My husband's family did not practice tithing, for many reasons. So during the early years of our marriage, we had a lot of fights about the amount of money we would give away. I felt quite self-righteous, accused my husband of not trusting God, and so on. I was, in Jesus' words, neglecting the more important matters. I cannot ignore Jesus' condemnation of the Pharisees, because they are also His words to me. They are included in the gospel story because they are His words to all human beings, flawed as we are.

Through this verse, Jesus gently reminded me that tithing is an important discipline, but the way that I treat people—including my husband—is equally important. And writing checks is only a small part of what it means to follow Him. Was I doing anything for victims of injustice? Was I being merciful, even to those I disagreed with? Was I being faithful to God's calling—not only with my money but also with my life?

FAITH STEP: *This verse tells us we should practice justice, mercy and faithfulness. Write down one specific action you will take this week in each of these areas.*

—Keri Wyatt Kent

DECEMBER 13

"Happy are you when people insult you and harass you and speak all kinds of bad and false things about you, all because of me. Be full of joy and be glad, because you have a great reward in heaven." Matthew 5:11–12 (CEB)

*A*lthough America is becoming an increasingly secular culture, we do not experience the level of persecution that many Christians endure. In countries all around the world Christians are jailed and beaten, raped, denied access to jobs, harassed and treated unjustly.

Jesus' point is not that we go out looking for persecution. Rather, we should ask whether we follow Jesus enough that we stand out from the culture around us. How do we handle the small struggles in our lives, or how do we react when things don't go our way? Are we faithful in small things?

Based on this verse, I wonder what sort of life Jesus was expecting His followers would live.

I have found that the greatest persecution I've endured—and it was minor, believe me—came from other Christians, from people who have publicly critiqued my theology, criticized what I've written, misunderstood and twisted my words, never coming to me personally to talk it over. I realize it goes with the territory of being a writer and sharing your ideas with the world, but it's still painful.

Many of us, myself included, go to great lengths to avoid suffering. We expend more energy avoiding suffering than it would take to simply endure it. What we forget is that suffering has the potential to transform us.

But suffering for its own sake is pointless. Jesus said suffering blesses us when we suffer "because of him." In *The Life You've Always Wanted*, John Ortberg writes, "Suffering alone does not produce perseverance, only suffering that is endured somehow in faith."

FAITH STEP: *Where have you faced insults and persecution because of Jesus? If this hasn't happened in your life, why do you think that is?*

—Keri Wyatt Kent

DECEMBER 14

"Now Moses was tending the flock of Jethro his father-in-law, the priest of Midian, and he led the flock to the far side of the wilderness and came to Horeb, the mountain of God. There the angel of the Lord appeared to him in flames of fire from within a bush." Exodus 3:1–2 (TNIV)

*M*oses actually spoke to God on a mountaintop and received his commission from the Lord. He had seen astounding things that both frightened and amazed him. Then he had to climb down the mountain, back to his ordinary life, and follow the instructions God had given to him. He made drastic changes, leaving his home and traveling to Egypt, overcoming his insecurities.

Peter, James and John also had their mountaintop experience with Jesus, seeing Him for who He truly is. Yet they had to go back to the other disciples, to the things that were still the same, even though they themselves were now different.

Have you had a mountaintop experience? Maybe at a retreat or a special place? Do you remember that feeling of being amazed and close to Jesus, of being transformed from the inside out?

But then you had to go back to your regular life. The mountaintop feeling faded. Your will to obey grew weaker. You faced obstacles and fear.

This happens to all of us, young and old alike. The trick is to not forget what you promised to Jesus while on that mountaintop, even when the feeling has faded, and then to keep your promise. This is the most important moment—not the moment you made the promise while on the mountaintop, but in this moment, if you'll decide to still do what Jesus asks, when things are hard.

FAITH STEP: *What was your last mountaintop moment? What did you decide in that moment? Has your resolve wavered? Strengthen it. Write down what you intend to do on an index card and keep it in your purse to remind you. Jesus still wants your obedience even when you're not on the mountaintop anymore.*

–Camy Tang

DECEMBER 15

"For to us a child is born, to us a son is given, and the government will be on his shoulders. And he will be called Wonderful Counselor, Mighty God, Everlasting Father, Prince of Peace." Isaiah 9:6 (NIV)

*W*hen my children were young, I sometimes despaired of peace. I'd set the supper table envisioning uplifting conversations about our day, but by the time I'd dished up the casserole, the battles began.

"His chair is too close to mine."

"She got more French fries than me."

"Tell him to stop breathing so loud."

"I get the computer first after supper."

Instead of the grace and love I hoped to instill in my family, my efforts to bring reconciliation and understanding usually resulted in more accusations, cries for justice and pouting.

My frustrating attempts to mediate family squabbles showed me how difficult it is to bring peace. On my own, I couldn't create peace between my children, or peace in my marriage, or even peace within my own thoughts. And I certainly couldn't create reconciliation with God.

Every interaction in my life makes me realize how much I need Jesus, the Prince of Peace. I love this description of the promised Savior in Isaiah. "Mighty" and "Everlasting" reflect His power, and "Counselor" reminds me of His gentle wisdom. Only Jesus has the perfect combination as both God and man to be the Prince of Peace. He's strong enough to solve the problems too big for me, and merciful enough to give His life to restore me.

FAITH STEP: *Is there a lack of peace in an area of your life? An inner conflict, strained relationship or even a barrier in your walk with God? Invite Jesus to be your Prince of Peace, and bring both His power and His love to that situation.*

—Sharon Hinck

DECEMBER 16

"Blessed is she who has believed that the Lord
would fulfill his promises to her!" Luke 1:45 (NIV)

As a child I pictured Jesus' mother as sweet, gentle, caring—nearly perfect. Out of all the women in the world God picked her, right? She had to be someone special. As I've spent more time in God's Word I've discovered she's special for one reason most of all: Mary believed. In a song from her heart, Mary says:

> "My soul glorifies the Lord
> and my spirit rejoices in God my Savior,
> for he has been mindful
> of the humble state of his servant.
> From now on all generations will call me blessed,
> for the Mighty One has done great things for me—
> holy is his name."
> Luke 1:46–49 (NIV)

Mary's belief was where it should have been: on God. She accepted her role. She thanked God for her mission. And because of her belief generations of people have called her blessed and have thought of her as someone special.

This makes me wonder what things my disbelief causes me to miss out on. Only one woman was chosen to be Jesus' mother, but God has great missions designed for each of us. We simply need to realize He loves us most of all, His plans are perfect, and we can be part of those plans if we focus not on what we're lacking but rather on what He's offering.

FAITH STEP: *No one is perfect, yet God wants to do great things through us if we choose to believe Him and follow His plan for us. What has Jesus asked you to do for Him? Are you willing to do it? To be called by God means He sees you as special in His sight. Have faith today to embrace Jesus' call and His special plan for you.*

—*Tricia Goyer*

DECEMBER 17

"When they saw the star, they were filled with joy! They entered the house and saw the child with his mother, Mary, and they bowed down and worshiped him. Then they opened their treasure chests and gave him gifts of gold, frankincense, and myrrh." Matthew 2:10–11 (NLT)

*O*ur culture, unfortunately, misunderstands giving. We think of it, honestly, as trading. I get you something, you get me something—hopefully we spend about the same amount of money so no one feels awkward. We all know that panicked feeling when a friend shows up at our door in December with a wrapped package in her hand, and we realize we didn't get anything for them. We now feel we "owe" them a gift. I've read articles in women's magazines that suggest keeping a wrapped stash of generic gifts in your front closet for such unexpected occasions. Kind of takes the meaning out of it, doesn't it?

Imagine if the wise men had thought this way: "I wonder what Mary and Joseph will give us. Do you think they'll know we got this frankincense on clearance at T.J. Maxx?" Of course not. And did Mary, seeing these strange gifts, think, "Okay, gold, that works for me. But spices you normally use for burial? What kind of baby gift is that? And it's so awkward that I have nothing to give them in return!"

Jesus and His family simply received their gifts without any concern for what they would give back. The Magi likewise seemed unconcerned with reciprocity—it was enough to find and worship a king they'd seen declared in the night sky years before.

In the same way, we can never give something equal in value to God's Christmas gift—Jesus. He is a gift we must humbly receive.

FAITH STEP: *Spend some time thinking about God's generous gift of His Son. How can you be generous to others in the way God has been generous to you?*

—Keri Wyatt Kent

DECEMBER 18

"And the shepherds returned, glorifying and praising God for all the things they had heard and seen, just as it had been told them." Luke 2:20 (AMP)

*E*ven though some of my best teen memories were of spring breaks spent at church youth camp, some of my worse experiences came in the months that followed. At camp, everyone loved Jesus—or so it seemed. We worshipped three times a day and heard messages of Jesus' love at least twice. I usually attended with other teens from my church, who were very different from my friends at school. Ones I wished I could be around every day. I experienced Jesus' love so strongly at camp, and returning to normal life was hard. It was like flying back to a Montana winter after a Florida vacation and trying to stay warm from the memory of the sunshine for months and months.

I can imagine the challenge the shepherds faced after they returned from seeing Jesus was a little like imagining the sun's warmth while shoveling snow on an overcast Montana day. The angel choir in the night sky was only a memory. They'd left the little baby back at a stable in Bethlehem. But, the one thing they did have was each other. "Do you remember?" "Can you believe it?" "Wow, the baby was there just like the angels said." "Seriously, the Son of God." I bet they glorified and praised Jesus the rest of their lives over that one.

It's a good reminder to surround ourselves with those who've experienced what we've experienced—the miracle of Jesus entering our lives. Experiences with Jesus shouldn't be spring-break high points. Instead they should be lived out and talked about with friends.

FAITH STEP: *Is there a special friend you haven't talked to in a while? Add his or her name to your to-do list and find a way to connect and to hear about what Jesus is doing in each other's lives.*

—Tricia Goyer

DECEMBER 19

"'The virgin will conceive and give birth to a son, and they will call him Immanuel' (which means 'God with us')." Matthew 1:23 (TNIV)

One summer, I did a Bible study on the names of God. The one name out of all of them that seemed especially important was Jesus' name, Immanuel. God had several names throughout history, but for His Son, He chose "God with us." He didn't choose "God who sees" or "the Lord my rock" or "God almighty."

Instead, He chose, "I am with you."

I am with you when you interview for that job. I am with you when you first fall in love. I am with you when you grieve over a lost loved one. I am with you when you celebrate your birthday. I am with you when you get into that car accident. I am with you when you hold your child in your arms—I am holding you too.

I am with you always, to the very end of the age.

There are times we feel all alone, but Jesus' name—His very essence—promises that He's with us, even if we don't feel Him. He's there to protect us. He's there to teach us. He's there to comfort us. He's there to guide us.

The way we live our lives should be different because Jesus is with us. We can be stronger, bolder, more loving. Our God is not up in the heavens looking down. Our God is right here with us.

FAITH STEP: *Are you feeling alone right now? Pray and ask Jesus to help you remember He's with you. Then write down things you can do to live more boldly because you know He's with you every step of the way.*

—Camy Tang

DECEMBER 20

" 'Choose life and not death!'... The people remained silent
and said nothing in reply, because the king had commanded,
'Do not answer him.' " 2 Kings 18:32, 36 (NIV)

*S*ad to say, but more and more we hear of bullies messing with kids at school. Bullies have been around forever, and they're not going anywhere soon, at least not until Jesus returns to destroy all wickedness and sin forever.

Sometimes bullies' actions can be blatant. But just as cruel, and more devious, are the ways some bullies twist words to get us doubting our faith and all we know to be true about Jesus. From the first bully—the serpent in the Garden of Eden—God's enemies have taken aim at His people by manipulating words to sound truthful. And those words can be more deadly than fists.

Eve allowed herself to get sucked into an entire conversation with her greatest enemy about what was really true. She had already heard the truth directly from God. What if she had turned her back on the serpent and refused to engage at his level? Unfortunately, she chose to hang around and chat, opening the door to be manipulated by something that sounded good.

Much later, but still back in Old Testament days, King Hezekiah showed great wisdom in commanding his people not to answer their enemies who tried to create doubt that God could save his nation. The people were vulnerable, having suffered horrendously during a long siege. They were desperate for their lives. But engaging the enemy's "wisdom" would have ended in devastation.

Like King Hezekiah, Jesus encourages people to choose life by choosing to believe in him: "I am the way and the truth and the life. No one comes to the Father except through me" (John 14:6, NIV).

Don't open the door to be deceived or manipulated by Satan's lies. Listen only to Jesus, the Source of truth.

FAITH STEP: *What lies have you heard that sound like truth? How does the Bible answer that "bully" of mistruth?*

—Erin Keeley Marshall

DECEMBER 21

"And have you completely forgotten this word of encouragement that addresses you as children? It says, 'My son, do not make light of the Lord's discipline, and do not lose heart when he rebukes you, because the Lord disciplines those he loves, and he chastens everyone he accepts as his child.'" Hebrews 12:5–6 (TNIV)

*I*f you never disciplined your child, he would be a spoiled rotten brat. He'd be destructive, whiney and all-around selfish. Your discipline teaches him consideration and kindness, and makes him into a better person.

It's the same way with us and Jesus. He needs to discipline us to help us become better people. Sometimes it's a word from someone to tell us when we've done something wrong. Sometimes it's a conviction by the Holy Spirit when we're reading the Bible or sitting in church. It's not pleasant, but it molds us into people Jesus can use.

I think that's why He talks about us taking His yoke upon ourselves. Being yoked to Jesus teaches us when we're going too fast or too slow, or when we're heading in the wrong direction. He's disciplining us so that we learn how to work with Him, yet at the same time, He's sharing the load because the yoke is on Him too.

So rather than complaining about our discipline or our hardships, why not try thanking Jesus for them? They're molding us into better children of God, and Jesus is bearing His share of our load too.

FAITH STEP: *Write down all the hardships you're going through right now. Then go down the list and thank Jesus for each one. Open your heart to what Jesus might be saying to you about these things.*

—Camy Tang

DECEMBER 22

"Have I not commanded you? Be strong and of good courage;
do not be afraid, nor be dismayed, for the Lord your God is
with you wherever you go." Joshua 1:9 (NKJV)

*A*s I prayed for a friend this morning the above verse came to mind, and the phrase, "with you" became my meditation. I'd been searching for a word of encouragement to share with my friend, and there it was, like a gentle whisper. Two words: With you.

My friend's son was injured by an IED explosion in Afghanistan this week. She called me after receiving the news, and hour by hour we've kept in touch as events unfolded and more information became available. After a couple of harrowing days of waiting, she flies out today to be with him at his bedside in a military hospital. Though so ready to be near him, she is afraid of what she will see when she walks into his room.

"With you" is a comfort on so many levels. As I shared these words with my friend, we marveled at how they express her soul's longing—just to be with her son, to rush to his side and pour into him every ounce of strength and love a mother's heart can hold. She is limited by what the military allows, and subject to military timing. And yet Jesus has no such limits. He is with her, and with her son—always.

FAITH STEP: *This promise gives my friend courage in her situation. As you spend this morning with Jesus, take courage in the promise that He is with you as well.*

—*Gwen Ford Faulkenberry*

DECEMBER 23

*"Let Your mercy, O Lord, be upon us, just
as we hope in You." Psalm 33:22 (NKJV)*

This morning I attended the funeral of an old high school friend. I remember him as a "teddy bear," the kind of guy who always smiled and joked, a person you just wanted to hug. Everybody loved him. And yet his death these twenty years after high school was a suicide. The act of one completely hopeless, utterly lost.

It has been years since I last saw him. Sitting in the funeral home today it was impossible for me to reconcile the jolly person I knew as a kid with this man in deep darkness. I looked into the faces of his children and felt anger, confusion and, most of all, sorrow. What pushes a person to the point of total despair?

Life can be hard. That's a given. I don't know the details of my friend's journey, but I suspect he had some difficult times along the way. I've heard drugs were a part of his recent demise, which seems consistent with a need to escape reality.

What became so clear to me as I processed his passing is that hope makes the difference between life and death. It's what my friend lacked— and what the whole world needs. I'm not talking about "dreams" or "wishes," those words that sound nice but slip through our fingers like sand when life lets us down. True hope, the kind that never disappoints, is found in Jesus. When it comes down to it, we can always count on Him.

FAITH STEP: *Have you lost hope in a certain area? Remember, Jesus will never fail you. Renew your hope in Him today, and see His mercy rain down over your life.*

—*Gwen Ford Faulkenberry*

DECEMBER 24

"But be sure to fear the Lord and serve him faithfully with all your heart; consider what great things he has done for you." I Samuel 12:24 (TNIV)

The other day, I drove to the grocery store, fought my way through the crowded parking lot, and slid my car into a stall. I tiptoed through water puddles and entered the store, picking up a basket at the side of the door as I walked toward a table loaded with brownie bites and apple streusel bars. And then I stopped.

I couldn't remember why I had needed to come to the grocery store.

Now I fully understood my parents' bemoaning how their memories were fading away the older they got. I stood in confusion just inside the front doors, then started wandering down the aisles, trying to remember. I knew it was important, but I couldn't even say if it was meat or vegetable or dairy that I needed. After twenty minutes, I drove home and then remembered I had needed to pick up sour cream for the beef stroganoff I was cooking for dinner. And yes, I drove back to the store to get it.

When I was younger, I didn't understand why God was constantly telling people to remember what He'd done for them. Now I do. It's easier than we realize for us to forget the spectacular blessings and work of the Lord. Even Jesus had to remind His disciples about feeding the five thousand with five loaves of bread, when I would have thought they'd surely remember.

FAITH STEP: *Take a moment now to remember what Jesus has done for you. Coming to earth in human form. The cross. Any momentous or minuscule things He's done in your life. Cling to those memories and use them to worship Him.*

—Camy Tang

DECEMBER 25

"But as for me, I will enter Your house through the abundance
of Your steadfast love and mercy; I will worship…in
reverent fear and awe of You." Psalm 5:7 (AMP)

I love that verse. And I think the reason I love it so much is that I often come to the Lord empty. Empty-handed, like a beggar clad in filthy rags, and also empty down in my soul, with a painful longing to be satisfied, and yet the knowledge that I have absolutely nothing to offer in the exchange. There's not a single, solitary reason He would want to let me enter His house. And yet. The Bible says I can enter through the abundance of His steadfast love and mercy.

I picture myself, this grubby pauper lifting a stained hand to knock on the door. But even before I can knock, the door is thrown open wide and my Father steps forward to greet me.

This relationship is a great mystery: how we can be loved with the familiarity of a family, totally secure knowing He is always with us and yet loved by a holy being who's so very different from us. His ways are past finding out. He is high and lifted up. He is totally different—beyond our comprehension. Bono, the lead singer of U2, said: "The idea that there's a force of love and logic behind the universe is overwhelming to start with…. But the idea that that same love and logic would choose to describe itself as a baby born in…straw and poverty is genius, and brings me to my knees, literally…. I am just in awe of that…. It's the thing that makes me a believer."

When I come to the Lord, one thing He gives me in exchange for my emptiness is awe. An awe that someone like Him would come to earth in order to save someone like me. What a mystery. What a Savior!

FAITH STEP: *Embrace the mystery and the miracle of Your Savior today. Remember You are a pauper no more—but a child of the King.*

—Gwen Ford Faulkenberry

DECEMBER 26

*"Therefore, since we have been made righteous through
his faithfulness combined with our faith, we have peace
with God through our Lord Jesus Christ." Romans 5:1 (CEB)*

I hate to admit this, but sometimes I nag God. Like an insistent mosquito buzzing in his ear, I whine and complain about my life. Ironically, one of the things I insistently ask for is peace.

By peace, though, I typically mean that I'd like Him to take care of things that are not easy for me, to change the behavior of people who annoy me, to get rid of my struggles.

Which probably just makes Him laugh. Jesus never promised an easy life; in fact, He told us we'd have troubles. But we can be at peace in the midst of those troubles because when our faith collides with His faithfulness, we're "made righteous" with God. He sees us differently. The things that would disrupt our relationship are gone. It is this unhindered relationship, not our circumstances, that gives us peace.

I'm learning to live in the peace that already exists in that relationship, and to pray for peace—not to erase conflict, but peace that will equip me to cope with less than ideal situations.

The word peace, which appears in all but two of the books in the New Testament, is most often used as a greeting: grace and peace to you! It describes not just an absence of conflict but harmonious relationships, and the contentment that comes from that relationship.

Jesus is the source of peace for our souls, and for our world. When we have peace in our hearts, we can be peacemakers in the world.

FAITH STEP: *Do you have peace with God through Jesus? If you have put your faith in Him, you do, even if you don't feel it all the time. What do you need to do today to live in that peace?*

—*Keri Wyatt Kent*

DECEMBER 27

"But the father said to his servants, 'Quick! Bring the best robe and put it on him. Put a ring on his finger and sandals on his feet. Bring the fattened calf and kill it. Let's have a feast and celebrate. For this son of mine was dead and is alive again; he was lost and is found.' So they began to celebrate." Luke 15:22–24 (NIV)

"There is a time for everything, and a season for every activity under the heavens: a time to be born and a time to die, a time to plant and a time to uproot, a time to kill and a time to heal, a time to tear down and a time to build," Ecclesiastes 3:1–3 (NIV)

*D*oes Jesus laugh?

There are certainly signs of His sense of humor. Parties and festivities were important in the Bible. He attended the happy affair of the wedding in Canaan and told the parable of the celebration the father threw when his prodigal son returned home. Joy is mentioned dozens of times in Scripture. I also like to think God smiled when He created the platypus.

Jesus is God but when He walked on earth He was also completely, utterly human. Why wouldn't He laugh? We are made in God's image and we have been created to laugh. It is a natural and innate thing we humans do. There's not a happier sound than that of children laughing. Surely Christians are meant to laugh, to be joyous and to celebrate the Savior who loves us.

FAITH STEP: *Bring joy and laughter into your Christian walk. Being a dour Christian does nothing to improve your witness. Let the joy of salvation that you feel on the outside, spill onto your lips and into your smile. You are saved and going to spend eternity with Jesus! Smile!*

— *Judy Baer*

DECEMBER 28

"His beloved Son, in whom we have redemption, the forgiveness of sins. He is the image of the invisible God, the firstborn of all creation." Colossians 1:13–15 (NASB)

I've always agreed with the DaySpring card that reads, "When you get down to it, all that really matters is Jesus." But who is Jesus, really? He's not easily definable; not someone we can put into a box.

C. S. Lewis writes in *The Lion, The Witch and The Wardrobe*, "[Jesus] is not a tame lion, but He's good."

The good part is easy, isn't it? It's the untamed nature of Jesus that can be a problem, at least for me. I've read a lot of writing about Jesus that comes across like a biology textbook in the sense that He seems like a fish to be dissected. If I approach Him this way He becomes so distinctly other—existentially—that the relationship we have is no longer personal.

The pendulum can also swing in the opposite direction. Some people's approach to Jesus is so personal I want to scream. I can't know another's heart or experience, but I know that Jesus is not my homeboy. He's not something I can contain. In other words, He's a good lion, but He's still a lion. And that fact demands that I approach Him with reverence and awe.

Like Lewis' Lucy Pevensie, I believe our approach to Jesus should be childlike faith. She recognized Aslan's power while still fully trusting in His goodness. At His invitation, she climbed on the back of the Lion and let Him take her wherever He wanted her to go. And it was a beautiful journey.

FAITH STEP: *Let Jesus, the Lion of Judah, take you wherever He wants you to go today.*

—Gwen Ford Faulkenberry

DECEMBER 29

*"You are the salt of the earth…. You are the light of the world.
A city on top of a hill can't be hidden." Matthew 5:13–14 (CEB)*

What does it mean to be salty? Salt flavors; salt irritates; salt disinfects. Salt actually changes things it comes in contact with: it melts ice, and it preserves food. It is not a neutral substance. Just the right amount makes food wonderfully savory, but too much renders food inedible. A salt scrub can get things clean, but salt in a wound can sting and even injure.

I want to live out this vision Jesus paints of what the lives of His followers should look like: to be salt and light. One of the biggest challenges to that is the hectic pace of our lives. For salt to change anything, it has to come in contact with it. When I keep myself too busy, I miss opportunities to be salt and light.

Imagine if someone was in darkness, and needed a light. If you had a light, but all you did was run past them on your way to church, waving your light, would that help them? Slowing down has enabled me to stop and shine the light of Jesus' love into people's lives.

One of the ways I've tried to be salt and light is to really get to know my neighbors, some of whom don't know Jesus. Serving on the PTA at my kids' grade school; joining the neighborhood bowling league or book club; taking time to just visit with my neighbors when we're out working in the yard—these provide opportunities to build relationships where I can be "salty," where I can shine light.

That doesn't mean preaching at them. It simply means loving them—by listening, by simply being a friend. Other times it might mean bringing a meal to someone who is sick. Other times, being salt and light means choosing not to do certain things—for example, to not gossip, not to bad-mouth others.

Does a light say "look at me"? Or does it simply shine?

FAITH STEP: *Spend some time in prayer and self-examination. Ask God to show you if there is any way in which you have snuffed out the light of His love or become unsalty.*

—*Keri Wyatt Kent*

DECEMBER 30

"How great is your goodness, which you have stored up for those who fear you, which you bestow in the sight of all on those who take refuge in you." Psalm 31:19 (TNIV)

*A*round New Year's, I sometimes choose a word or phrase that is my theme for the year. One year that word was fear.

People were confused because who wants to be fearful? But I wanted to know what it was to fear the Lord.

Fear means something slightly different today than in biblical times, but I learned that it's essentially the same sort of deep, trembling reverence. Sort of the same respect you give to a shark or a whale—something powerful and very different from yourself. Every time I saw the word fear in my Bible reading, it enhanced my understanding of how we are to *fear* God.

When Jesus calmed the storm on the lake, His disciples were both amazed and fearful of Him. They understood that He wasn't an ordinary man. They still loved Him, respected Him, followed Him, argued with Him, abandoned Him, denied Him and worshipped Him. Jesus was still their master and their friend, but they also feared Him. Their fear was part of the complexity of their relationship with Him, and it should be that way with us too.

FAITH STEP: *Do you fear Jesus, or has your relationship with Him become too comfortable? Do you have the kind of deep reverence and respect for Jesus that you need to have? Whether in an e-book version of the Bible or online, look up passages with the word fear, so you can better understand what it is to fear Him.*

—Camy Tang

DECEMBER 31

"Which of you, if your son asks for bread, will give him a stone? Or if he asks for a fish, will give him a snake? If you, then, though you are evil, know how to give good gifts to your children, how much more will your Father in heaven give good gifts to those who ask him!" Matthew 7:9–11 (NIV)

$\mathcal{D}$id you ever beg for a bicycle when you were in grade school? Then, in one of those dream-come-true moments, you woke up on your birthday morning and there it was: bright, shiny, red, with plastic tassels on the handlebars.

You walked it down the front porch and aimed for the sidewalk. The bike was bigger than you'd realized. You tried out the seat and the bike tilted from side to side. Much scarier than you had expected. The ground looked a long way off.

When my first novel was released, my editor called me to say, "I'm holding your book. Would you like to come and get one?" I was off the phone and into my car in a flash, zipping down the road to my publisher's office. There it was. My dream-come-true moment. Bright, shiny, red, with raised lettering and the delicious smell of ink.

The euphoria passed as a realization hit me. People would be reading it. Strangers who might not like it. Reviewers and critics. What if the book totally flopped? Could I handle the disappointment? Plus, I was contracted to write more. What if I couldn't? What if the words dried up? The whole idea of writing novels was scarier and bigger than I'd expected. I felt wobbly and way too far from the ground. How could I pedal this big, beautiful gift?

With the book on the passenger seat, I drove home subdued. "Lord, I know this is a gift, but it also scares me."

Jesus' words from Luke came to mind. God's gifts are good. If He gives us a bike, He will also hold the handlebars and keep us balanced. He runs alongside us and teaches us how to ride. He doesn't give gifts that come back to bite us. His gifts are beyond what we can ask and imagine. And even though they sometimes bring new responsibilities and challenges, we can pedal down the block without fear.

FAITH STEP: *As you unwrap the gift of a new year, if it feels a little big and frightening, ask Jesus to guide you and help you keep your balance as you face each new adventure.*

—Sharon Hinck

JUDY BAER was born and grew up on a farm on the prairies of North Dakota. She graduated from Concordia College, Moorhead, Minnesota with majors in English and education and a minor in religion. Judy is married, lives in Minnesota, and has two daughters and three stepchildren. She is the author of more than 75 books.

GWEN FORD FAULKENBERRY lives and writes in the mountains of Ozark, Arkansas. She and her husband, Stone, have three children. Gwen teaches English at Arkansas Tech University-Ozark Campus, and is the author of two novels and three devotional books. Check out her Facebook page at Gwendolann Adell Ford Faulkenberry.

TRICIA GOYER has written more than 25 books. Her intention is to serve ordinary women by encouraging extraordinary things with God's help. In addition to writing, Tricia enjoys sharing Jesus' love with local teenage moms and frequently goes on missions trips. She lives in Arkansas with her husband, John, and their four wonderful children.

SHARON HINCK is a wife and mother of four who loves spending mornings—and all day—with Jesus. She has an MA in Communications, and her award-winning novels explore ordinary women on extraordinary faith journeys. Sharon welcomes visitors to her website at sharonhinck.com

KERI WYATT KENT is the author of many devotionals, including *Simple Compassion* and *Rest*; she writes and speaks to help people slow down so that they can listen to God. Keri is a member of Willow Creek Community Church, where she has volunteered for more than two decades. She and her husband, Scot, live with their teenage son and daughter in Illinois.

ERIN KEELEY MARSHALL is the author of *Navigating Route 20-Something* and *The Daily God Book*. She was raised in Chicago's western suburbs and graduated from Taylor University in Indiana. Erin enjoys hanging out with her husband, Steve, and their two children, Paxton and Calianne. Find her on Facebook, Twitter, and at erinkeeleymarshall.com.

CAMY TANG grew up in Hawaii and now lives in San Jose, California, with her engineer husband and rambunctious mutt, Snickers. She is a staff worker for her church youth group and leads one of the Sunday worship teams. Camy has authored many Christian novels. Visit her website at camytang.com to read short stories and subscribe to her quarterly newsletter.

A Note from the Editors

Mornings with Jesus was created by the Books and Inspirational Media Division of Guideposts, a nonprofit organization that touches millions of lives every day through products and services that inspire, encourage and uplift. Our magazines, books, prayer network (OurPrayer.org) and outreach programs help people connect their faith-filled values to daily life.

Your purchase of *Mornings with Jesus* makes a difference. When you buy Guideposts products, you're helping fund our many outreach programs to military personnel, prisons, hospitals, nursing homes and educational institutions. To learn more about our outreach ministry, visit GuidepostsFoundation.org.

To find out about our other publications and to enjoy free online resources such as inspirational newsletters, blogs, videos, Facebook and Twitter links, visit us at Guideposts.org.